CONSUMER GUIDE RESTAURANTS IN IRELAND

For the first time an Irish restaurant guide *for* consumers *by* consumers

An up-to-date guide written by consumers dealing with almost three hundred restaurants all over Ireland. Unbiased information on food, service, ambience, *and* value for money.

Includes basic information such as: location, opening hours, meals served, drinks, credit cards accepted, disabled access, service charge.

All the concerns of the ordinary consumer are carefully taken into account. The book deals with a wide price range, restaurants for that special occasion, travelling, holiday or simply when you want to fill a gap!

A truly frank and independent guide of unrivalled credibility. Based on reports by subscribers to *Consumer Choice* magazine.

Expresses the tastes and needs of ordinary consumers.

The Consumers' Association of Ireland is a wholly independent, non-government, non-profit making organisation, working exclusively in the interests of consumers. It is linked to Consumer associations in Britain, the USA and elsewhere.

CONSUMER CHOICE GUIDE TO RESTAURANTS IN IRELAND

Consumers' Association of Ireland

THE O'BRIEN PRESS
DUBLIN
Distributed in Great Britain by
HODDER & STOUGHTON

First published 1989 by The O'Brien Press Ltd.
20 Victoria Road, Rathgar, Dublin 6, Ireland

Copyright © The Consumers' Association of Ireland Ltd.,
publishers of *Consumer Choice* magazine

All rights reserved.
No part of this book may be reproduced or utilised
in any form or by any means, electronic or mechanical, including
photocopying, recording or by any information storage and retrieval
system without permission in writing from the publisher. This
book may not be sold as a remainder, bargain book, or at a
reduced price without permission in writing
from the publisher.

We do not allow the use of any Guide material in any form
of advertising, sales promotion or publicity.

British Library Cataloguing in Publication Data
Consumer guide to restaurants in Ireland
1. Restaurants, lunch rooms, etc. Ireland
Directories
647'.95417

ISBN 0-86278-184-1

10 9 8 7 6 5 4 3 2 1

Editor: Ide ní Laoghaire
Book design: Michael O'Brien.
Cover Design: The Graphiconies, Dublin
Typeset in Palatino at The O'Brien Press.
Computer Manager: Ivan O'Brien
Cover Photograph: Lucy Johnston
Illustrations: *regional drawings* Rory Campbell
decorations Orlagh Murphy
maps Consumers' Association of Ireland
Printing: The Guernsey Press Co. Ltd.,
Guernsey, Channel Islands

Contents

Introduction 6
How to Use This Guide 7

DUBLIN CITY and COUNTY
Dublin City 13
Dublin County 35

EAST
County Kildare 55
County Meath 60
County Wicklow 63

SOUTH EAST
County Carlow 74
County Kilkenny 75
County Waterford 76
County Wexford 81

CORK CITY and COUNTY
Cork City 90
Cork County 97

SOUTH WEST
County Kerry 116
County Limerick 120
County Tipperary 124

WEST
County Clare 131
County Galway 136
County Mayo 144

NORTH and NORTH WEST
County Cavan 152
County Donegal 152
County Leitrim 154
County Louth 154
County Monaghan 157
County Sligo 158

MIDLANDS
County Laois 164
County Longford 165
County Offaly 166
County Roscommon 167
County Westmeath 169

Report Forms from 171

Introduction

This guide to a large selection of restaurants in the Republic of Ireland is unique. No hotel, restaurant, café, nor pub has been included in it unless it has been favourably reported on by members of the Consumers' Association of Ireland — subscribers to its monthly magazine, *Consumer Choice*. Restaurants were visited during the course of the ordinary social or business activities of the 'reporters'. As our membership is countrywide, the guide embraces a wide spectrum of catering establishments. For the sake of convenience we refer to them all as restaurants.

GOOD FOOD, GOOD VALUE

Value for money is the natural watchword of *Consumer Choice*. Reports on establishments where members estimated they had got good food at good value prices form the basis of this Guide. Our 'reporters' visited the restaurants concerned perhaps for a special evening out, perhaps on a journey across the country, perhaps on business in a city or town, but never in any sense as inspectors. They reported on restaurants which they had recently visited; they did not visit them in order to report. Their comments reflect the experience of ordinary, reasonably critical restaurant users, with no connection, personal or commercial, with the places on which they have reported. It may be noted in passing that they tended to patronise middle-price restaurants rather than those at the top end of the price range! *Consumer Choice* has taken every possible step to ensure the independence and objectivity of all recommendations in this Guide. *Consumer Choice* magazine never carries advertising, nor do its publishers — the Consumers' Association of Ireland — receive funding from any commercial source. We are therefore totally free of obligation towards any business concern and can without regard to any economic link publish our assessments. Every report used in the compilation of this Guide has carried a signed declaration that the person reporting has no connection with the owner or the manager of the establishment.

GETTING INTO THE GUIDE

Assessments are as up-to-date as possible, members having been asked to report only on places recently visited, and the dates of such visits checked on the report forms, the earliest of which were submitted in February 1988, the latest in November 1988. In no case has a restaurant been included on the basis of one favourable report only, since we realise that in an isolated case a false impression, for better or for worse, could be gained. We have required that a restaurant anywhere in the country should have received *at least two favourable reports*. The only material furnished by restaurant managements is the purely factual information relating to such matters as opening hours and prices.The greatest possible discretion has been exercised in the analysis of reports. Any adverse report received has been counted against a favourable report on the same restaurant, the total number of positive recommendations gained by that restaurant being accordingly reduced. Requests from restaurants for report forms to distribute to their customers were refused; we issued them only to individual consumers. We have checked as far as possible that all establishments in our guide were complying, at the time of going to press, with the Food Hygiene Regulations. For all these reasons our guide is selective.. The principle of including only those restaurants recommended by our 'reporters' was rigidly adhered to, and no restaurant, no matter how well known or of what high repute, has been included unless the required minimum number of favourable reports has been received for it. It is a guide by consumers, for consumers.

If you know of any restaurant that you feel is worthy of recommendation, let us know. There are forms at the end of this guide for doing this. We would welcome these for our next edition.

We are glad to see that a number of pubs are serving meals, many of which are excellent value; we would hope to see more in the future. Next time round, indeed, we would like to widen our scope, and, for instance, to see Northern Ireland represented. We welcome reports from readers on restaurants in any part of Ireland.

Sláinte – Good Eating!

How to Use This Guide

The country has been divided into eight regions. In each, the counties comprising them have been placed in alphabetical order; the towns are in alphabetical order in their counties, as are, in their turn, the restaurants in those towns. For convenience, in the Cork and Dublin sections, Cork City and Dublin City have been placed at the beginning of the sections.

The data which open and conclude each assessment are self-explanatory except for our pricing code. The symbols have the following significance:

£ — under £10 for a table d'hôte dinner

££ — £10 to £16 for a table d'hôte dinner

£££ — £16 to £22 for a table d'hôte dinner

££££ — over £22 for a table d'hôte dinner

If a restaurant does not offer a table d'hôte dinner, the price has been computed on the average cost of three courses from the à la carte menu. In those few cases where only lunch is served, the symbol has been allocated by comparison with the lunch prices of restaurants serving both meals.

DUBLIN CITY AND COUNTY

DUBLIN AS A GEOGRAPHICAL ENTITY was known from very early times under the name of the Ford of the Hurdles (in Irish, Baile Atha Cliath). One of the great highways crossed the River Liffey here, near the present Christ Church Cathedral; and it was in the area of that crossing that the Vikings built their fortified settlement, naming it Dubh Linn (Black Pool). The Normans arrived from England in the twelfth century, and from then until 1922 Dublin was the centre of the fluctuating English power in Ireland.

Growing affluence in the eighteenth century saw the rise of magnificent public and private buildings, setting off fine squares and thoroughfares. The Bank of Ireland in College Green, originally built as the Parliament House, the façade of Trinity College opposite, the Custom House, and the Four Courts all belong to that period, and have managed to survive vandals, philistines, and commercial greed. The Custom House and the Four Courts were extensively damaged in the Civil War of the early 1920s but have been restored. The Royal Hospital in Kilmainham, built as a home for veteran soldiers, is a noteworthy example of recent restoration. It is some distance from the city centre, in the general area of Heuston Station. Within easy walking distance of the centre are all the other buildings which have been mentioned, as well as Dublin Castle, where the State Apartments are open to the public, St. Patrick's and Christ Church Cathedrals, and Leinster House. A guide to the city is essential for visitors, and there are many such publications readily available in the city's many bookshops, and in the tourist offices.

Culturally, Dublin has a lot to offer. The National Gallery in Merrion Square is one of the major art galleries in Europe. North of the Liffey the Municipal Art Gallery in Parnell Square has a good collection of Impressionists as well as other modern art. There are also several commercial galleries. Keep a special eye out for the Millennium sculptures in the city centre which portray typical 'Dubs', past and present. In Trinity College the Book of Kells (an illuminated copy of the four Gospels, dating from around A.D. 800) draws queues of sightseers daily. An increasing interest in recent years for overseas visitors of Irish extraction has been the tracing of their ancestral roots, which calls for a visit to the Genealogical Office in Kildare Street.

Theatre is available not only in the internationally known Abbey and Gate Theatres, but also in the Olympia and the Gaiety, which provide a good mix of commercial theatre; there are also several fringe establishments. Dublin bookshops are of a high standard; in addition to the sale of new books, second-hand bookshops flourish, and a secondhand book fair, attended by sellers from all over Ireland, is held monthly in the Mansion House. Informal entertainment in Dublin tends to centre round pubs, the evening papers usually carrying advertisements for planned 'gigs', and impromptu sessions springing up in many places. The National Concert Hall in Earlsfort Terrace is used extensively to provide music, from classical to folk.

Although suburbia threatens to overwhelm the small towns of County Dublin, the area in general is of great interest. Old castles are numerous, having been built to protect the settlers of 'The Pale' from the wild Irishry, and there are many fine residences, two of which are Newbridge House near Donabate on the north side and Marley Park near Rathfarnham on the south. Both of these are in public ownership and have extensive parkland attached to them. Another fine park on the north side is St. Anne's in Raheny, which has beautiful rose gardens, and of course there is also the Phoenix Park with its herds of deer. Dublin Zoo is in a corner of the Phoenix Park.

Dublin is splendidly situated between the sea and the hills. One of the best ways to appreciate this is to take the Dart coastal railway between Bray on the south side and Howth in the north. At Howth, Dalkey, and Killiney you will find the best coastal scenery; in general the sandy beaches are on the north side, from Portmarnock to Balbriggan. The hills are opened up by many forestry areas affording pleasant walking. Other outdoor activities in Dublin include golf on one of the many courses, and tennis in well-developed municipal parks, which also provide adventure playgrounds for children.

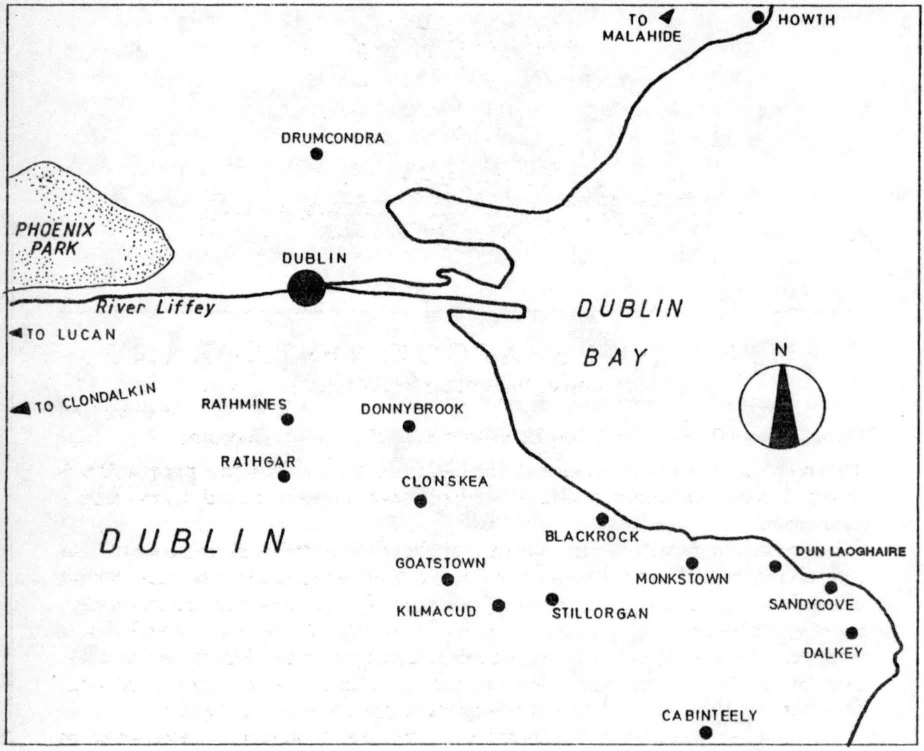

Dublin City

ANTE ROOM SEAFOOD RESTAURANT
20, Lower Baggot Street, Dublin 2.
Tel. 01-604716 ££ Service 10%
Open 12.30-14.00 Mon-Fri, 18.30-22.30 Mon-Sat. *Closed* 22-31 December.

This restaurant is in the basement of a Georgian house. To some people, it has 'buzz', is small, intimate, and convivial; others see it as cramped. It specialises in seafood.

Reporters had both lunch and dinner there, with the menus more or less interchangeable. They sampled oysters, crab claws in garlic butter, cockle and mussel pie, duck and pork pâté and chowder for starters. For the main dish there was fillet steak with prawns, roast pheasant, steak topped with pâté, sole with prawns. Desserts included chocolate truffle cake and lemon cheesecake. The cheese board featured Irish farmhouse cheeses. The house wine was satisfactory; the prices of the list wines were good value for money.

Cooking was excellent, well presented, with good sauces; vegetables were cooked *al dente* and thoughtfully selected.

Service was good and friendly.

•*Drinks* wine licence •*Meals* lunch (AC+T d'H), dinner (AC+T d'H) •*Cards* Access, Visa, American Express, Diners •*Cater for* children

ANVIL RESTAURANT
AND GOAT LOUNGE BAR
Goatstown, Dublin 14. (At principal Goatstown crossroads.)
Tel. 01-984145/983216 ££ Service 10%
Open 12.00-15.30/18.00-23.00 daily. *Closed* Christmas Day, Good Friday.

At The Goat complex, the new, purpose-built Anvil Restaurant serves lunch and dinner, while the lounge bar serves lunches, and has an à la carte menu available all day. The Anvil looks rather like a modern church, all glass and wood. As it has only recently been built it has not had time to acquire a distinctive personality.

Our reporters had the bar lunch, as well as lunch and dinner in The Anvil. Oysters, chicken salad, apple tart, and fruit salad were chosen for the bar lunch. At lunch in The Anvil, starters were seafood pancakes, goujons of sole, and soup; main dishes were breaded plaice, black sole, turbot, and fillet steak, with a selection from the cheese board to follow. An unusual starter at dinner was a very good black pudding; black sole and pheasant were main dishes, and Gaelic coffee was chosen instead of dessert. Wines, chosen from an extensive list, were very good.

Cooking, in general, came in for praise, with a couple of reservations — pheasant was underdone, fillet steak overdone. Service was very attentive.

•*Drinks* full licence •*Meals* lunch (AC + T d'H), dinner (AC + T d'H) •*Cards* all major •*Cater for* children, wheelchair (not to toilets), non-smokers

---

ASHTON'S
11, Vergemount Terrace, Clonskea, Dublin 6.

Tel. 01-698982   £   *Service* nil
Open 12.30-14.15 Mon-Sat. *Closed* Christmas Day, Good Friday.

Ashton's is a pub which serves lunches. It is an old roadside pub renovated and pleasantly laid out and decorated. It is divided by seat backs and the bar counter, so that it does not seem as large as it is. The car park attached to it cannot accommodate all the patrons' cars, but the road around this part of Clonskea is wide enough to permit safe parking on both sides.

Lunch is collected from a self-service counter, with a choice of hot dishes and well prsented salads, rolls and a choice of gâteaux for dessert. Our reporters had cream of spinach soup, pasta and mixed salads, tuna salad, meat pies, and lamb casserole with vegetables. Coffee was good, and of course a full range of drinks was available.

Cooking was very good, presentation excellent, the staff friendly and competent.

•*Drinks* full licence •*Meals* lunch (AC) •*Cards* Access, Visa, Diners

---

THE BAD ASS CAFE
9/10 Crown Alley, Dublin 2. (Between Dame Street and Aston Quay.)

Tel. 01-712596   £   *Service* nil
Open 9.00-24.00 daily. *Closed* two days at Christmas, New Year's Day, Good Friday.

The Bad Ass Café you either hate or love. It is well described in the words of its proprietor: 'Real pizzeria, great buzz, capacity 100, music, video juke box.' One reporter advised visitors not to go there if they are over 40 and to bring along ear plugs. A little like a disused factory in decor, it is bright and spacious, the walls decorated with posters. It is considered arty and trendy and very popular with young people. It is a good place too for families with young children and it is open on Sundays.

Our reporters ate there at various times of the day. They started with coleslaw, minestrone soup, salad with bread, or sautéed mushrooms. For the main course there was lasagne — 'good but portions small' — burgers with french fries, Mexican chilli and pizzas. For dessert there was pear melba, knickerbocker glory, banana split and vanilla sundae. The kids adored the sparklers in the ice creams. The cooking was thought to be good, especially the pizzas; the service good, friendly, if a little amateur — most of the people working in the Bad Ass are students. A special feature of the café is the overhead wire transporter used to send orders and receipts. The final comment: 'Noisy, unglamorous, good food, friendly service, value for money'.

•*Drinks* wine licence •*Meals* all day including breakfast and inclusive tourist menu •*Cards* Visa, Access, American Express •*Cater for* children, non-smokers

BERKELEY COURT HOTEL
(BERKELEY ROOM)
Lansdowne Road, Dublin 4.

Tel. 01-601711 £££ Service 15%
Open 12.30-14.30/18.30-22.30 daily.

The Berkeley Court Hotel is decorated in sumptuous style, with elegant, comfortable furnishings, and the Berkeley Room Restaurant is in keeping with the rest of the hotel. It is a place for a special occasion.

Our reporters, who had dinner and Sunday lunch there, chose as starters prawn and avocado, melon and Parma ham, salmon mousse, and prawn cocktail, with roast beef, rack of lamb, roast duckling, and fillet steaks for main dishes. There was a wide selection on the dessert trolley, two of the sweets chosen being profiteroles — 'beautifully luscious' — and pears cooked in wine. House wine, red and white, was very good.

Cooking was excellent, and service was friendly and attentive.

•*Drinks* full licence •*Meals* lunch (T d'H), dinner (T d'H) •*Cards* all major

BERKELEY COURT HOTEL
(CONSERVATORY GRILL)
Lansdowne Road, Dublin 4.

Tel. 01-601711 ££ Service 15%
Open 07.30-23.30 daily.

The Conservatory Grill is part of the luxurious Berkeley Court Hotel, with a more reasonably priced menu than the Berkeley Room, dealt with above.

Reporters ate in the Grill at lunch-time and in the evening, choosing for starters egg mayonnaise, smoked mackerel, pâté, and 'Molly Malone' platter (seafood). Main dishes were steak, roast duckling, plaice, and kebabs, with Irish Mist soufflé as a dessert. House wine was adequate.

Cooking was generally good, but the steak was tough, and baked potatoes soapy. Service was good and friendly, with personal attention from the manager.

•*Drinks* full licence •*Meals* breakfast, lunch (AC), dinner (AC) •*Cards* all major

BESHOFF'S
7, Upper O'Connell Street, Dublin 2.

Tel. 01-743223 £ Service nil
Open 11.30-24.00 Mon-Thur, 11.30-01.00 Fri-Sat, 12.30-24.00 Sun.

Beshoff's is an upmarket self-service fish and chip restaurant; it has a newly decorated 'old shop front'. Inside, it is fresh and bright, with marble tables, also stools at shelves. Prices for the various combinations of food are set out very clearly above the self-service counters.

The fare is, of course, fish and chips, with several varieties of fish, and soft drinks, tea, and coffee.

Cooking is excellent, both fish and chips cooked to the right degree. The staff are helpful and competent.

•*Drinks* soft •*Meals* **continuous fish and chip menu** •*Cards* none •*Cater for* **children**

BROPH'S RESTAURANT
15, Merrion Road, Ballsbridge, Dublin 4.
Tel. 01-605288/602366   £££   *Service* 10%
Open 19.00-23.00. *Closed* bank holidays.

Broph's, an evening dinner restaurant, is on the first floor over Le Cirque Dining Club. The interior is elegant and cosy, 'tasteful with a good atmosphere'. Customers like the way the chef mingles with the guests.

Starters for our reporters included sweetbreads, mussel salad, warm kidney salad, crab with avocado, duck tart and warm prawns with garlic. For the main course there was pheasant with watercress in wine sauce, veal with spinach, fish and beef. The 'crispy vegetables' were complimented. Desserts included rhubarb fool, crème brûlée, blueberry profiteroles and strawberry millefeuilles. Wine chosen from the list was good.

Cooking was excellent, as was the service. One reporter of French origin said the service was 'French', — the ultimate compliment!

•*Drinks* wine licence •*Meals* dinner (T d'H), pre and after theatre supper menu •*Cards* all major •*Cater for* groups of up to forty by arrangement

BURLINGTON HOTEL (SUSSEX ROOM)
Upper Leeson Street, Dublin 4.
Tel. 01-605222   ££   *Service* 15%
Open 12.30-23.30 Mon-Sat, 12.30-21.30 Sun.

This is a spacious, pleasantly-lit restaurant on the ground floor of the large Burlington Hotel.

Reporters had dinner there, choosing for starters tuna fish salad, melon, and fruit juice. Main courses were roast beef, chicken supreme, and savoury omelette. Ice cream, gâteau, and cheesecake were desserts. Wine was satisfactory.

Cooking was in general good, particularly of main course dishes. Salads, however, were mediocre. Service was courteous and attentive.

•*Drinks* full licence •*Meals* lunch (AC + T d'H), dinner (AC + T d'H) •*Cards* all major

CAPTAIN AMERICA'S
1st Floor Grafton Court, Grafton Street, Dublin 2.
Tel. 01-715266   £   *Service* nil
Open 12.00-00.30 Mon-Fri, 12.00-01.00 Sat, 12.00- 24.00 Sun. *Closed* three days at Christmas, Good Friday.

This American style fast-food restaurant is principally for the young or for parents with children. It specialises in hamburgers, barbecue, and 'tex-mex' meals. The restaurant has a bar, and people waiting for tables are directed there until a table becomes available.

Our reporters had steak with salad and chips, a Mexican dish of minced meat, onions, beans and peppers, burgers, and chicken Kiev, with apple tart to follow. Drinks were mainly selected from the bar; the house wine was not so good.

Cooking was in the main good, although the chicken was somewhat dry. Service was fast, friendly, and efficient.

•*Drinks* full licence •*Meals* lunch (AC), dinner (AC) • *Cards* all major • *Cater for* children

CARRICK HALL
69, Orwell Road, Rathgar, Dublin 6.

Tel. 01-960444 £ *Service* 12.5%
Open 12.30-15.00/18.00-24.00 weekdays, 12.00-21.00 Sun.

Carrick Hall is an old-fashioned Victorian house converted to a guest-house, restaurant, and bar. The interior is pleasantly decorated in an old fashioned way, with an old-world atmosphere. Snack lunches and dinners are available there as well as full meals, and the restaurant uses home-grown herbs and vegetables.

All our reporters had dinner there. Home-made soup, smoked mackerel salad, egg mayonnaise and leek soup were starters; for the main course there were, among other dishes, bacon and cabbage, grilled lemon sole, turkey and ham, roast pork, and sea trout with almonds. Irish Mist cold soufflé was a delicious dessert; also sampled were strawberry cheesecake, sherry trifle, and Bailey's mousse. French house wine was acceptable; there was also a full range of drinks from the bar.

Cooking, especially of fish and vegetables, was in general good — just one reservation, that the food was a little bland. Service was good, even though some of the staff were inexperienced.

•*Drinks* full licence •*Meals* lunch (AC + T d'H), dinner (AC + T d'H) •*Cards* Visa, Access, American Express, Diners •*Cater for* children, wheelchair

CASPER AND GIUMBINI'S
Glendenning House, Wicklow Street, Dublin 2.

Tel. 01-794347 ££ *Service* nil
Open 12.00-24.00 daily. *Closed* two days at Christmas, Good Friday.

This is a bar-cum-restaurant decorated in Edwardian style, serving food ranging from American brunch to more traditional lunches and dinners. There is a resident pianist and an atmosphere of buzz. Our reporters ate a variety of food there — lunches, dinners, brunch and snacks — the majority having dinner. As the dishes for the full lunch and dinner seem interchangeable, they are described together here. Seafood chowder, onion soup, and breaded mushrooms (the last very popular) were starters, with salmon Hollandaise, moussaka, scampi, Gaelic steak, and chicken Kiev as main dishes. The choice of desserts included hot fudge sundae, meringues, ice cream, and profiteroles. Drinks were chosen from the bar. Snacks were hamburgers and salads.

Casper and Giumbini's is a much frequented eating place, and it is only right that we should say that, while we received many reports on it, a number were unfavourable on various points related to the cooking. In general it earned approval, but several people found the main dishes disappointing: Gaelic steak sauce tasted more of cornflour than of whiskey, salmon Hollandaise was too bland, the coating on chicken Kiev was too heavy and a bit overcooked. Service was generally friendly and attentive.

•*Drinks* full licence •*Meals* brunch, lunch, dinner, snacks (all AC) •*Cards* Visa, Access, Diners, American Express •*Cater for* wheelchair (not to toilets)

THE CEDAR TREE
11A, St. Andrew Street, Dublin 2.

Tel. 01-772121   ££   *Service* 12.5% (dinner only)
Open 12.00-15.00 1 Mar-31 Dec, 17.30-23.30 all year. *Closed* one week at Christmas.

The Cedar Tree is a Lebanese restaurant in a basement, with Middle Eastern decor and atmosphere. In addition to Lebanese cuisine, it provides several vegetarian dishes.

Our reporters had gone there to experience something different and were pleased. They had lunch and dinner, dealt with together here. For starters they tried feta cheese, stuffed vine leaves — 'delicious' — vegetable nibbles with dips and hummus, all with hot pitta bread. One reporter had a starter which consisted of eight to ten different dishes with sauces and pitta bread. For the main course there was falafel, beef, lamb and chicken in sauces. There was also a Lebanese Mesa (similar to an Indonesian Rijstafel) made up of many dishes such as hummus, falafel, cracked wheat, chicken and salads. For dessert, home-made cassata and baclava. Reporters found the wine good, a Mommesin at £8 a bottle recommended. One reporter found the traditional Lebanese drink, arak, delightful and different.

The cooking met with general approval and the service was friendly.

•*Drinks* wine licence •*Meals* lunch (AC + T d'H), dinner (AC + T d'H) •*Cards* Access, Visa, American Express, Diners •*Cater for* children (up to 20.00 hrs), vegetarians

---

COFFERS RESTAURANT
6, Cope Street, Dublin 2. (Off Dame Street, behind the Central Bank.)

Tel. 01-715900/715740   ££   *Service* 10%
Open 12.30-15.00/18.00-23.30 weekdays, 18.00-23.30 Sun. *Closed* three days at Christmas.

Coffers is a small intimate restaurant in an old building with a shop front appearance. Inside, it gives the impression of warmth, as it is pleasantly decorated and has an open fire effect. It serves an 'executive' lunch, as well as à la carte, and evening dinners. There is a private room available for special occasions.

All our reporters had lunch there. For starters they chose pâté maison, Stilton-stuffed mushrooms (in which the Stilton was scarcely detectable) and tomato and mushroom soup (home-made, with good taste and substance). Main dishes were seafood Mornay, grilled pork chop, and escalope of salmon. Desserts were Bailey's ice cream and orange soufflé. There was unlimited coffee. House wine was acceptable, and there was an adequate wine list.

Cooking was in general good, meat and fish well flavoured and of good texture; the exceptions were the Stilton mushrooms already mentioned, and the orange soufflé, which lacked an orange 'tang'. Service was satisfactory.

One reporter expressed the reservation that the executive lunch at £7.75 did not compare well with the à la carte menu, as choice was limited — three starters, three main dishes, and two desserts — and portions were not very generous.

•*Drinks* full licence •*Meals* lunch (AC + T d'H), dinner (AC + T d'H) •*Cards* all major

THE COLONY RESTAURANT
7, Johnson's Court, off Grafton Street, Dublin 2.

Tel. 01-712276 ££ Service 10%
Open 09.30-18.30 daily, 19.30-23.30 Wed-Sat. *Closed* bank holidays, three days at Christmas.

There is nothing remarkable about the outside of this restaurant. Inside is an eclectic collection of styles — a jungle theme, oilcloth table cloths. It serves lunch every day, dinner Wednesday to Saturday, and provides home-made food.

All our reporters had dinner there, sampling Caesar's salad, deep-fried mushrooms, mussels in garlic, seafood pasta, fettucine and soup for starters. For the main dish there was chicken teryaki, monkfish kebabs, cheese and spinach-stuffed sole, pork escalopes, fillet of beef in marsala sauce, entrecôte steak. Most chose home-made ice cream for dessert. When it came to wine it was felt that the Colony gave good quality at competitive prices.

Cooking was good, the portions generous. The consensus on service — casual but nice. 'The staff care,' said one reporter. The Colony has good food, reasonable prices and live music most evenings.

•*Drinks* wine licence •*Meals* lunch (AC), dinner (AC) •*Cards* Visa, Access
•*Cater for* children, wheelchair (not to toilets), large parties

CONNACHT RESTAURANT
13/14, Dame Court, Dublin 2.

Tel. 01-793550/793547 ££ Service 10% (dinner only)
Open 11.30-20.30 p.m. Tues-Sat, 11.30-15.30 Mon. *Closed* public holidays.

The outside of this restaurant is attractive; it has even been called 'distinguished looking'. Inside, the surroundings are comfortable, warm and pleasant.

There is a lasting impression of cleanliness.

Our reporters had lunch and dinner, trying seafood chowder, home-made soup, shrimp cocktail or pâté for starters. Main dishes featured salmon trout, pork in sauce, turkey breast with ham and cheese stuffing, and breast of chicken. Reporters who didn't have to worry about their waistlines went for pavlova with kiwi, vanilla ice, fresh raspberries and chocolate gâteau for dessert. The house wine was good.

The cooking was excellent, with presentation getting full marks. Service was friendly, and the general impression was of a 'homely, warm place'.

•*Drinks* wine licence •*Meals* lunch (T d'H), dinner (AC + T d'H) •*Cards* Access, Visa, American Express •*Cater for* children

THE COURTYARD
Belmont Court, Belmont Avenue, Donnybrook, Dublin 4.
Tel. 01-838815/839172 £ *Service* nil
Open 12.00-24.00 weekdays, 12.00-15.00/17.00-23.00 Sun. *Closed* two days at Christmas, Good Friday.

This is a purpose-built restaurant looking out on to a landscaped courtyard. The tables are set in cubicles, giving privacy, but the seating is a little cramped for anyone of a big build. You don't have to book for the Courtyard. On a busy evening this can be a drawback: you can have a long wait for a table. It is best to arrive early — before 19.30 — on weekend evenings.

Our reporters had both lunch and dinner. For starters they sampled prawn cocktail, stuffed mushrooms, spiced beef salad, egg mayonnaise and soup. Main dishes included lasagne, spinach roulade, chicken Kiev, fillet steak, fish, liver and bacon. Desserts were the usual fare: fruit salad, cheesecake. Banana and apple fritters offered something a little different. The house wine was pleasant and inexpensive.

Cooking and service were good. The general consensus: a pleasant place with reasonable food at a reasonable price.

•*Drinks* wine licence •*Meals* lunch (AC + T d'H), dinner (AC), tourist menu 12.30-14.30/16.30-21.00 Mon-Thur, 17.00-23.00 Sun •*Cards* none •*Cater for* children (children's menu 12.00-19.00), vegetarians

DILLON'S RESTAURANT
21, Suffolk Street, Dublin 2.
Tel. 01-774804/774310 ££ *Service* nil
Open 08.00-24.00. *Closed* two days at Christmas.

Dillon's restaurant is open all day; in addition to lunch and dinner it serves breakfast and morning coffee up to 12 noon, afternoon tea from 15.00-17.00 hours.

Our reporters had both lunch and dinner there and found it a good mid-range restaurant. 'Good for anyone watching pennies' and 'good value', were the type of comments made. Starters included pâté, corn on the cob, home-made soup, egg mayonnaise. Steak tournedos, scampi, chicken Kiev, lasagne, double burgers, roast beef with Yorkshire pudding and chicken in white sauce were some of the dishes on offer for the main course. For dessert there was banana split, chocolate gâteau, knickerbocker glory and cheesecake. Specially recommended was the house wine, Piat d'Or, for £6.30 a bottle.

Cooking was very satisfactory; the food was good and wholesome, and cooked as ordered. Service was efficient and friendly, with a personal touch.

•*Drinks* wine licence •*Meals* breakfast, lunch (AC + T d'H), dinner (AC + T d'H), tourist menu all day daily •*Cater for* children, wheelchair (not to toilets)

EASTERN TANDOORI
34/35, South William Street, Dublin 2.
Tel. 01-710428/710506 ££ Service 12.5%
Open 12.00-14.30/18.00-23.30 daily. Closed two days at Christmas, Good Friday.

'When you pass through the door you leave Ireland and enter the heart of India.' That is how one person described Eastern Tandoori, an Indian restaurant offering both north and south Indian cuisine.

An authentic atmosphere is created with life-size brass statues of Buddha, and by Indian music and perfumes. It is relaxing and peaceful.

Reporters had both lunch and dinner there. Poppadums and a small mixed salad were already on the table when people arrived. Starters included chicken Tandoori, baked in a clay oven, shish kebab, chicken shashlik, vegetable samosa. For the main course there was murghi (chicken) — done in a paprika sauce — lamb pasanda in a creamy almond sauce, chicken chilli massala and many other Indian dishes, all served with nan bread. Desserts included a small selection of Indian sweets; deep-fried honey balls, cold rice with cinnamon, mango, almond cake, lychees. The house wine was very acceptable.

Overall the cooking was excellent: 'best quality used', 'tasty and distinctive', were some of the comments. The service was commended: it gave 'attention to every whim'. One reporter thought it was ' the best Indian restaurant in Dublin.'

• *Drinks* wine licence • *Meals* lunch (AC + T d'H), dinner (AC + T d'H)
• *Cards* all major • *Cater for* children, non-smokers

ERNIE'S RESTAURANT
Mulberry Gardens, Donnybrook, Dublin 4.
(Donnybrook Mews, off Main Street, behind block of shops and pub.)
Tel. 01-693300 £££ Service 10% (lunch), 12.5% (dinner)
Open 12.00-14.30 Tues-Fri, 19.00-22.00 Tues- Sat. Closed week at Christmas, bank holiday weekends.

One point on which all reports on this upmarket restaurant agree is that it is very hard to find: it is a renovated mews, (not signposted from the street) in a pleasant courtyard, floodlit at night. The interior decor is very attractive, with the owner's collection of Irish paintings around the walls; and the atmosphere is relaxed and welcoming; it is luxurious but not too formal. All our reporters had dinner there. Starters included smoked salmon mousse, cold seafood platter, quail, and lobster bisque. Main dishes were fillet steak, veal in white wine, lobster, and scallops with side salad. Profiteroles, a selection of home-made ice cream, and meringue with fresh strawberries were among the desserts. There was an extensive wine list, but prices were somewhat high. Cooking was 'perfect' — 'the best food I have ever eaten in Dublin'. Service was helpful, friendly, and 'not without humour'. The owner/chef visits each table towards the end of the night for an informal chat. This is a restaurant for a special occasion.

• *Drinks* wine licence • *Meals* lunch (AC + T d'H), dinner (AC + T d'H)
• *Cards* Visa, Access, American Express, Diners • *Cater for* wheelchair

FLANAGAN'S RESTAURANT
61, Upper O' Connell Street, Dublin 1.

Tel. 01-731388 £ *Service* nil
Open 12.00-24.00 daily. *Closed* two days at Christmas.

Flanagan's is a restaurant with coffee shop and pizzeria, specialising in steaks, chicken, and fish dishes. It meets a need between the many fast food outlets in the area and the more expensive downtown restaurants. It has an exterior shop-front appearance and inside it is somewhat lacking in space, but the backs of the seats are high and this divides up the restaurant and gives a sense of privacy.

All reporters had dinner there. Starters included garlic mushrooms, egg mayonnaise, house pâté and soup. For the main course there was sirloin steak, farmhouse griddle, chicken Kiev, plaice and lasagne. Meringues, ice cream, and apple pie were the favourite desserts. House wine (Piat d'Or) was good.

Cooking was good in the main, although a 'well-done' steak was still pink inside, and in one case potatoes were soggy. Desserts and coffee were highly recommended. Service was pleasant and in general efficient, but somewhat slow at times.

•*Drinks* wine licence •*Meals* lunch (AC + T d'H), dinner (AC + T d'H), tourist menu daily •*Cards* Access, Visa •*Cater for* children, wheelchair (not to toilets)

FRANSEL'S BISTRO
306, Lower Rathmines Road, Dublin 6.
(Junction of Upper and Lower Rathmines Roads.)

Tel. 01-972362 ££ *Service* nil
Open 18.00-23.30 Mon-Sat. *Closed* Christmas Day, two days after Easter, two weeks in August.

This restaurant is pleasant, quaint, and attractive. It serves evening dinner only and generally has a special inclusive Dinner for Two offer.

To begin with, our reporters tried soup, deep-fried squid, cheese puffs, and garlic mushrooms. Main dishes included T-bone steaks, sole stuffed with prawns, and prawns and lychees with mushrooms in a curry sauce. Desserts featured fruit cocktail, profiteroles, meringues, Black Forest gâteau or Bailey's syllabub mousse. Wine was satisfactory; a bottle of wine is supplied with the Dinner for Two and this was found to be very good value.

Cooking was excellent, service unobtrusive but attentive.

•*Drinks* full licence •*Meals* dinner (AC +T d'H) •*Cards* Access, Visa •*Cater for* wheelchair (not to toilets)

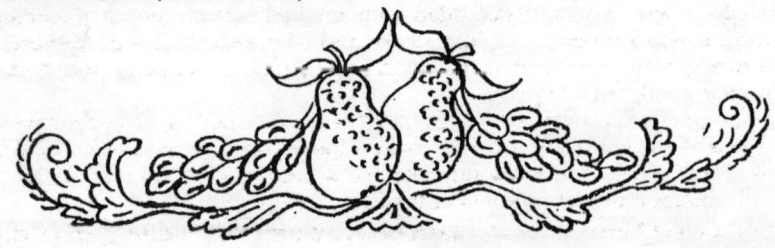

LES FRERES JACQUES
74, Dame Street, Dublin 2.

Tel. 01-794555 £££ Service 12.5%
Open 12.00-14.30/19.00-22.30 Mon-Fri, 19.00- 22.30 Sat. *Closed* bank holidays, and a week at Christmas.

The outside of this restaurant is painted a dark subdued elegant green; looking inside through the window one can see plenty of plants and copperware. The bar and dining area downstairs is small; upstairs there is more room. It specialises in French cuisine, and has a pleasant ambience with watercolours of French rural scenes on the walls.

Our reporters, who all had dinner, liked the dignified welcome they received from the patron and his staff and thought the set five-course dinner for £18 a good idea. The first course is soup, followed by a choice of smoked salmon, oysters, pâté, lamb kidneys in wine sauce, or sweetbreads. One reporter who found the kidneys overdone and tough had this charge removed from the bill. The main course gave a choice of saddle of lamb, duckling, steak, crayfish, or pheasant. For dessert there was crêpes flambées, crême brûlée, chocolate mousse, followed by a selection from the cheese board. The house white wine was thought mediocre but the other wines served, a Sancerre, a 1983 Hermitage, a Gigondas, a Côte du Rhône, were high quality and were properly served.

Cooking was 'delicious', 'first class', 'superb', and service was attentive.
•*Drinks* wine licence •*Meals* lunch (AC + T d'H), dinner (AC + T d'H)
•*Cards* Visa, Access, American Express

FXB'S RESTAURANT
1A Lower Pembroke Street, Dublin 2.

Tel. 01-764606/767721 ££*Service* nil (12.5%, parties of 10 and over)
Open 12.30-14.30/17.30-23.30 Mon-Fri, 17.00- 23.00 Sat-Sun. *Closed* Christmas Day, Good Friday and bank holiday mornings.

As an offshoot of the well-known Dublin butchers, F.X. Buckley, one can expect this restaurant to have the best in meat. It has a small courtyard in front; the inside is pleasant, having been renovated in the last few years.

Reporters had both lunch and dinner there. The starter at lunch was home-made soup, with plaice in a tasty house sauce and fillet steak to follow. At dinner, starters included brie cheese in a light pastry case — 'well garnished and presented, unusual and delicious' — vegetable rolls, carrot and orange soup which our reporters thought could be hotter and thicker, breaded mushrooms, or spring rolls. Main dishes included fillet of chicken breast with avocado in wine sauce, plaice filled with smoked salmon, poached salmon with orange and lemon sauce, fillet steaks, and T-bone steaks. For dessert there was rum gâteau, described as delicious, and chocolate mousse. White house wine was good, red adequate.

Although this is considered a specialist beef restaurant our reporters were happy with the way their fish was cooked. Steaks were done as ordered. The service was efficient and friendly and the waiters gave good advice. Some people thought the restaurant 'a little pricey' for lunch.
•*Drinks* wine licence •*Meals* lunch (AC), dinner (AC), tourist menu daily 17.30-19.30 •*Cards* Visa, Access, Diners, American Express

GALLERY 22
22, St. Stephen's Green, Dublin 2.
Tel. 01-686169 £££ Service nil
Open 12.15-14.30 Mon-Sat, 18.15-22.45 Tues-Sat. *Closed* public holidays.

This is a basement restaurant, with a somewhat shabby entrance, but with a comfortable interior and an open fire. While it is a popular venue for business lunches, the closeness of the tables does not facilitate confidential conversation.

Our reporters had both lunch and dinner there. Starters were cauliflower and bacon soup, garlic mushrooms, and seafood pancakes. Papillotes of sole, lamb Wellington, game pie, and baked cod were the main dishes, with gâteau in orange sauce, carrot cake, and oranges in caramel sauce as desserts. The house wine was satisfactory.

Cooking was, in the main, good, although sauce with the game pie was too rich, and vegetables disappointing. Service was attentive at the tables, but there was no reception service (hanging-up of coat, etc.), at least at lunch time.

•*Drinks* wine licence •*Meals* lunch (AC + T d'H), dinner (AC + T d'H) •*Cards* all major

---

GRESHAM HOTEL (ABERDEEN ROOM AND TERRACE RESTAURANT)
23, Upper O'Connell Street, Dublin 1.
Tel. 01-746881 ££ Service nil
Open 07.15-23.30 weekdays, 07.15-22.30 Sun. *Closed* Christmas Day.

The Aberdeen Room and Terrace Restaurant are at the back of the Gresham Hotel, through the foyer. The first thing to strike the visitor is the unusual, tasteful, grey and pink colour scheme. This is carried through the restaurant; walls, curtains, table linen, uniforms, carpet all toning in. The atmosphere is relaxing. Well designed lighting gives a bright feel to the windowless room in daylight hours, a romantic subdued mood in the evenings.

Our reporters had lunch and dinner. For starters they had avocado and smoked salmon, cream of asparagus soup, poached oysters with Pernod and spinach, avocado slices with raspberry and mint sauce, carrot and potato soup. Main dishes included roast beef, plaice, noisette of lamb in green pepper sauce, breast of chicken in sauce, ham and mushroom omelette. For dessert there was a selection from the trolley, including fresh pineapple, chocolate mousse, fresh fruit salad. The house wines were satisfactory, the white served properly chilled.

Food was appetising and artistically presented, the service attentive and pleasant. Many were surprised at such good value with high quality in a city centre hotel.

•*Drinks* full licence •*Meals* breakfast, lunch (AC + T d'H), dinner (AC + T d'H) •*Cards* all major •*Cater for* children

THE GREY DOOR
23, Upper Pembroke Street, Dublin 2.
Tel. 766011 £££ *Service* 12.5%
Open 12.30-15.00/18.00-23.00 Mon-Fri, 18.00- 23.00 Sat. *Closed* bank holidays.

This is an upmarket restaurant, in a Georgian house. It is decorated and furnished in appropriate style, but tables are somewhat small and close together. Herbs and some vegetables are grown personally by the head chef. The restaurant specialises in Scandinavian and Russian cuisine; as one person put it: 'All dishes are described by exotic titles which have to be explained by the waiter.'

Reports came to us on both lunch and dinner; if anything, the menu sampled for the former was more elaborate. The starters were smoked herring and salmon with a little caviar, salmon soup, and mushrooms. Main dishes were lamb kidney and tagliatelle, steak, and trout. For dinner, smoked fish was a starter, with veal as a main dish. Desserts were pineapple on pastry and Bailey's Irish mousse; these were judged the weakest part of the meal.

Wine — Muscadet, red wine, and port — was good.

Cooking was excellent and service very good; there was a general air of good management about the establishment.

•*Drinks* wine licence •*Meals* lunch (AC + T d'H), dinner (AC + T d'H)
•*Cards* Access, Visa, Diners, American Express

HALLINS RESTAURANT
Moore Mall, Ilac Centre, Moore Street, Dublin 1.
Tel. 01-729111/729070 £ *Service* nil
Open 08.00-17.30 Mon-Sat. *Closed* public holidays.

Hallins is a good restaurant for lunch, or to rest weary legs in the middle of a shopping trip. The tables are well spaced, and lots of plants give a feeling of restfulness. The restaurant is self-service, but the staff give help to carry trays to tables.

Reporters had lunch and a snack. In a lunch of roast chicken, the only item that came in for criticism was reconstituted mashed potatoes. Cooking was in general good and service pleasant and efficient. The restaurant has a wine licence but our reporters, on business bound, did not indulge.

While by no means a gourmet restaurant, Hallins provides a useful, adequate eating facility in a busy shopping area.

•*Drinks* wine licence •*Meals* lunch (AC), tourist menu 11.30-17.30 all year
•*Cards* none •*Cater for* children, non-smokers

THE INDEPENDENT PIZZA CO. LTD.
46, Lower Drumcondra Road, Dublin 9.

Tel. 01-302957 £ Service nil
Open 12.00-03.00 Mon-Thur, 12.00-03.30 Fri-Sat, 14.00-03.00 Sun. Closed four days at Christmas, Good Friday.

This is a pizza restaurant and take-away, a young person's place, with pop music, clean and modern. Pizzas were excellent — the pizza special had a little of everything — and the wine which accompanied them was good, at £1.30 a glass. Coffee and minerals are also available. Service was fair.

•*Drinks* wine licence •*Meals* pizzeria menu •*Cards* none •*Cater for* children

INTERNATIONAL CHINESE RESTAURANT
109, Lower Rathmines Road, Dublin 6.

Tel. 01-974452 ££ Service 10%
Open 12.30-14.15 Wed-Fri, 17.30-24.30 Mon-Sat. Closed bank holidays.

The outside of this restaurant is a tinted plate glass window; the inside is pleasantly decorated and welcoming. The tables are rather close together, and are often too small to take all the dishes.

Our reporters had both lunch and dinner there. The most popular starter was spare ribs — the ribs were meaty and came in good-sized portions. Other starters were spring rolls and soup. For the main course they chose duck, chicken in orange sauce, sweet and sour pork, sweet and sour chicken, roast duckling, chicken curry. Most opted for ice cream for dessert. House wines were acceptable.

Cooking was excellent, the ingredients fresh, the food good and hot. Service was good too.

•*Drinks* wine licence •*Meals* lunch (AC), dinner (AC) •*Cards* Access, Visa, Diners •*Cater for* children

IT'S NATURAL
71, Dame Street, Dublin 2.

Tel. 01-795015 £ Service nil
Open 10.00-22.30 weekdays. Closed bank holidays.

This is what is termed a 'demi-veg' restaurant. Plenty of fresh salads and vegetarian dishes are available, a little chicken and fish but no red meat. Organically grown vegetables are used. Outside it looks bright and exposed, inside it has tubular steel furnishing, with plenty of plants to soften the lines. The restaurant covers the ground floor and basement. A nice touch is the rack holding Irish daily papers, ideal for a person eating alone. Meals are available all day.

Our reporters had soup, a vegetarian pasta dish, vegetable strudel with salmon samosa and salad, and fish pie. The fish pie was delicious. For dessert there was apple crumble, or a giant cookie. The house wine was termed 'just about all right.'

The cooking was good, interesting, tasty, the salads beautifully fresh. Although it is a self-service restaurant the staff are friendly, and available when needed.

•*Drinks* wine licence •*Meals* lunch (AC), dinner (AC) •*Cards* none •*Cater for* children, wheelchair (not to toilets)

KAPRIOL RESTAURANT
44, Lower Camden Street, Dublin 2.

Tel. 01-751235/985496   ££££   *Service* 12.5%
Open 19.30-24.00 Mon-Sat. *Closed* four days at Christmas, three weeks in August.

The Kapriol is an Italian restaurant, serving evening dinner. Seating only 28, it is intimate, high partitions making for privacy. There are hand-painted plates covering almost every square inch of the walls and jugs hanging from the ceiling which give the restaurant a quaintness and a certain charm. The proprietor takes a personal interest in the well-being of his guests. The restaurant is family run, specialising in Italian cuisine, and growing its own herbs. It has an extensive wine list, the proprietor being a member of the Irish Guild of Sommeliers.

For starters our reporters tried mixed salad with Italian dressing, home-made minestrone soup, spaghetti carbonara, prawn salad, cold meats. Main courses included veal Cordon Bleu and Dublin Bay prawns in lemon, brandy and cream sauce. The house white wine was recommended; other wines chosen were Muscadet and a white Soave.

The Italian cooking was excellent; it was obvious only fresh ingredients had been used. Desserts included ice cream, crème caramel, cassata, and zabaglione.

Service was first class, with flexibility allowed in ordering.

•*Drinks* wine licence •*Meals* dinner (AC) •*Cards* Access, Visa, Diners, American Express •*Cater for* wheelchair (not to toilets)

KILMARTIN'S WINE BAR
19A, Upper Baggot Street, Dublin 2.

Tel. 01-686674   ££   *Service* 12.5%
Open 12.30-14.30/18.00-23.00 Mon-Fri, 18.00-23.00 Sat. *Closed* two days at Christmas, two days at New Year, Good Friday.

Kilmartin's looks like a shop from the outside; inside, it reminds one of a French wine bar. It has a simple decor, with plenty of plants, and it is cosy.

Our reporters dined there for lunch and dinner. Soup was the most popular starter, a potato and onion soup, served with a dash of cream, and brown bread and butter being particularly commended. A very popular main course was chicken, stuffed with salmon, in a tangy lemon sauce. Desserts chosen were chocolate mousse, and fresh raspberries with cream. House wine was good quality, and properly served. Service was friendly and efficient even when the place was busy.

•*Drinks* wine licence •*Meals* lunch (AC), dinner (AC) •*Cards* all major

LOCK'S RESTAURANT
1, Windsor Terrace, Portobello, Dublin 8.
01-543391/538352   £££   Service 10%
Open 12.30-14.00 Mon-Fri, 19.15-23.00 Mon-Sat. *Closed* one week at Christmas.

This upmarket restaurant is in an old converted building overlooking the Grand Canal, near Portobello Bridge. It has timber beams and an open fire. There is crisp white table linen and gleaming cutlery and glasses. The attitude of the staff is attentive and welcoming. The restaurant uses cuisine moderne, has its own herb garden, and serves game in season.

While both lunch and dinner are served, all our reporters had dinner. Some of the starters chosen were pasta with mussels and mushrooms — 'too much pasta, too few mussels and mushrooms' — black pudding, warm salad with chicken livers and bacon, beignets of cheese with raspberry sauce. Main dishes included seafood au gratin, snipe, and hake — 'fish of the day'. Desserts selected were chocolate mousse and fresh fruit salad. Wines were selected from the wine list; a house wine is also available.

Cooking and presentation were of a high standard. Service was professional, and the wine waiter was knowledgeable.

•*Drinks* full licence •*Meals* lunch (AC +T d'H),dinner (AC + T d'H) •*Cards* Visa, Access, American Express, Diners •*Cater for* children (before 21.00)

MARTHA'S VINEYARD
Powerscourt Townhouse Centre, Dublin 2.
01-791517   ££   Service nil
Open 12.00-15.00/17.00-22.00 daily. *Closed* bank holidays.

Martha's Vineyard is a bistro-type restaurant and wine bar, in the stylish Powerscourt Townhouse Shopping Centre. It serves lunch, afternoon snacks, and dinner. It is warm, clean and comfortable with a casual atmosphere.

Our reporters, who all had dinner, sampled pâté maison, mushroom soup, mussels in cream sauce as starters. For the main dish they chose Gaelic steak in whiskey sauce, plaice, tournedos Rossini. Desserts included pineapple fritters, Black Forest gâteau, chocolate mousse. Wine, chosen from the wine bar list, met with approval. The cooking was very good, the food hot, tasty and well presented, the steaks done precisely as requested. Service was prompt and attentive, but unobtrusive.

•*Drinks* wine licence •*Meals* lunch (AC + T d'H), dinner (AC + T d'H) •*Cards* Visa, Access, American Express •*Cater for* children, wheelchair

MITCHELL'S CELLARS
21, Kildare Street, Dublin 2.
Tel. 01-680367   ££   Service nil
Open 12.30-14.30 Mon-Sat. *Closed* bank holiday weekends, Saturdays June-September, Good Friday, week at Christmas.

This bistro-style restaurant is open for lunch only, serving home-cooked style food and using organically grown produce where possible. It is in converted wine cellars.

Smoked chicken with green salad, asparagus quiche, and filleted haddock in white wine sauce were enjoyed by our reporters. Blackberry pudding was pronounced delicious (the restaurant specialises in desserts) and there was also a cheese board.

There was an adequate wine list, and the red house wine was good. Cooking was excellent, service relaxed but prompt.

•*Drinks* wine licence •*Meals* lunch (AC only) •*Cards* Access, Visa, American Express, Diners •*Cater for* children

MONTROSE HOTEL

Stillorgan Road, Dublin 4. (Service road to left of N11 dual carriageway.)
Tel. 01-693311　　　　　　　££　　　　　　　Service 15%
Open 06.30-23.00 weekdays, 06.30-15.00/18.00-22.00 Sun.

This is a medium-sized, busy hotel, in which the dining areas have recently been tastefully redecorated.

Reporters had both lunch and dinner there. Starters included egg mayonnaise, soup, and prawn cocktail — this last recommended for the ample supply of prawns without too much sauce. Main dishes were omelette, scampi, and generous portions of first class roast beef. Desserts — meringue and pineapple, apple tart, fruit salad — did not arouse much enthusiasm; one reporter thought them 'banal'. House wine was pleasant and the price reasonable.

Cooking and presentation of the food gave the impression that time and care had been devoted to them. Service was relaxed but efficient. The Montrose 'is the kind of place where you can eat well, even on a budget'.

•*Drinks* full licence •*Meals* breakfast, lunch (AC +T d'H), dinner (AC + T d'H) •*Cards* all major •*Cater for* children, wheelchair

NICO'S RESTAURANT
53, Dame Street, Dublin 2.
Tel. 01-773062　　　　　　　££　　　　　　　Service nil
Open 12.30-14.30 Mon-Fri, 18.00-24.00 Mon-Sat.

Nico's is an Italian-Irish restaurant, small and busy with plenty of 'buzz'. It has a good atmosphere, and pleasant lighting, but tables are rather close together and there is scarcely enough room on the tables for two to take all the dishes.

Our reporters all had dinner there. Starters included prawn cocktail, lobster bisque, minestrone soup, pâté maison, and melon. For the main dish there was sole stuffed with prawns in garlic butter, veal chasseur, cannelloni, fettucine, spaghetti bolognese and spaghetti carbonnade. The dessert menu was criticised as offering a poor selection, most being one or other form of ice cream. The house wine was good.

Cooking was commended, especially of traditional Italian dishes. Service varied; on one occasion it was attentive but not obtrusive, on another 'more

businesslike than friendly'. The overall impression was of a pleasant, unassuming restaurant — good value for money.
•*Drinks* wine licence •*Meals* lunch (AC), dinner (AC) •*Cards* Visa, Diners, American Express

---

O'DWYER'S
8, Lower Mount Street, Dublin 2.

Tel. 01-761718 £ *Service* nil
Open 12.00-24.00 daily.*Closed* Christmas Day and Good Friday.

This is a bar/restaurant/pizzeria offering food all day. One enters down a narrow stairs, beside the pub entrance. The atmosphere is pleasant. Neapolitan pizzas with salads are the staple menu. Our reporters also had minestrone soup, and garlic bread. The house wine was very good. All drinks are available from the pub.

The quality of the pizzas was excellent, and service was efficient and friendly.

•*Drinks* full licence •*Meals* continuous pizzeria menu •*Cards* Access, Visa, American Express •*Cater for* children

---

OLD DUBLIN RESTAURANT
90/91, Francis Street, Dublin 8.

Tel. 01-542028/542346 £££ *Service* 12.5%
Open 12.30-14.15 Mon-Fri, 19.15-23.00 Mon-Sat. *Closed* bank holidays.

The Old Dublin, in the Liberties, is an upmarket restaurant with lots of character, an open fire, and a feeling of comfort. It offers Russian and Finnish cuisine. There are parking facilities, and two small private dining-rooms for parties.

Our reporters, who all had dinner there, sampled blinis (Russian pancakes with various fillings), gravlax (thin slices of cured salmon), hot smokies, shellfish in sauce, and consommé. Main courses chosen were casserole of monkfish in wine, rack of lamb, salmon en croûte, sole in cream sauce. Desserts featured profiteroles, strawberry shortcake, cheesecake, and ice cream; there was also a varied cheese board. White Burgundy house wine was very good, and a German wine recommended by the waiter was just the right accompaniment to the chosen dish.

Cooking was excellent — the dishes were unusual, perfectly prepared, and delicious. Service was attentive.

•*Drinks* wine licence •*Meals* lunch (T d'H), dinner (T d'H) •*Cards* Access, Visa, American Express, Diners

---

THE ORCHID SZECHUAN
120, Pembroke Road, Ballsbridge, Dublin 4.

Tel. 01-600629 ££ *Service* 10%
Open 12.30-14.15 Mon-Fri, 18.00-24.00 daily. *Closed* three days at Christmas.

The Orchid specialises in cooking from China's Szechuan region. Silk wall hangings and mirrors create an exotic atmosphere once inside this basement restaurant.

Our reporters had both lunch and dinner there. For starters they ordered spare ribs, spring rolls, crispy duck, soup. The main course featured chicken, prawns, duck with chow mein, sweet and sour chicken, sweet and sour prawns, pork in hot garlic sauce, beef in bean sauce. For dessert there was fresh fruit salad, and apple pie. House wine was a good quality and fair price. Cooking and service were very good, the only complaint being that some dishes got cold very quickly.

•*Drinks* wine licence •*Meals* lunch (AC), dinner (AC) •*Cards* all major •*Cater for* children (over 5), wheelchair (not to toilets)

PASTA PASTA
27, Exchequer Street, Dublin 2.
Tel. 01-792565 ££ *Service* 10% (parties of 5 and over)
Open 12.00-15.30/17.30-23.30 weekdays. *Closed* bank holidays.

Pasta Pasta is a bright modern Italian restaurant; an excellent place for basic Italian pasta dishes, home-made by the proprietor.

Our reporters had dinner there. The starters were raw vegetables with a dip, parma ham stuffed with cream cheese, soup. For the main course they chose escalopes of pork steak, breaded scallops and mushrooms, lasagne, cannelloni with spinach and ricotta cheese, a chicken dish, steak, cannelloni with seafood. The favourite dessert was profiteroles. The house wine was acceptable.

Cooking, especially of pasta, was good, but it was felt by more than one person that the amount of pasta added to a dish smothered the main feature. Service was excellent.

•*Drinks* wine licence •*Meals* lunch (AC), dinner (AC) •*Cards* Visa, Access, Diners, American Express •*Cater for* children, wheelchair (not to toilet)

PATRICK GUILBAUD
46, James' Place, Lower Baggot Street, Dublin 2.
Tel. 01-601799/764192 £££ *Service* 15%
Open 12.30-14.00 Mon-Fri, 19.30-22.00 Mon-Sat. *Closed* bank holidays.

Patrick Guilbaud's is in James' Place, in among garages and car repair workshops, not the type of area where you would normally expect to find a top class French restaurant.

The restaurant, however, is attractive both inside and out. There is a modern spacious feel to the place, an abundance of plants, and intelligent lighting. It was thought that the restaurant looks its best in daylight when the unusual natural lighting effects can be seen to advantage. One person described it as 'an oasis of tranquillity'. Patrick Guilbaud dishes are mostly nouvelle cuisine. Some people love this, 'the portions are small so you feel good after a meal.'

Reporters had both lunch and dinner there. For starters there was prawn pasta, game salad, asparagus, fish terrine, or duck pâté. Unusually for nouvelle cuisine the portions of duck pâté were too large. Main dishes included lobster, pan-fried beef with wild mushrooms in burgundy sauce, fillet of trout stuffed with salmon mousse wrapped in a pancake in butter sauce, kidneys in red wine sauce, breast of wild duckling. Desserts featured chocolate mousse, warm sliced apples in sauce, home-made mint ice cream or kiwi, lemon and peach sorbet.

The cooking was deemed to be imaginative, superb, top quality French.

Service was excellent too. People were not as happy with the wine. Many thought it over-priced; one person said that the fine wines were expensive and the choice in other wines limited.

•*Drinks* full licence •*Meals* lunch (AC +T d'H), dinner (AC + T d'H) •*Cards* Visa, Access, Diners, American Express, Airplus

PERIWINKLE SEAFOOD BAR
Unit 18, Powerscourt Town House Centre, Dublin 2.
Tel. 01-794203 £ *Service* nil
Open 10.30-17.00 Mon-Sat. *Closed* Christmas, Easter, bank holidays.

This restaurant specialises in seafood and is not open in the evenings. It is in what was the cellar of the converted Powerscourt Town House, has pine decor and quarry tile floors.

The food was 'distinctly home-made'; our reporters had seafood chowder, seafood sandwich, and a mixed seafood platter, with chocolate fudge cake (carrot cake and walnut meringue were also available) with pleasant La Gravette, a medium dry, French white wine.

Cooking was highly approved 'up to cordon bleu standard — the fish dishes were very tasty.'

Self service was quick moving even with long queues.

•*Drinks* wine licence •*Meals* lunch (AC + T d'H) •*Cards* none •*Cater for* non-smokers

RAJDOOT RESTAURANT
26, Clarendon Street, Dublin 2.
01-794274/794280 £££ *Service* 12.5%
Open 12.00-14.30/18.30-23.30 Mon-Sat. *Closed* for lunch on public holidays.

This is an Indian restaurant, with a well appointed and comfortable spacious interior. It provides vegetarian dishes as well as other standard north Indian cuisine.

Our reporters had dinner there. A starter was charcoal-grilled mackerel; vegetarian dishes and chicken tandoori were main courses, with a dessert based on rice, and fresh fruit salad to follow. The house wine was very pleasant.

Cooking and presentation were good; the flavour of the food was excellent. Service was deferential and efficient.

•*Drinks* wine licence •*Meals* lunch (T d'H), dinner (AC + T d'H) •*Cards* all major

ROYAL GARDEN RESTAURANT
Westbury Centre, off Grafton Street, Dublin 2.
Tel. 01-791397 ££ *Service* 10%
Open 12.30-14.30/18.00-24.00 Mon-Fri, 12.30-24.00 Sat 13.00-23.30 Sun. *Closed* three days at Christmas, Good Friday.

This Chinese restaurant, specialising in Cantonese cuisine, is uninspiring from the outside but spacious, well decorated, and relaxing inside.

Our reporters all had dinner there. For starters there was spare ribs, prawn toast with sesame, prawn dumplings, soup. For the main course they tried sizzling prawns with green peppers and black bean sauce, a chicken and duck dish, sweet and sour pork, chicken with cashew nuts, scallops with bamboo shoots and water chestnuts, roast crisp duck and pineapple. Desserts included fresh fruit salad and banana fritters. There was a good choice of wine; Graves dry, Châteauneuf du Pape, and Chablis were all good. The cooking and presentation were voted excellent; the food arrived at the tables lovely and hot as well. Service was very attentive and efficient.

•*Drinks* wine licence •*Meals* lunch (AC + T d'H), dinner (AC + T d'H) •*Cards* all major •*Cater for* children

SHAY BEANO
37, Lower Stephen Street, Dublin 2.

Tel. 01-776384   £££   Service nil
Open 12.30-14.30/19.00-22.30 Mon-Sat. *Closed* bank holidays.

Shay Beano's is a French restaurant, described by our reporters as a 'serious restaurant' and as 'giving few concessions to Irish taste'. The general impression of this establishment is that the surroundings do not match the excellence of the food.

Our reporters had both lunch and dinner there. They started with wild rabbit, mussels, white fish in pastry envelope, soup (described as very good by everyone), sweetbreads, lamb kidneys sautéed. For the main course there was veal, lamb, chicken in lemon sauce, beef in burgundy wine. Desserts included chocolate mousse gâteau which was said to be very good, lemon tart which had a good piquant sauce, choux pastry with chantilly and gooseberry sauce. Red house wine was excellent, but the white was not highly approved.

Cooking was 'superb', service attentive and efficient.

•*Drinks* wine licence •*Meals* lunch (AC), dinner (AC + T d'H) •*Cards* none •*Cater for* wheelchair

STOKERS RESTAURANT
16, Harcourt Street, Dublin 2.

Tel. 01-782441   ££   Service 12.5%
Open 12.30-14.30 Mon-Fri, 18.00-22.00 Tues-Sat.

This restaurant is in a converted basement, granite steps leading down. Inside it is comfortable without being remarkable, the tables well spaced.

Our reporters, most of whom had dinner, started with pâté, soup, pigeon breast, smoked salmon crêpes with walnut sauce. For the main dish they tried monkfish with melon and ginger, roast duck, sea trout, sirloin steak in wine sauce. Desserts featured fresh fruit salad, meringue with walnut purée, ice cream, Bakewell tart. House red and white wines were recommended for value and quality.

Cooking was above average, the portions adequate, the food well presented, with the sauces adding to rather than smothering the food. Service was good, and fast during lunch hour.
• *Drinks* wine licence • *Meals* lunch (T d'H), dinner (AC + T d'H) • *Cards* all major

TROCADERO
3, St. Andrew Street, Dublin 2.
Tel. 01-775545/792385 ££ *Service* 12.5%
Open 18.00-00.30 Mon-Sat, 18.00-23.30 Sun. *Closed* two days at Christmas, Good Friday.

The Trocadero, serving evening dinner only, has a traditional theatre decor and clientèle. The walls are decorated with signed photographs of theatrical personalities; it is a warm, cosy place with plants, and candles on the tables. It is the kind of restaurant people keep coming back to; one of our reporters has been going there for the last twenty years.

Reports featured fried garlic mushrooms in batter, crabmeat and spinach, broccoli soup, warm salad with avocado, and home-made pâté. Some of the main dishes were peppered steak, lasagne, cannelloni, salmon, monkfish, and chicken Maryland. As well as chocolate pudding, rhubarb fool, and pavlova for dessert, there was an unusual Bailey's and blackcurrant syllabub. The house wine was good.

Cooking was in the main very good, but cannelloni and lasagne 'tasted leathery, and as though they had been kept warm for a number of hours'. Service was friendly and efficient
• *Drinks* wine licence • *Meals* dinner (AC only) • *Cards* Visa, Access, Diners, American Express

WESTBURY HOTEL (RUSSELL ROOM)
Off Grafton Street, Dublin 2.
Tel. 01-791122 £££ *Service* 15%
Open 12.30-14.30/18.30-22.30 weekdays, 12.30- 14.30/18.30-21.30 Sun. *Closed* Christmas Day evening.

The Russell Room is the main restaurant of the Westbury, and its pleasant decor is that of a high-grade international hotel. Quite a few of our reporters felt they had been given good value for money in the Westbury; some had lunch, others dinner.

Starters included soup, melon, prawn cocktail, fish chowder and pâté. During a French week there was salad of young pigeon with prawns and parcel of smoked salmon with sorrel sauce. Main dishes included 'run of the mill' beef, roast duck, plaice, lamb, roast chicken and ham, but also soufflé of sole with white wine sauce, tournedos in fresh grapes and wine. For dessert there was almond cake, chocolate Cointreau gâteau, fruit salad. The house wine was acceptable.

The cooking was good, as was service.
• *Drinks* full licence • *Meals* lunch (AC + T d'H), dinner (AC + T d'H) • *Cards* all major

WHITE'S ON THE GREEN
119, St. Stephen's Green, Dublin 2.
Tel. 01-751975/751181 £££ Service 12.5%
Open 12.30-14.30 Mon-Fri/19.00-22.30 Mon-Sat. Closed bank holidays.

White's on the Green looks quite modest on the outside, somewhat like an elegant shop. It is modest inside too; as one person described it — 'it has high standards but no showing off'. It does, however, use beautiful china. The restaurant serves cuisine moderne.

Both lunch and dinner were the subject of reports. At lunch, starters were prawns and soup, with wild duck and quail as main dishes, and crêpes for dessert. Starters at dinner included grapefruit and mango salad, gravlax (salmon), oysters, and warm duck and quail salad. Main courses were medallions of veal, lobster in the shell, loin of lamb, sea bass in sauce. Desserts included strawberry flan and peach and grapefruit sorbets. There was an impressive wine list, and the 'very cheapest' were excellent; house red and white wine were good.

Cooking was in general highly rated, with the exception of the medallions of veal, which were not very tender. Service was good. The general verdict on White's is that, while undoubtedly expensive, it is a good restaurant for entertaining a special guest or for a celebration.

•*Drinks* wine licence •*Meals* lunch (AC + T d'H), dinner (AC + T d'H)
•*Cards* Visa, Access, Diners, American Express, Airplus

County Dublin

BLACKROCK

PARK RESTAURANT
26, Main Street, Blackrock, Co. Dublin.
Tel. 01-886177 £££ Service 12.5%
Open 12.30-14.15/19.30-21.45 Tues-Fri, 19.30-21.45 Sat. Closed Tuesdays after bank holidays.

The outside of the Park is discreet — plain but classy. The inside is unostentatious, elegant, warm and comfortable.

Everyone who visits the Park seems to be driven to superlatives. The cooking was described as excellent, memorable, 'as good as any tasted here or abroad' and 'hard to see how it could be improved'. For starters our reporters, who nearly all had dinner, chose such dishes as seafood pasta with shellfish sauce, cream of codling soup with saffron, crab salad, melon with blackberries, game terrine, orange sorbet. Main courses included carbonnade of beef and lamb in oyster sauce (at lunch) and, at dinner, sole on the bone, pheasant, mallard and game chips, and baked stuffed sea trout in filo pastry. For dessert there was chocolate mint soufflé, ginger pudding, orange surprise, meringues, and mousse. Guests could have as many cups of coffee as they wished at no extra charge. The cheese board gave a good selection. The wine list was very comprehensive, the house red at £8 a bottle deemed first class. Service was very professional.

Our reporters liked the Prix Fixe menu at £19.50 (plus service charge and drinks), the space between the tables, the clean white linen, and the absence of muzak. Everyone said they would recommend this restaurant without hesitation.

•*Drinks* wine licence •*Meals* lunch (T d'H), dinner (AC + T d'H) •*Cards* all major

SPARKS STEAK HOUSE
63, Main Street, Blackrock, Co. Dublin.

Tel. 01-882008 ££ *Service* nil
Open 12.30-14.30/18.00-23.00.

To some people Sparks Steak House is open and spacious, for others a little spartan. It is not the type of place you go to for a romantic dinner; on the other hand the food is good and children are welcome. Because of Blackrock's one-way traffic system, you have to approach Sparks by car from the Dun Laoghaire end; it is opposite the library.

All our reporters had dinner there. The rack of baby pork ribs was particularly praised as a starter. In fact, some people found it very filling. Other favourites were garlic mushrooms, teryaki beef, chowder and farmhouse pâté. In main dishes the charcoal chicken breasts got a special mention; all the steaks were cooked exactly as requested. Other dishes on offer were lamb, swordfish, duckling. Desserts included profiteroles, cheesecake, ice cream, apple pie. Australian house wine was excellent; there was a good wine list.

Cooking was good, the food very well flavoured. Service was pleasant and attentive. A good place in its price range.

•*Drinks* wine licence •*Meals* lunch (AC), dinner (AC) •*Cards* Access, Visa, American Express •*Cater for* children

CLONDALKIN

HEALY'S BLACK LION INN
Orchard Road, Clondalkin, Co. Dublin. (Centre of village, off Main Street.)
Tel. 01-574814/574253 £ *Service* nil
Open 11.30-24.00 weekdays, 12.30-23.00 Sun. *Closed* one week at Christmas.

Healy's Black Lion is a pub-cum-restaurant, and its old-inn appearance has been maintained in good order. It is a lounge-type restaurant, which is comfortable with a relaxed and informal atmosphere. Steaks and seafood are its specialities.

Most reporters had dinner there, but two people who had lunch in the lounge were amazed at the range of food on offer — 'vast, enticing, and interesting' — from which they chose tacos and Southern Fried Chicken, with a drink. Home-made pâté was a firm favourite as a starter for dinner; there was also smoked trout, soup and egg mayonnaise. Beef bourguignon, deep-fried plaice, sirloin steak and chicken Kiev were among the main dishes. Desserts included Knickerbocker glory, pavlova, lemon meringue, and fruit salad. House white wine was good; other drinks were chosen from the bar.

Cooking was excellent, service pleasantly attentive but not obtrusive.

•*Drinks* full licence •*Meals* lunch (AC + T d'H), dinner (AC +T d'H), tourist menu (Mon-Sat 15.00-21.00) •*Cards* Access, Visa, American Express •*Cater for* children (before 20.00), wheelchair

DALKEY

NIEVE'S RESTAURANT
26, Castle Street, Dalkey, Co. Dublin.

Tel. 01-856156 ££ Service 10%
Open 18.30-24.00 daily. *Closed* Good Friday.

Nieve's is an evening dinner restaurant. Outside, it has a pleasant old-fashioned appearance; there is a large window with a heavy curtain on a brass rail at eye level. Inside it is warm and homely, with a coal-effect fire and live piano music.

It specialises in modern Irish style cookery.

Starters chosen by our reporters were melon cocktail, garlic mushrooms, house pâté, and home-made soup. Some of the main dishes were pheasant, chicken en croûte, duckling in orange sauce, trout in wine sauce, and fillet steak. Among the desserts selected from a trolley were fresh fruit salad and chocolate gâteau. The French house wine was agreeable.

Cooking was excellent, including that for a cheaper rate table d'hôte dinner. Service was pleasant, prompt, and efficient.

•*Drinks* wine licence •*Meals* dinner (AC + T d'H), tourist menu daily 18.30-19.30 •*Cards* Visa, Access, Diners, American Express •*Cater for* children

DUN LAOGHAIRE

CAPTAIN AMERICA'S WEST
Unit 216, Dun Laoghaire Shopping Centre, Co. Dublin.

Tel. 01-804688 £ Service nil
Open 12.00-01.00 Mon-Sat, 12.00-24.00 Sun. *Closed* three days at Christmas, Good Friday.

'Everyone to his fancy,' said the farmer kissing his cow. To young people Captain America's is interesting, modern, trendy, cheerful and loud. It is great for families with young children, with high chairs, crayons, and kids' menus. For people over a certain age, Captain America's is ear-muff territory.

For starters our reporters tried potato skins with chilli sauce — the chilli sauce was HOT. For the main course most opted for hamburgers, some had steaks. The food was well cooked; the only complaint, that baked potatoes were soapy. The children's chicken portion was deboned and easy to manage. For dessert there was banana split, mocha cheesecake, chocolate nut sundae,

the last described as delicious. Service was helpful, cheerful, and prompt with a keenness to please. A baby's bottle was heated without hesitation, meals held while young children were fed first. Red and white house wine were drinkable, but one reporter said the 'freshly ground coffee' was awful.
•*Drinks* full licence •*Meals* lunch (AC), dinner (AC) •*Cards* all major •*Cater for* children

PIER 3
Marine Parade, Dun Laoghaire, Co. Dublin.
Tel. 01-842234/5/6 ££ *Service* nil
Open 12.30-14.00 Tues-Fri, 18.30-22.30 Tues-Sat. *Closed* bank holidays.

A brisk walk down the pier at Dun Laoghaire on a cold day will put you in the right mood for the welcoming fire at Pier 3. It is situated on the seafront past the East Pier in the direction of Sandycove. Pier 3 is a typical nineteenth-century Dun Laoghaire terraced house. Its interior, recently renovated, is not particularly impressive, but there is an atmosphere of personal welcome. The restaurant specialises in gourmet food at reasonable prices, using cuisine naturelle, with home grown herbs.

All our reporters had dinner. They enjoyed seafood éclair — a light pastry filled with seafood plus a sauce — seafood terrine which had a lovely creamy flavour, mushrooms stuffed with blue cheese in a batter, and home-made fennel and pepper soup for starters. The main course included stuffed chicken breasts in sauce, salmon steak, monkfish in vol au vent cases with sauce, an Italian vegetarian dish, venison in brandy sauce and chicken with seafood stuffing. Surprisingly, some people still had room left to try brandy snaps — voted excellent — chocolate éclairs, meringue with chocolate mousse and home-made ice cream. Wine was satisfactory, with the house red Rioja getting a special mention. The cooking was excellent with vegetables particularly remarked on. All reports indicate that this is a restaurant with a desire to please, welcoming, and serving very high quality food.

•*Drinks* wine licence •*Meals* lunch (AC + T d'H), dinner (AC + T d'H) •*Cards* Visa, Access •*Cater for* children, wheelchair

ROYAL MARINE HOTEL
Dun Laoghaire, Co. Dublin.
Tel. 01-801911 ££ *Service* 10%
Open 12.30-14.30/18.00-21.30 daily.

This hotel has an ornate Victorian appearance, overlooking Dun Laoghaire harbour in well-kept grounds. It is attractive and comfortable inside.

Most of our reporters had dinner. One had the bar lunch, consisting of braised pork chops with vegetables — good, with generous helpings. At dinner, starters were seafood pancakes and soup, with salmon and roast beef to follow, and fresh fruit salad and apple pie with ice cream for dessert. The house wine was satisfactory.

Main courses were well cooked and presented, but starters and desserts were not up to the same standard. Service was friendly and attentive.

•*Drinks* full licence •*Meals* lunch (T d'H), dinner (AC + T d'H) •*Cards* all major

---

SOUTH BANK RESTAURANT
1, Martello Terrace, Dun Laoghaire, Co. Dublin.
Tel. 01-808788 ££ *Service* nil
Open 19.00-22.30. *Closed* Christmas Day, Good Friday.

The South Bank is in a terraced house, in among other restaurants, along the seafront. It is smart and stylish, and serves evening dinner only. It has a low ceiling which tends to make the restaurant very noisy when it is full.

For starters, our reporters tried chicken livers in whiskey and cream sauce, melon with blackberries and champagne, duck and spinach soup. For the main course there was peppered steak, monkfish in cream and garlic sauce, and turkey fillet with peaches. Desserts featured fresh fruit salad, gâteau Diane, and cheesecake; there was also a good selection on the cheese board. House wines, a red Bordeaux and a white Rheinwein, were good.

Cooking and presentation were commended. Service was in the main good, although more than one reporter found it slow in the early stages of the meal.

•*Drinks* wine licence •*Meals* dinner (AC) •*Cards* all major •*Cater for* wheelchair

HOWTH

ABBEY TAVERN
Howth, Co. Dublin
Tel. 01-390282/322006 £££ *Service* nil
Open 19.00-23.00 Mon-Sat. *Closed* Good Friday, Christmas Day.

This is a pub-cum-restaurant serving evening dinner and providing traditional Irish music and entertainment. As such it is a Mecca for tourists in the season. It has an old-world tavern aspect and is warm and inviting. Traditional Irish fare is served and home produce, including locally-landed fish, is used whenever possible.

Starters for our reporters included bisque, smoked salmon, mussels, and prawn cocktails. Some of the main dishes were salmon, sole, duck, and monkfish, with pavlova, fruit salad, strawberries, and crème caramel as dessert. Children in one party had corn on the cob, chicken, and ice cream. Drinks were chosen from the bar.

Cooking was very good, and service excellent, with particular attention to children.

•*Drinks* full licence •*Meals* dinner (AC only) •*Cards* Access, Visa, Diners, American Express •*Cater for* children (with parents), non-smokers

HOWTH LODGE HOTEL
Howth, Co. Dublin.

Tel. 01-390288 ££ Service 5% (for parties over 8)
Open 12.30-14.30 Mon-Fri and Sun, 19.00-21.30 Mon- Sat. Closed three days at Christmas, Good Friday.

Howth Lodge has the appearance of an old-fashioned seaside hotel; it backs on to Claremont Beach, and is painted black and white.

Our reporters said that, while this may not be considered an haute cuisine restaurant, the food was good. For starters they tried melon, soup, hot garlic mussels in bread crumbs, prawn salad — all with home-made brown bread. Reporters who had the bar lunch chose chicken casserole and lasagne; those having dinner ordered turbot, monkfish, plaice, breast of chicken, sirloin steak cooked on charcoal. For dessert there was raspberry and cream, fruit salad, baked Alaska, chocolate mousse, cheesecake, apple flan. The house wine was acceptable.

Everyone was happy with the quality of the cooking. The bar lunch was more imaginative than most such lunches, the vegetables served for dinner different to the usual run-of-the-mill and well cooked. Service was friendly and good, one reporter receiving decaffeinated coffee, and Flora instead of butter, without a fuss. Plus points for Howth Lodge are direct access to the beach and the well-lit supervised car park.

•*Drinks* full licence •*Meals* lunch (AC), dinner (AC), bar food •*Cards* Access, Visa, Diners, American Express, Airplus, JCB •*Cater for* children, wheelchair (not to toilet)

KING SITRIC
East Pier, Howth, Co. Dublin.

Tel. 01-325235/326729 £££ Service nil
Open 12.30-14.30 Mon-Fri, 18.30-23.00 Mon-Sat. Closed ten days at Christmas, bank holidays.

The King Sitric occupies a former Harbour Master's house, carefully restored. The entrance is somewhat cramped, but the restaurant is very clean and has spotless, good quality table linen. As befits its proximity to a major fish landing area, it specialises in local seafood, also serving game in season.

Reporters had both lunch and dinner there, dealt with together here. Starters included smoked salmon, fried fish cake — 'rather bland but not unpleasant', — and crab; main dishes were monkfish, grilled hake, and sole. Fresh fruit, ice cream and almonds, and meringue with chocolate sauce were the desserts. House wine was excellent. Gewürztraminer, chosen from the wine list, cost £13 a bottle.

Cooking was highly acclaimed, both fish and vegetables being cooked to the right degree. Service was efficient.

•*Drinks* wine licence •*Meals* lunch (AC + T d'H), dinner (AC + T d'H)
•*Cards* Visa, Access, American Express, Diners •*Cater for* children, wheelchair

RUSSELLS
1, Harbour Road, Howth, Co. Dublin.

Tel. 01-322681/2 £ *Service* nil
Open 12.30-14.30 Tues-Fri, 18.30-23.00 Sat-Mon.

Russells in Howth is a restored harbour warehouse. The natural granite stone and rafters have been exposed and cleaned, the floors are of natural wood. Overlooking scenic Howth Harbour, Russells gives a beautiful view on a summer's evening. Downstairs it has a bar with an open fire; the restaurant is upstairs with a balcony above the restaurant. Russells is within walking distance of Howth Dart station. As befits a harbour-side restaurant, it offers a variety of fish dishes daily.

Nearly all our reporters had dinner; one sampled the lunch, which did not differ significantly. For starters they chose smoked salmon with spinach roulade, pork ribs in barbecue sauce, soup. The spinach roulade was the most popular. For the main course there were medallions of pork, veal, chicken Mimosa, peppered fillet steak, roast duck, scallops, fillet of plaice, and chicken. For dessert the orange flan was pronounced unusual and good; there were also profiteroles, apple pie, chocolate éclairs, gâteau with chocolate sauce.

Reporters who ordered a Muscadet, Rioja, Mouton Cadet, were well satisfied. The house wine was thought a little harsh.

In the main the cooking was good, just one or two disappointments: veal was tough, and soup rather tasteless. When it came to service many reporters felt they were waiting far too long for their tables, even when they had booked well in advance. Some had to return their food because it was not warm enough.

•*Drinks* full licence •*Meals* lunch (AC + T d'H), dinner (AC + T d'H), high tea on Sun •*Cards* Visa, Access, Diners •*Cater for* children, non-smokers

ST. LAWRENCE HOTEL
Howth Harbour, Howth, Co. Dublin.

Tel. 01-322643 £ *Service* nil
Open 12.30-14.00/18.30-22.30 daily. *Closed* Christmas Day and Good Friday.

From this hotel you can see Howth Harbour with its yachts and fishing vessels, the island of Ireland's Eye and Howth lighthouse. In the dining-room the tables are rather close together, and it can be difficult to manoeuvre with hot plates.

At the St. Lawrence Carvery you serve yourself: you can take as little or as much as you like. There are various sittings at lunch hour and in the evenings. Reporters ate there both at lunch-time and in the evening. Starters included soup and a wide range of salads. For the main course there was pork, ham, roast beef, chicken, fish, with potatoes cooked in various ways, and vegetables. Meat was very good, beef and bacon getting a special mention. Vegetables did not fare so well: 'overcooked' was the word used most often to describe them. There was a selection of desserts such as trifle, pears, jelly, pavlova. One reporter thought the desserts didn't taste as good as they looked. The house wine was good.

•*Drinks* full licence •*Meals* breakfast, lunch (T d'H), dinner (T d'H) •*Cards* Visa, Access, American Express, Diners •*Cater for* children (half-price under 8 years), wheelchair

LUCAN

FINNSTOWN HOUSE HOTEL
Newcastle Road, Lucan, Co. Dublin. (1.5km from Lucan off N4.)
Tel. 01-280644   £££   Service nil
Open 12.30-14.30/19.00-22.00 daily.

Finnstown House is a modernised eighteenth-century country house in wooded grounds (where there are squirrels and peacocks). It incorporates a health farm, but restaurant patrons need not fear that this implies a restricted diet for them. Some of its more unusual specialities are kid goat, goose, lobster, and suckling pig. Fresh local vegetables and herbs from the garden are used. It is advisable to telephone in advance of a visit.

Our reporters visited Finnstown House for both lunch and dinner. At lunch, starters were cream soup, and beef and vegetable soup, neither of which aroused much enthusiasm. A main course of poached salmon in white wine with dill batter, chosen from an extensive menu, was, however, excellent. At dinner, avocado with prawns, and shellfish bisque were starters; among the main courses were roast rack of lamb, fillet steak, roast kid goat, and monktail medallions. The dessert trolley provided a wide selection; as an alternative, there was a cheese board. The house wine was good, but soda water and lime were considered expensive. Apart from the lunch-time soup, cooking was excellent, and service very good.

•*Drinks* full licence •*Meals* lunch (T d'H), dinner (T d'H) •*Cards* Access, Visa, Diners, American Express •*Cater for* children, wheelchair, non-smokers

SPA HOTEL
Lucan, Co. Dublin.
Tel. 01-280494   ££   Service nil
Open 07.30-09.45/12.30-14.45/18.00-22.00 daily.

The Spa Hotel, built in a vaguely Victorian Gothic style, has a commanding position above the Dublin-Galway road. Inside, it has recently been refurbished and is clean and bright.

Our reporters had dinner and Sunday lunch and for starters tried egg and kiwi salad, avocado and prawns, breaded mushrooms in garlic, and soup. For the main course there was roast leg of lamb with mint sauce, fillet steak with Bearnaise sauce, roast beef, grilled fresh salmon. Desserts were 'run-of-the-mill': fresh fruit salad, sherry trifle, meringue and ice cream, home-made ice cream. House wine was acceptable.

Generally the cooking was of a high standard, the food hot, nicely presented. One reporter was given a very tough fillet steak but this was changed to very good roast beef on complaint. Service was good.

•*Drinks* full licence •*Meals* breakfast, lunch (AC + T d'H), dinner (AC + T d'H), tourist menu 18.00-21.00 throughout the year •*Cards* Access, Visa, American Express

MALAHIDE

BONNE CHERE
5, St. James Terrace, Malahide, Co. Dublin.
Tel. 01-453171/403107 ££ *Service* 12.5% (Sunday lunch only)
Open 18.00-23.00 weekdays, 12.30-15.00/18.00-23.00 Sun. *Closed* two days at Christmas, Good Friday.

This restaurant is in the basement of a Georgian terraced house, serving Sunday lunch and evening dinner. It is small and cosy, with a pleasant relaxing atmosphere.

Reports dealt both with dinner and with Sunday lunch. At lunch, starters were cream of vegetable soup and mushroom beignets, with main dishes of roast lamb, roast beef, and chicken nuggets for children. Desserts were apple pie and meringues, both with ice cream. There was a wide choice of starters for dinner, including avocado with raspberry and walnut dressing, garlic mushrooms, soused herrings, Dublin smokies (trout, salmon, and mackerel), and iced melon. Main dishes chosen were entrecôte steak, escalope of veal, seafood pancake, and veal, pork, and beef medallions.

Meringues and apple and raisin pie were home-made desserts selected. House wine was commended at both lunch and dinner.

Cooking was very good, service friendly and attentive.

•*Drinks* wine licence •*Meals* Sunday lunch (AC + T d'H), dinner (AC + T d'H), tourist menu (daily 18.00- 20.00) •*Cards* Access, Visa, Diners, American Express •*Cater for* children, wheelchair

THE GRAND HOTEL
Malahide, Co. Dublin.
Tel. 01-450633 ££ *Service* 12.5%
Open 12.30-14.15/18.00-22.15 weekdays, 12.30- 14.15/18.00-20.00 Sun. *Closed* three days at Christmas.

The small town of Malahide has managed to keep its character despite the ever-advancing urban sprawl from Dublin. The Grand is at the edge of the town on the road to Portmarnock, overlooking the bay with its yachts bobbing in the water.

You may not get haute cuisine in the Grand Hotel but you will get a good meal, well cooked. Our reporters who had lunch and dinner there chose asparagus soup for starters. For main dishes the preferences were ribs of beef, roast beef and fillet of plaice. Desserts included baked Alaska, hot apple pie, and ice cream.

House wine was good value for money.

Cooking was excellent, and service good from a staff who were anxious to help. Overall, a comfortable place with a genial atmosphere.

•*Drinks* full licence •*Meals* lunch (AC + T d'H), dinner (AC + T d'H) •*Cards* Access, Visa, Diners, American Express •*Cater for* children, wheelchair

JOHNNY'S
9, St. James Terrace, Malahide, Co. Dublin.
Tel. 01-450314/452206   £££   *Service* nil
Open 19.30-24.00 Tues-Sat. *Closed* Christmas week, Easter week, 1 Sept-14 Oct.

Johnny's is an upmarket restaurant, with an owner/chef, and situated in the basement of an old-style terraced house. It is pleasantly decorated and has a log fire in winter.

For starters, reporters had spinach pancake Mornay, fish soup, avocado with prawns, and Parma ham with melon. Main dishes were queen scallops with rice, veal, and scallops Provençale, with chocolate gâteau and blackberries to follow, selected from a dessert trolley. White house wine was good; other wines were chosen from the list.

Cooking was excellent and service very good.

• *Drinks* wine licence • *Meals* dinner (AC + T d'H), dinner at £12.50 served as an option Mon-Fri • *Cards* Access, Visa, Diners, American Express • *Cater for* wheelchair (not to toilet)

OSCAR TAYLOR'S
Coast Road, Malahide, Co. Dublin.
Tel. 01-450399   £   *Service* 10%
Open 17.30-23.30 weekdays, 12.30-20.00 Sun and bank holidays. *Closed* three days at Christmas, Good Friday.

This purpose-built restaurant is part of the Stuart Hotel, on the first floor, overlooking Malahide beach, with its own entrance. It specialises in steaks, and serves a family lunch on Sunday as well as evening dinner. It is brightly lit; partitioned cubicles give a feeling of privacy.

Reporters all had dinner, all but one having various steaks including a 15oz. serving; the odd man out had sea trout. Starters included pâté, mushrooms in batter, prawn cocktail, and soup. Desserts were Knickerbocker glory, meringue Chantilly, and apple tart and cream.

Piat d'Or house wine was very good. Everyone was pleased with the quality of the cooking; the steaks were done exactly as requested. Service was friendly and attentive.

• *Drinks* full licence • *Meals* Sunday lunch (AC), dinner (AC) • *Cards* none • *Cater for* children (special menu)

MONKSTOWN

BARRELS TRATTORIA
Over Goggin's Pub, Monkstown, Co. Dublin.
Tel. 01-801992   ££   *Service* 10%
Open 18.30-23.30 Mon-Sat.

Barrels, an upstairs restaurant serving evening dinner, is small but comfortable. Tastefully decorated, a notable feature is the block-mounted theatre posters from Dublin and London. It is a place with plenty of 'buzz'.

To begin with, our reporters chose tagliatelle with cream and garlic sauce, stuffed peppers, mussels in garlic sauce, whitebait, breaded mushrooms in

garlic mayonnaise. Main dishes included veal in breadcrumbs stuffed with spinach, turkey saltimbocca, seafood Provençale, sole in prawn sauce, scampi, fillet steak Napoli. For desserts there was fresh fruit salad, chocolate gâteau, and crème de menthe ice cream — the latter described as 'mouthwatering'. The house wine was standard. Cooking and service were both excellent.
•*Drinks* wine licence •*Meals* dinner (AC) •*Cards* all major

---

THE BRASSERIE
Monkstown Crescent, Monkstown, Co. Dublin.
Tel. 01-805174/800546　　　　　££　　　　　Service 10%
Open 10.00-23.00 Mon-Sat. *Closed* Christmas Day, Good Friday.

The Brasserie has a warm and inviting atmosphere, with pleasant background music. Paper tablecloths, however, struck a jarring note in the otherwise agreeable ambience.

Reporters had both lunch and dinner there. Pâté, macaroni cheese, and home-made vegetable soup were starters at lunch; at dinner, they were smoked salmon, tagliatelle, seafood crêpes, and garlic mussels. Main dishes at lunch were chicken Kiev and poached salmon; those at dinner were peppered steak, prawns Provençale, and black sole on the bone. Irish coffee mousse was highly commended as a dessert. Vegetables — stuffed tomatoes, Brussels sprouts — were excellent. Red and white house wine were very good.

The cooking was praised, and the service was very pleasant and very efficient.
•*Drinks* wine licence •*Meals* lunch (AC + T d'H), dinner (AC + T d'H), tourist menu 12.00-15.00, 1st May-31st Oct •*Cards* all major

---

COOPER'S WINE BAR
8, The Crescent, Monkstown, Co. Dublin.
Tel. 01-842037　　　　　££　　　　　Service 10%
Open 12.00-15.00/18.00-23.30 weekdays, 12.00-18.00 Sun. *Closed* Christmas and Good Friday.

The stone walls and pillars, the open fire, give Cooper's an old-fashioned congenial feel, a welcoming atmosphere. On the ground floor there is a bar with seats at the counter and windows; further back, a restaurant, with another upstairs. Outside, a small cobbled courtyard sets the tone. It is a busy restaurant, with lots of bustle, and a piano player.

Our reporters ordered crab bisque, seafood vol-au-vent, spare ribs, blue cheese in pastry and spring roll, as starters. For the main course they selected jumbo prawns, chicken Tandoori, Chinese fillet beef with blackbean sauce, peppered steak, and duckling. The prawn and duckling dishes were enthusiastically recommended. Cooper's gave a wide choice of French, Chinese, Indian, and Irish cuisine, and carried it off successfully. For desserts there was chocolate mousse, brown bread ice cream — pronounced lovely — and banoffi (toffee, banana and cream on shortbread). The house wine was good, and the mark-up on wine generally quite reasonable. Service was courteous and friendly.
•*Drinks* wine licence •*Meals* lunch (AC), dinner (AC), bar food all day, tourist menu 12.00-19.30 Mon-Fri

RATHFARNHAM

KILLAKEE HOUSE RESTAURANT
Killakee Road, Rathfarnham, Dublin 14. (At the foot of the Dublin Mountains.)
Tel. 01-932645 £££ *Service* 12.5%
Open 19.00-22.30 weekdays. *Closed* bank holidays.

Killakee House is a rambling old farmhouse in the foothills of the Dublin mountains. Down through the years it has had associations with the Hellfire Club, which adds an air of mystery. It is said to be haunted by a black cat. The restaurant serves evening dinner only.

The choice in starters included avocado salad, seafood pancake, spinach ravioli, home-made soup, pâté. For the main course there was Wicklow lamb, roast duckling, pheasant, steak with garlic sauce. The desserts were run-of-the-mill: apple pie, fresh fruit salad, cheesecake, strawberry mousse. Red house wine was fine, white wine disappointing.

Cooking was very good, particularly that of the duckling and pheasant. Service, while not particularly rapid, was attentive and pleasant; one reporter who brought a guest suffering from coeliac disease said that the person's dietary needs were looked after graciously and without fuss.

•*Drinks* wine licence •*Meals* dinner (AC + T d'H) •*Cards* all major

SANDYCOVE

OLIVE RESTAURANT
34, Glasthule Road, Sandycove, Co. Dublin.
01-841027 ££ *Service* 10%
Open 18.30-23.00 Tues-Sat, 18.30-22.00 Sun.

You could pass by the Olivé without noticing it; it is upstairs over a boutique, and the entrance is round a corner. Inside, it is quite small, decorated with paintings and plants, and has linen tablecloths on the individually-lit tables. Dinner only is served.

For starters our reporters chose goujons of plaice, pigeon breasts, garlic stuffed mushrooms, and French onion soup. Main courses were fried chicken in breadcrumbs, duckling, rack of lamb, vermicelli with seafood, sea trout, and sirloin steak. Vanilla ice cream in chocolate sauce, raspberry mousse, peach gâteau, meringue, and pavlova were desserts. House wine at £8 a bottle was of fine quality. There was an extensive wine list.

Cooking was excellent, one person holding that it was as good as in any of the French restaurants in Dublin. The only part of the menu which evoked criticism was the desserts, described as lacking in imagination. A pleasing aspect of the attentive service was that the exact composition and method of cooking of unfamiliar dishes were explained to the customers when they were placing their orders.

•*Drinks* wine licence •*Meals* dinner (AC + T d'H), tourist menu Tues-Thur •*Cards* Access, Visa, Diners •*Cater for* children(up to 21.00hrs)

RUSSELL'S RESTAURANT
56, Glasthule Road, Sandycove, Co. Dublin.
Tel. 01-808878/805118 ££ Service nil
Open 18.30-23.00 Mon-Sat. Closed Christmas Day, Good Friday.

This restaurant, open for dinner only, is on the first floor, over a hairdressing salon. It is a comfortable place, although the tables are rather too close together.

Starters for our reporters included such dishes as seafood terrine, parsnip fritters, walnut fritters and aubergines, and the general consensus on the starters was 'nothing special'. The main courses were better. There was roulade de volaille, saumon au beurre — 'good, with good helpings' — chicken with Stilton, medallions of pork in grape sauce and Armagnac, deemed 'excellent', pheasant, fillet of steak — 'cooked as requested and good' — and sea trout. The only complaint was about the pheasant which was 'dry, overdone'. Desserts showed imagination, featuring poached pears in red wine, fresh oranges with Grand Marnier, as well as old faithfuls like profiteroles and chocolate roulades. House wine was palatable.

Cooking was good in general, vegetables — cauliflower, ratatouille and red cabbage — being particularly well cooked. Service was friendly and efficient.

Russell's early evening table d'hôte menu — available up to 20.00 — is very good value. The overall impression is of 'a jolly, lively atmosphere'.

•*Drinks* wine licence •*Meals* dinner (T d'H) •*Cards* Access, Visa

SANDYFORD

BROWNE'S RESTAURANT
Balally Shopping Centre, Sandyford, Co. Dublin.
Tel. 01-954380 ££ Service nil
Open 08.30-18.00 Mon-Sat, 18.00-21.30 Thur-Sat. Closed bank holidays, four days at Christmas, first two weeks in August.

Browne's is a small family-run restaurant in a shopping centre on the edge of the Sandyford Industrial Estate. It is purpose-built, and decorated in bistro style. Everything is made on the premises, using herbs and fruit from the proprietors' own gardens.

All reporters had dinner there. Starters were mussels in garlic butter, avocado with blue cheese, prawn cocktail, home-made pâté, and soup. Chicken Kiev, steak chasseur, and kidneys in red wine were some of the main dishes, with home-made ice cream and raspberry meringue among the desserts. Wine was 'fair'. Decaffeinated coffee was available.

Cooking and presentation were very good, service attentive and well paced.

•*Drinks* wine licence •*Meals* breakfast, lunch (T d'H), dinner (T d'H), tourist menu (lunch 12.00-18.00, dinner 18.00-19.30) •*Cards* none •*Cater for* children, wheelchair (not to toilets)

SKERRIES

THE RED BANK
7, Church Street, Skerries, Co. Dublin.
Tel. 01-491005 £££ *Service* nil
Open 19.00-22.00 Tues-Sat. *Closed* three days at Christmas, Good Friday, last fortnight October.

The Red Bank is a family-run, evening dinner restaurant in the north Dublin fishing port of Skerries. The husband is chef, and his wife manages the restaurant. The Red Bank was formerly a bank building, so outside it is good and solid. Inside it has the appearance of the dining-room of a 'Big House'. It is intimate, with only eight tables.

You can hear the sea from the Red Bank; it is not surprising that fish is an important part of the menu. Our reporters started with dressed crab, casserole of piping hot mussels in garlic, and a dish of crab claws and prawns; for non-fish eaters, warm salad of lamb kidneys, mushrooms. The main course featured fillet of hake with horseradish, steak, salmon and brill in two sauces, black sole stuffed with mussels in a prawn sauce, as well as entrecôte steak. For dessert there was pavlova, fresh fruit salad, or half a pineapple filled with fresh fruit salad and a liqueur of your choice.

Our reporters thought the menu inventive, the cooking superb. One couple who regularly go to France said the fish here was as good as they have had anywhere. The service was first class, people enjoyed having the chef/proprietor come out and talk to them about the meal and explain how it had been cooked. The wine cellar is in the former bank vault, a nice touch. The house red, a Rioja, was good and good value at £8.25 a bottle.

•*Drinks* wine licence •*Meals* dinner (AC) •*Cards* Visa, Access, Diners, American Express •*Cater for* children (over 12), wheelchair

STILLORGAN

BEAUFIELD MEWS
Woodlands Avenue, Stillorgan, Co. Dublin. (Off dual carriageway N11, righthand side coming from city.)
Tel. 01-880375/886945 ££ *Service* 12.5%
Open 18.30-22.00 Tues-Sat. *Closed* public holidays.

Beaufield Mews is a converted coach house, with an old-world ambience, and relaxed atmosphere. It serves evening dinner only, and has an attached antiques shop, open until 21.00hrs.

As well as everyday starters such as mushrooms and melon, Beaufield Mews served our reporters parsnip and walnut soup, celery and almond soup, devilled crab. Main courses featured venison in wine sauce, grilled salmon, duck a l'orange and pheasant. For dessert there was orange soufflé, orange liqueur gâteau, and lemon mousse. The house wine was very acceptable.

Cooking was in general excellent, the food very well presented. The only complaint was that the pheasant was dry and tough. Service was attentive and efficient.

•*Drinks* full licence •*Meals* dinner (T d'H) •*Cards* all major •*Cater for* special parties, wheelchair, non-smokers

BLAKE'S RESTAURANT
Stillorgan, Co. Dublin. (Off N11 dual carriageway,
near Stillorgan Shopping Centre.)
Tel. 01-887678 £ *Service* nil
Open 12.00-24.00 daily. *Closed* Christmas Day, Good Friday.

Blake's is a large building of utilitarian aspect, not incongruous with its location beside a car sales depôt and a busy traffic route. It is spacious inside, and the cubicle-type seating affords privacy. It is a place where one can bring children.

This restaurant has no pretensions to haute cuisine; one person summed up what it has to offer as 'reasonably priced eating in pleasant surroundings'. Menus for both midday and evening were found somewhat 'run-of-the-mill' by our reporters. Typical dishes were scampi, steak, mixed grill, and chicken, with the inevitable Black Forest gâteau, cheesecake, trifle, and ice cream for dessert. The wine list was adequate — a good choice, not expensive. House wine met with approval.

Cooking was good, service fast and courteous.

•*Drinks* wine licence •*Meals* lunch (AC + T d'H), dinner (AC + T d'H)
•*Cards* none •*Cater for* children

SICHUAN RESTAURANT
4, Lower Kilmacud Road, Stillorgan, Co. Dublin.
Tel. 01-884817/889560 ££ *Service* 10%
Open 12.30-14.30/18.00-23.30 Mon-Fri, 13.00- 14.30/18.00-23.00 Sat-Sun. *Closed* three days at Christmas.

There is nothing remarkable about the outside of this restaurant, part of a row of shops. Inside, it has a fountain and a small fish-pond. Seating in the eating booths can be slightly uncomfortable.

Reporters had both lunch and dinner there. Starters included spring rolls, chicken and sweet corn soup, spare ribs, and — particularly recommended — hot and sour soup. Some of the main dishes were king prawn curry, sliced beef in sauce, lamb with cashew nuts, sweet and sour pork, roast duck with pancakes. Lychees, pineapple fritters, and rose cake were chosen from a somewhat limited dessert selection. Chinese tea was very good, and the house wine adequate; there is a satisfactory wine list.

The cooking was very good, the food being prepared with great care and well presented. Service was pleasant and efficient, but some people found the wait between courses long.

•*Drinks* wine licence •*Meals* lunch (AC + T d'H), dinner (AC + T d'H)
•*Cards* all major •*Cater for* children, vegetarians

SWORDS

OLD SCHOOLHOUSE

Coolbanagher, Swords, Co. Dublin. (Down sidestreet of Swords village, to the left travelling north.)

Tel. 01-402486/404160 ££ *Service* nil
Open 12.30-14.30 Mon-Fri, 19.00-22.30 Mon-Sat. *Closed* bank holidays.

Situated beside a river, this is an old national school, and both inside and outside the original building has been maintained; the inside is co-ordinated in a schoolhouse theme. A conservatory has been added to the building and our reporters found this lovely in the summer but a little chilly for pre-dinner drinks in the winter.

All our reporters had dinner there. For starters they had mussels in garlic, mushrooms in garlic butter, home-made soup, chicken liver pâté, salmon mousse, avocado and strawberry vinaigrette. The last two were recommended for their attractive presentation. For the main course there were such dishes as chicken in white wine sauce, scallops and prawns in sauce, sole stuffed with mussels, monkfish with scallops or poached brill. Desserts included chocolate mousse, pavlova, fresh fruit salad, and cheesecake. The house wine was good.

Cooking was excellent. Service was in the main friendly and efficient, but in some cases a trifle too fast.

•*Drinks* wine licence •*Meals* **lunch (AC + T d'H), dinner (AC + T d'H), lunchtime tourist menu (Mon-Fri)** •*Cards* **Visa, Access, Diners, American Express, Airplus, Luncheon Vouchers** •*Cater for* **children, wheelchair (not to toilets)**

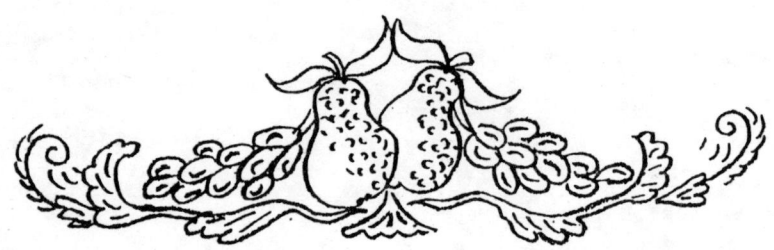

EAST

Counties Kildare, Meath, Wicklow

MEATH IS A COUNTY rich in historical and archaelogical interest. Newgrange, near the Boyne, is probably Ireland's best-known National Monument. The information and tourist centre which has been built across the road from the great passage grave blends in well with the landscape. Although there are huge numbers visiting Newgrange in the tourist season, they are admitted to the megalith in small batches without undue delay. The interior has been lit by electricity without losing its character. The tomb at nearby Knowth is closed because of on-going excavation, but that at Dowth, also in the vicinity, is open to the public. A much less well known but striking passage grave 'cemetery' is on the Loughcrew Hills (Sliabh na Calliagh) near Oldcastle, in the west of the county.

On the Hill of Slane, near Newgrange, St. Patrick is reputed to have lit the Paschal fire on the first Easter day after he landed in Ireland. Slane is on a hilly site beside the Boyne; between there and Navan the river has many scenic stretches, notably at Beauparc. To the north, Kells, where the famous Book of Kells originated, is an attractive inland town, with a round tower, ancient crosses, and St. Columba's oratory. The Hill of Tara, off the Navan-Dublin road, was the seat of the High Kings of Ireland. The earthworks, which are all that remain of the former dwellings, give an idea of the extent of this royal fortress. West of Tara lies Trim, a Norman town with the ruins of an immense castle on the banks of the Boyne. Downstream from Trim is Bective, the home of the writer Mary Lavin whose literary career began with her *Tales from Bective Bridge*. Another literary personage connected with County Meath is Francis Ledwidge, who lived near Slane and whose promising talent was cut short by his death in the First World War.

The roads of Meath have many signposts for stud farms and racing stables. Fairyhouse, near Ratoath, and not far from Dublin, is noted especially for its Easter week race meetings, when the roads converging on it are packed with cars and buses. Horses are, of course, associated with County Kildare. Road signs near the Curragh warn drivers of 'Horses Crossing', and strings of horses out for training make a fine sight in the mornings. The National Stud near Kildare town is open all summer.

The Liffey is County Kildare's river; one may walk along its banks at Kilcullen and Newbridge, and near Sallins is the Leinster Aqueduct, where the Grand Canal is carried over the river. The towpaths of the canal provide walks, as long or as short as you wish, many of them having been way-marked to constitute the 'Kildare Way'. There are barge trips on the canal in summer from Robertstown. From Lowtown, near there, a branch of the canal runs south to link up with the River Barrow. At Monasterevin and Athy there are walks along the river. Ballitore, in the neighbourhood of Athy, was a Quaker settlement, where Edmond Burke went to school. Near Ballitore is Moone, with its carved high cross. Near to Dublin, Maynooth has grown greatly in recent years, both as a dormitory town for Dublin and in its own right as a university town. Celbridge has Castletown House, an enormous eighteenth-century Georgian mansion open to the public; at the opposite end of the village is the grey pile of Celbridge Abbey, where Dean Swift used to visit his Vanessa.

Kildare merges into Wicklow near the Blessington lakes; many people are surprised to learn that these were artificially created in the early 1940s to serve the hydro-electric scheme at Poulaphouca. Apart from its scenic value, this large stretch of water now provides canoeing, sail board, and water ski-ing facilities. Near here is Russborough House, where the Beit family's art collection, china, and furniture are on display at weekends in summer. The granite Wicklow Mountains divide west Wicklow from the east. Apart from their beauty, the mountains are a wonderful recreation area on Dublin's doorstep. Even in the height of summer, there are few places other than Glendalough which could be deemed in any way crowded. Traffic congestion in Glendalough has been greatly eased by the opening of a big new car park, with picnic sites and a visitor centre, on the Laragh side of the monastic ruins. The ruined monastery, round tower, and Lower and Upper lakes are a constant attraction for tourists and 'natives' alike. Many contend that Glenmalure, over a mountain ridge from Glendalough, is at least the scenic equal of Glendalough. Glenmalure was the stronghold of the O'Byrnes, the stand of Fiach Mac Hugh O' Byrne against Elizabethan forces being commemorated by a tablet on a large boulder. Rathdrum is not far from Glenmalure, and there is found Avondale, once the home of Charles Stewart Parnell. The grounds of Avondale are now a forest park, and part of the house is maintained as a Parnell museum. Further down the Avonmore river from Avondale is the Meeting of the Waters, where Thomas Moore is reputed to have composed 'Sweet Vale of Avoca'. Truth to tell, the Vale of Avoca is nowadays marred by the spoil heaps of disused mines, and, nearer to Arklow, the Nitrigin Eireann factory.

Between Arklow and Wicklow town are many pleasant beaches, the largest being Brittas Bay. On the main N.11 road which leads south through County Wicklow from Dublin are Mount Usher Gardens on the banks of the River Vartry at Ashford. The wonderful variety of shrubs and trees makes these gardens well worth a visit. Near its source, at Roundwood, the Vartry has been flooded to make the big reservoir of the Roundwood lakes.

Co. Kildare

CASTLEDERMOT

DOYLE'S SCHOOL HOUSE
Main street, Castledermot, Co. Kildare.

Tel. 0503-44282   £££   Service 10%
Open 19.30-23.00 Tues-Sat, 12.30-14.00 Sun.

As its name suggests, this restaurant is a converted school-house. It looks well on the outside, with decorative window boxes. Inside, it has antiques and old furniture. The waiting area is a comfortable sitting-room. The atmosphere is relaxed and friendly, and guests are not hurried over their meals. It serves evening dinner from Tuesday to Saturday, and lunch on Sunday.

Cooking is country-house style, using locally produced herbs, cheese, and vegetables, and hormone-free beef.

Reporters all had dinner, and found the menus innovative. Lambs' brains with garlic mayonnaise, smoked salmon and savoury pancakes were some starters. Main dishes included wood pigeon, pork fillet, pheasant with calvados, poached salmon with orange and ginger sauce, and roast lamb. There was a large choice of unusual desserts from a trolley, including gooseberry tart, home-made profiteroles, and Bailey's and Grand Marnier ice cream.

House wine at £7.75 a bottle was enjoyable. Côtes du Rhône, Muscadet, sherry and Smithwicks were also approved. Service was attentive and friendly, but unobtrusive.

• *Drinks* wine licence • *Meals* dinner (AC + T d'H), Sunday lunch (T d'H) • *Cards* all major

CELBRIDGE

MICHELANGELO RESTAURANT
Main Street, Celbridge, Co. Kildare.

Tel. 01-242086   ££   Service 10%
Open 18.00-24.30 Mon-Sat. *Closed* three days at Christmas, Good Friday.

This is a small stone-faced building, with a cosy interior. As the name suggests, Michelangelo's specialises in Italian food, serving evening dinner only. The restaurant has a homely and pleasant atmosphere, there is generally music, and it has been described by one person as a place where one has 'every need catered for and you feel as if you are a celebrity customer'.

Some of the starters our reporters chose were Parma ham with melon, minestrone soup with Parmesan cheese, and sorbet. Cannelloni with

ratatouille, tortellini (pasta with smoked salmon and cream), fillet steak, veal, and prawns in white wine sauce were main dishes. Desserts were all based on ice cream. House wine at £7.50 a bottle was acceptable; Villa Antinori was also chosen, as was grappa, an Italian brandy. Cooking was excellent — 'food has a home-cooking quality about it'. Service was friendly and professional.
•*Drinks* wine licence •*Meals* dinner (AC) •*Cards* all major

KILDARE TOWN

SILKEN THOMAS
The Square, Kildare.

Tel. 045-21695   £   *Service* nil
Open 12.30-14.30/18.00-22.00 daily (except 21.30 Sun). *Closed* five days at Christmas, Good Friday.

This pub-cum-restaurant is at the hub of the town, and while there is a certain amount of parking space in the square, traffic here tends to be congested and it is as well to use another area. The pub is named after a prominent member of the Norman Fitzgerald family, whose stronghold was in Kildare, and who led a rebellion against Henry VIII. It is nicely decorated inside and out, with wood predominating, an open fire, and a collage in the lounge depicting the history of Silken Thomas. There is a pleasant, friendly air about the place.

Reporters had both lunch and dinner there. Melon, roast beef, and strawberries and cream were chosen at lunch. For dinner, the starter was home-made vegetable soup. T-bone steak and Dover sole were the main dishes, with banana splits as dessert. None of the reporters had wine with the meal, but one had 'a good pint' before it.

Cooking was, in general, very good; steak was done exactly as requested, and vegetables cooked to just the right degree. The roast beef, however, could have been more tender.

Service was pleasant, and well-timed. Hot food was served hot. One person enthused about Silken Thomas as 'a good place that does not cost the earth'.
•*Drinks* full licence •*Meals* lunch (AC), dinner (AC) •*Cards* Access, Visa
•*Cater for* children (up to 20.00 hrs), wheelchair

LEIXLIP

SPRINGFIELD HOTEL
Lucan Road, Leixlip, Co. Kildare.

Tel. 01-244926   ££   *Service* nil
Open 12.30-22.30 daily. *Closed* two days at Christmas.

This is a pleasant country-house style hotel, with modern decor inside, and a large parking area.

Both lunch and dinner were the subject of reports; they are dealt with together here, as there was little difference between the menus. Starters were melon, pâté, and soup, with roast lamb, roast beef, and an assortment of vegetables to follow. A good choice of desserts included soufflé and ice cream. The house wine was satisfactory.

Cooking was described as 'good plain cooking', but vegetables were only average.

Service was fast and well-organised. One reporter, there with a party in which there were three elderly members, remarked on how pleasant and attentive the staff were to the older people.

•*Drinks* full licence •*Meals* lunch (AC+ T d'H), dinner (AC+ T d'H), tourist menu 18.30-22.00, year round •*Cards* Access, Visa, American Express

MAYNOOTH

LEINSTER ARMS
Main Street, Maynooth, Co. Kildare.

Tel. 01-286323 ££ *Service* nil
Open 08.00-15.00/17.00-22.00, bar snacks 10.00-22.00. *Closed* Christmas Day, Good Friday.

This is a lounge-bar-cum-restaurant, in an attractive stone-faced building, with ample off-the-street car parking. It serves carvery and snack lunches in the lounge (which is divided into several comfortable alcoves) and dinner in The Plough restaurant (which specialises in steaks). As it is on the main Dublin-Galway road, it does a brisk passing trade, as well as catering for local people and for those with business in Maynooth, for example at the mart and the college.

Reporters had the carvery lunch, and dinner. Roast beef and breasts of chicken were chosen at lunch time, with roast potatoes, chips, and a selection of vegetables. At dinner, starters were eggs rémoulade and French onion soup, with entrecôte steak to follow. Desserts were ice cream, chocolate gâteau, and Swiss apple tart. Drinks were selected from the bar, and coffee was of good quality.

Cooking was very good — the meat and vegetables were 'just right' — and service was pleasant and efficient.

•*Drinks* full licence •*Meals* breakfast, lunch (AC), dinner (AC + T d'H) *Cards* Access, Diners, American Express •*Cater for* children, non-smokers

NAAS

MANOR INN
South Main Street, Naas, Co. Kildare.
Tel. 045-97471 £ *Service* nil
Open 12.00-23.00 weekdays, 12.30-14.30/17.00-23.00 Sun. *Closed* two days at Christmas, Good Friday.

This is a pub which serves meals throughout the day. It is well patronised by the racing fraternity, and is a popular place for lunch. It is decorated in tasteful fashion and gives an air of welcome.

Most of our reporters had lunch there. The favourite starter at that meal was soup — vegetable or consommé. Chicken and mushroom pie, gammon steak, trout, and pork, were some of the main dishes, with ice cream, fruit salad, apple pie, and meringue glacé among the desserts. At dinner, starters were oyster bisque, mushrooms, and garlic mussels; main dishes were fillet steak and fish pie. Portions were generous.

House wine at £1.50 a glass was average; while few of our reporters drank, there was, of course, a wide choice of drink available from the bar.

Cooking was generally good, summed up by one person as 'not *haute cuisine*, but a good feed'.

Service from a young, efficient staff, who were very nice to children, was both helpful and fast.

•*Drinks* full licence •*Meals* lunch (AC), dinner (AC) •*Cards* Visa, Access, American Express, Diners •*Cater for* children

NEWBRIDGE

HOTEL KEADEEN
Newbridge, Co. Kildare. (Just outside the town, on the main road to the Curragh and Cork.)
Tel. 045-31666 £££ *Service* nil
Open 12.30-14.30/18.00-22.00.

This hotel is an attractive, well-furnished establishment — an old house with modern extensions, in its own grounds. The dining-room is well divided, and there is a comfortable seating area adjacent to it. The overall impression is one of a hotel with high standards. While our reports relate to both lunch and dinner, it must be said that we are not recommending the Keadeen as a quick stop for a cheap lunch en route to Cork or Limerick; rather, as it is quite expensive, it is a venue for an occasion.

Fish featured prominently in our reporters' choices for both lunch and dinner. As these menus were almost indistinguishable, the two meals are dealt with together here. Seafood cocktail, smoked salmon, deep-fried mushrooms, and pâté were some of the starters, with salmon (both grilled and cooked in a wine sauce), fillet of pork, veal, and steak as main dishes. There was a good selection of vegetables. Desserts included lemon soufflé, fruit salad, syllabub and apple pie. A 'delicious dry French wine' was one of the house wines.

Cooking was very good, with lightly cooked, fresh vegetables. Service was friendly, and, in the main, good, even under pressure of numbers.

•*Drinks* full licence •*Meals* lunch (AC + T d'H), dinner (AC + T d'H) •*Cards* all major

PROSPEROUS

TWIN GABLES
Prosperous, Co. Kildare. (On Prosperous-Naas road, about 0.5km from Prosperous.)
Tel. 045-68771 ££ *Service* nil
Open 19.30-23.00 Tues-Sat. *Closed* two days at Christmas.

Twin Gables is a family-owned restaurant serving evening dinner only. It is an attractive renovated cottage in its own grounds, with ample parking. The décor is a pleasant kitchen type, and the atmosphere is friendly and homely — 'like visiting a friend for a meal and a chat'.

Starters for our reporters included mussels in garlic butter, smoked salmon, mushrooms in cream sauce, and potato and leek soup. Main dishes were T-bone and sirloin steak, rack of lamb, stuffed pork steak, and baked salmon. Fresh fruit salad was the favourite dessert — no doubt reflecting the fact that the starters were very generous and left little room for what was to follow, as one reporter claimed. Wines were Black Tower, Côtes du Rhône, and Rioja.

Cooking was very good overall, the only reservation being about a T-bone steak chasseur, which was disappointing.

Service was pleasant but not professional.

•*Drinks* wine licence •*Meals* dinner (T d'H) •*Cards* none •*Cater for* children, wheelchair

STRAFFAN

BARBERSTOWN CASTLE HOTEL
Straffan, Co. Kildare. (4.5km from Celbridge, on the Clane road.)
01-288154/288206 ££ 10%
Open 19.00-22.00 daily, 12.30-15.00 Sun only. *Closed* last week in December.

Part of this hotel is a very old building, the castle keep having been built in 1172, and one of the wings being Elizabethan. The main dining room is on the ground floor of the keep. Notwithstanding its age, the interior is warm and welcoming with open fires. The restaurant uses fresh farm produce, vegetables and herbs in its menus.

All reports related to dinner. Avocado with mussels and grapefruit and melon were starters, with mushroom soup and prawn bisque. Main dishes included chicken Kiev and baked trout with almonds; and orange roulade and gâteau were among the chosen desserts. House wine was quite good and pleasant.

Cooking was very good and service excellent.

•*Drinks* full licence •*Meals* dinner (AC + T d'H), Sunday lunch(T d'H) •*Cards* Visa, Access, American Express

Co. Meath

KILMESSAN

STATION HOUSE HOTEL
Kilmessan, Co. Meath. (9.5km from Navan.)
Tel. 046-25588/25239 ££ Service nil
Open 18.00-22.30 weekdays, 12.30-21.30 Sun.

The Station House is off the beaten track but repays the trouble of finding it, according to our reporters — who advise people to travel to Navan and follow Kilmessan signs from there. It is part of a restored railway station (on a closed line). Children can play on the old platform while parents enjoy a drink. It serves Sunday lunch and evening dinners. There is a resident pianist.

Reporters had both Sunday lunch and dinner there. Starters were breaded mushrooms, soup, seafood salad, and egg mayonnaise. Duckling, roast beef, roast lamb, steak, and trout were some of the main dishes, with crême caramel, raspberry pavlova, and ice cream for dessert. The house wine was good.

Cooking was highly praised, the only criticism of the meals being that main course portions were rather too large. Service was unobtrusive and competent.
•*Drinks* full licence •*Meals* Sunday lunch (T d'H), dinner (AC + T d'H), tourist menu 17.00-19.00, 1 Apr-30 Sept •*Cater for* children

NAVAN

ARDBOYNE HOTEL
(TERRACE RESTAURANT)
Dublin Road, Navan, Co. Meath. (Just outside the town.)
Tel. 046-23119 ££ Service nil
Open 12.30-14.30/17.00-22.00 weekdays, 12.30-15.00/17.30-21.00 Sun. *Closed* three days at Christmas.

The Terrace Restaurant is in a modern hotel, set off by a well-kept flower bed and shrubbery, with an adequate car park. The modern style combines comfort and freshness. There is a general air of welcome. Fresh produce is used in the restaurant. The hotel, of course, serves both lunch and dinner, but all our reporters went there in the evening. Some of the starters they chose were cucumber soup, mussels, pancake with cheese. Fillet of pork, poached salmon, and beef Stroganoff were among the main dishes. Bordeaux and Vinho Verde were two wines deemed satisfactory.

Cooking was generally very good, although sauté potato came in for criticism as being greasy. UHT milk served in little cartons with coffee detracted from its presentation.

Service was prompt and helpful.
•*Drinks* full licence •*Meals* breakfast, lunch (AC + T d'H), dinner (AC + T d'H), tourist menu 18.30- 22.00 •*Cater for* wheelchair, children

BEECŒMOUNT HOTEL
Trim Road, Navan, Co. Meath.
Tel. 046-21553 ££ Service nil
Open 18.30-23.00 daily, 12.30-14.30 Sun only. Closed Christmas Day, Good Friday.

The outside of the Beechmount Hotel is not very impressive, but it has a large car park. Inside, it is tastefully decorated, creating a warm, cosy atmosphere. It serves evening dinner and Sunday lunch.

Reporters had both lunch and dinner there. There was a wide choice on the menu, and children's meals were equally imaginative, 'not just the usual chicken and chips'. Fish starters were in demand — eel, smoked salmon, prawns and avocado, crab meat salad, and shrimp and pineapple cocktail. Peppered steak, veal escalopes, roast beef, and poached salmon were some of the main dishes. Desserts were strawberries and cream, profiteroles, home-made butterscotch ice cream, and cheesecake. House wine was pleasant.

Cooking, especially of meat and fish, and presentation were very good; vegetables were just right. Service was efficient and friendly.

•*Drinks* full licence •*Meals* breakfast, lunch (AC + T d'H), dinner (AC + T d'H) •*Cards* Access, Visa, American Express, Diners •*Cater for* children, wheelchair (not to toilets)

DUNDERRY LODGE
Dunderry, Robinstown, Navan, Co. Meath. (Between Navan and Athboy.)
Tel. 046-31671 ££ Service nil
Open 19.30-21.30 Tues-Sat (1 Nov-19 Dec and 15 Feb-31 Mar); 12.30-14.00/19.30-21.30 Tues-Sat (1 Apr-31 Oct). Closed 20 Dec-15 Feb, Easter week.

Dunderry Lodge is a converted farm building and our reporters' feelings about its character were mixed. ' It's very different, very romantic' was one opinion, while another said it was an 'insignificant, well-kept barn at the end of an unnaturally large car park'. The interior is pleasantly decorated, with an open fire and white linen tablecloths, and the atmosphere is friendly and relaxed.

Both lunch and dinner were the subject of reports. At lunch, starters were fish chowder and mussel soup, with a fish platter and turbot as main dishes. At dinner, starters included warm winter salad, crab pâté, scallops, and cream of artichoke soup. Some of the main dishes were wild duck, pigeon breasts, venison, goujons of monkfish, and veal. Desserts chosen were floating islands, chocolate mousse, ginger ice cream, raspberry macaroon meringue, and damsons in red wine. The house wine was very palatable.

Cooking was excellent, and service professional, relaxed, and efficient.

•*Drinks* wine licence •*Meals* lunch (AC + T d'H), dinner (AC + T d'H)
•*Cards* Access, Visa, American Express

RATOATH

RYAN'S PUB AND RESTAURANT
Ratoath, Co. Meath. (In the village, opposite the Catholic Church.)
Tel. 01-256201 £ *Service* nil
Open 12.30-15.00/17.00-22.00 weekdays, 17.30-22.00 Sun. *Closed* Christmas Day, Good Friday.

This is a comfortable, well-furnished pub and restaurant with a pleasant, rural atmosphere. Ratoath is the nearest village to Fairyhouse racecourse, and the decor of Ryan's reflects this in its photographs of horses adorning the wood-panelled walls. The tables are rather small when occupied by four people. Its own car park is miniscule, but fortunately there is plenty of room for roadside parking.

Reporters had both lunch and dinner there. For lunch, they chose roast lamb and curried chicken, both with chips, and sherry trifle — the only dessert on offer that day — to follow. At dinner, a starter of egg mayonnaise was chosen; chicken Maryland was among the main dishes, but far and away the most popular was steak. There were several desserts — trifle, cheesecake, and ice cream among them — but the main course was too satisfying to permit of their being sampled. Coffee was thought by one party at lunch to be the weak point of the meal.

Cooking received high praise. Chips were crisp, the roast lamb succulent, and steaks cooked to perfection — each to the degree ordered. One man in a party of five having sirloin steaks said that their only comments on the food were; 'I wish herself would cook like this!' Service was friendly and efficient. In essence, Ryan's is a pleasant unpretentious country pub/restaurant with few 'frills' but good value in food.

•*Drinks* full licence •*Meals* lunch (AC), dinner(AC) •*Cards* none •*Cater for* children (up to 19.00 hrs)

SLANE

CONYNGHAM ARMS HOTEL
Slane, Co. Meath.
Tel. 041-24155 ££ *Service* nil
Open 12.30-14.30/18.00-21.45 weekdays, 12.30-14.30/18.00-19.45 Sun, 10.30-19.00 coffee bar. *Closed* five days at Christmas, Good Friday.

The Conyngham Arms is a recently renovated old village hotel. The local poet Francis Ledwidge is commemorated in its interior decoration. In addition to the restaurant, there is a coffee bar serving snacks, pastries, and sandwiches throughout the day, and the people who had a snack thought it very good value.

Reporters who had lunch and dinner there chose home-made soup, melon, and egg mayonnaise for starters. Main courses were roast beef, escalopes of pork stuffed with ham and cheese, grilled plaice, and pan-fried chicken in garlic. Desserts included fresh fruit salad, trifle, and apple tart. House wine was satisfactory.

Cooking was very good, as was presentation. Three beef eaters in one party marvelled at the way their personal tastes for rare, medium, and well-done meat were all perfectly satisfied. Service was pleasant and well but unobtrusively supervised.
•*Drinks* full licence •*Meals* lunch (AC + T d'H), dinner (AC + T d'H), tourist menu 18.00-20.00 June-Sept •*Cards* none •*Cater for* children (up to 20.00 hrs)

TRIM

WELLINGTON COURT HOTEL
Trim, Co. Meath.

Tel. 046-31108   ££   Service 10%
Open 12.30-14.30/18.30-21.30 daily. *Closed* Christmas Day, Good Friday.

This hotel, near the centre of Trim town, is a lovely period building with a spacious courtyard providing parking, and a stone archway over its entrance. The interior is attractively decorated and it has been described as 'a very pleasant place to have a meal'.

Lunch and dinner were sampled by our reporters. At lunchtime, the starter was soup, with boiled ham and roast beef to follow, and apple tart as dessert. Dinners were more adventurous; consommé and melon were among the starters, and pork steak en croûte was a popular main course choice, as well as roast lamb. Portions were 'unusually large — no room for desserts'. Red and white French and German wines were good.

Cooking was excellent, and service competent.
•*Drinks* full licence •*Meals* breakfast, lunch (AC + T d'H), dinner (AC + T d'H), tourist menu 12.30- 14.30/18.30-21.30, 1 May-30th Sept •*Cater for* children

Co. Wicklow

AUGHRIM

LAWLESS'S HOTEL
Aughrim, Co. Wicklow.

Tel. 0402-36280   ££   Service nil
Open 12.30-14.30/17.30-22.00 Tues-Sat, 17.30-21.00 Sun-Mon. *Closed* two days at Christmas, Good Friday.

This is a small, family-run hotel on the banks of the River Ow in a scenic area of south Co. Wicklow. It has been refurbished in a simple, tasteful style; food is available in the bar at lunchtime, and lunch and dinner in the well-appointed restaurant with crisp tablecloths and attractive china. The hotel uses local lamb, venison, trout, and veal.

Both lunch and dinner were the subject of reports. Home-made vegetable soup was a starter at lunch, with poached salmon and roast chicken to follow. At dinner, crabs, mushrooms in garlic sauce, and mussels were some of the starters; steaks cooked in various ways were the favourite main dish, and the cooking of these earned special commendation. Desserts included mint ice cream, profiteroles, apple tart, and lemon meringue pie. The house wine was pleasant.

Cooking was consistently good, and service friendly, courteous, and competent.

•*Drinks* full licence •*Meals* lunch (AC + T d'H), dinner (AC + T d'H), tourist menu lunch Mon-Sat •*Cards* Access, Visa, American Express, Diners, Airplus •*Cater for* children, wheelchair

BLESSINGTON

POULAPHOUCA HOUSE
Poulaphouca, Ballymore Eustace, Co. Wicklow. (29km from Dublin on main Blessington-Baltinglass road.)
Tel. 045-64412/64418 ££ Service 12.5%
Open 12.30-23.30 daily. *Closed* Christmas Day, Good Friday.

Poulaphouca House is a lounge-bar-cum-restaurant on the Kildare-Wicklow border on a corner of the Blessington lakes. It is an old house, attractively refurbished, with a lounge commanding a view of a well laid-out garden, and a comfortable, well-appointed dining-room.

Reporters had both Sunday lunch and dinner there. For starters, they selected melon and satsuma cocktail in a tangy sauce, home-made cream of chicken soup, smoked salmon, and prawn cocktail. Main dishes chosen were roast beef and roast Wicklow lamb; and desserts, selected from a varied sweet trolley, included cheesecake, fresh fruit salad, and apple tart and ice cream. Coffee, which was good, was frequently replenished. Drinks were chosen from the bar and from a comprehensive wine list.

Cooking was excellent; chicken soup was 'the real thing', and both beef and lamb were well flavoured and tender. Service was friendly, attentive, and prompt.

•*Drinks* full licence •*Meals* lunch (AC + T d'H), dinner (AC + T d'H), tourist menu 12.30-14.30 Mon-Sat •*Cards* Access, Visa •*Cater for* children, wheelchair, non-smokers

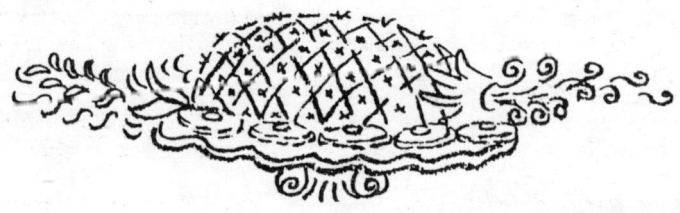

BRAY

PIZZAS 'N CREAM
9B, Albert Walk, Bray, Co. Wicklow. (Near Dart station.)
Tel. 01-861606 £ Service nil
Open 12.00-24.00 daily/12.00-00.30 Fri, Sat. *Closed* two days at Christmas, New Year's Day, Good Friday.

This is a pizzeria in a renovated mews. There is an open fire in cold weather and a patio garden for warmer days. Seating is basic inside, and there is a large room upstairs for larger parties. It is an ideal venue for a fine summer's evening and equally ideal for children, who are welcome.

Needless to say, pizzas are the bill of fare and you can watch them being made. There is 'a great choice of bases and toppings'. For those who were able for them, desserts included home-made ice cream and cheesecake. There was also a cheese board available. Wines were a little limited in choice but served at just the right temperature, and red house wine was thought good value at £6.75 a bottle.

The quality of cooking elicited remarks such as 'best pizzas we've ever had'. Service, however, was a trifle slow, particularly in clearing tables after previous occupants.

• *Drinks* wine licence • *Meals* pizzeria menu all day • *Cards* none • *Cater for* children, wheelchair

BRITTAS BAY

JACK WHITE'S INN
Brittas Bay, Co. Wicklow. (N11 Dublin-Wexford road, at main junction for Brittas Bay.)
Tel. 0404-7106 £ Service nil
Open 10.30-23.00 weekdays, 12.30-22.00 Sun. *Closed* Christmas Day, Good Friday.

This has an old inn-type exterior; inside, it is divided into several alcoves, which, with an open fire in the middle, gives a cosy feeling in cold weather. There are tables outside for summer use. It is a pub serving food, catering alike for passing Dublin-Wexford-Rosslare traffic and for visitors to nearby Brittas Bay — it is on the corner of the road leading down to the main Brittas Bay car park.

Our reporters stopped for lunches only and commented on the excellent value. Toasted sandwiches, home cooked ham, steak and lasagne, and a good variety of salads, were on offer along with home-made soups. Drinks were chosen from the bar.

Cooking was 'excellent'. One report stated, 'The owners certainly know how to look after tourists.' Another said, 'Best place I have been in for a long time!' Service was prompt and pleasant.

• *Drinks* full licence • *Meals* lunch (AC), dinner (AC) • *Cater for* children

DELGANY

THE WICKLOW ARMS
Delgany village, Co. Wicklow.
Tel. 01-874611 ££ Service 10%
Open 19.00-24.30 Mon-Sat. *Closed* bank holidays.

This bar-lounge-restaurant, right in the centre of Delgany village, has good car-parking facilities and lovely gardens where drinks can be taken in fine weather. In appearance the outside is like a rustic inn, and the inside is very cosy with open fires in two of the three bars. It is possible to eat in one of the bars as well as in the restaurant, where dinner is served in the evenings.

All our reports related to dinner. The menus showed imagination, with stuffed mushrooms, seafood chowder and home-made soups for starters. Seafood crêpes, veal à la crème and scampi were just a few of the main dishes. Portions were very generous for both courses. Desserts were 'exquisite' — home-made chocolate and orange cheesecake, lemon meringue pie, crème caramel, and ice creams. House wine was 'passable'; other drinks were selected from the bar. The food was well cooked and presented, and the service was very pleasant and efficient, but not always speedy.

•*Drinks* full licence •*Meals* bar lunches (AC), dinner (AC) •*Cards* Access, Visa, Diners

DUNLAVIN

RATHSALLAGH HOUSE
Dunlavin, Co. Wicklow. (3km from Dunlavin, on road to Grangecon.)
Tel. 045-53112 £££ Service 10%
Open 20.00-20.30 Tues-Sat, 14.30 Sun.

Rathsallagh's slogan 'not a hotel' is well suited to this beautiful old-world country house, standing in 500 acres of parkland. It is well signposted for miles around and is easily found. It uses home-grown fruit, vegetables and beef, and everything is fresh and home-made. It serves evening dinner and Sunday lunch.

Our researchers ate dinner there and were lavish in their praise of everything — the atmosphere, the character, the cooking, the service, and the Australian wines!

They tried starters like twice-baked cheese soufflé in cream, which 'was delicious.' Rack of lamb and roast beef were main dishes. The desserts from the trolley were 'exotic', with chocolate roulade, meringues and home-made ice creams. Australian Chardonnay and Château Trimulet St Emilion wines earned high commendation.

The quality of the cooking was described as 'excellent' and 'perfect' — tributes not often given. Efficient and friendly service was personally supervised by the owner.

•*Drinks* wine licence •*Meals* Sunday lunch (AC), dinner (AC) •*Cards* Access, Visa, Diners •*Cater for* wheelchair

ENNISKERRY

THE MEWS
Church Hill, Enniskerry, Co. Wicklow.
Tel. 01-863514 ££ Service 12.5%
Open 12.30-17.30/19.30-22.00 Tues-Sun.

The Mews is situated in the village of Enniskerry just below the Garda Station. An archway leads into the courtyard and the building looks quaint and inviting. Inside it is cosy with well-appointed tables and a pleasant outlook to a patio and garden. The open fire adds to the welcome and the overall impression is of 'a place one looks forward to visiting'.

Our reports were for lunch only: smoked trout pâté with home-made brown bread was a popular starter as was home-made soup. Fish featured in the main courses too. Our reporters tried baked trout, sole on the bone and roast sirloin of beef. Desserts included apple tart, fresh pineapple with Irish Mist, meringue and ice cream. The house wine was deemed very good.

Cooking was 'very good' and service was friendly and competent.

•*Drinks* wine licence •*Meals* lunch (AC + T d'H), dinner (AC + T d'H) •*Cards* all major

GLEN OF THE DOWNS

GLENVIEW HOTEL
Glen of the Downs, Co. Wicklow. (On Dublin-Wexford N11 road, 27km south of Dublin.)
Tel. 01-877600/877083 ££ Service nil
Open 12.30-14.15/18.00-21.15 weekdays, 12.30- 14.00/18.00-21.00 Sun. Closed two days at Christmas.

This hotel has an enviable location perched on a hill overlooking the Glen of the Downs, with beautiful grounds and the Sugarloaf mountain as a backdrop. The inside is tastefully decorated and spacious. Bar food is available in the evening and soup and sandwiches at lunch time, as well as the restaurant meals.

Reports dealt with both lunch and dinner in the restaurant. Potato and leek soup was a starter at lunch, with Wicklow ham to follow, and apple pie and ice cream for dessert. At dinner, after soup, pheasant was sampled, and fruit salad as well as apple pie were desserts. Red house wine was of good quality.

Cooking was very good, the food wholesome and appetising. Service was attentive and unobtrusive at dinner but a reporter who had lunch there found it 'prompt but clinical and detached'. £9.75 for the table d'hôte lunch seems somewhat excessive for ordinary lunch fare; dinner is relatively better value.

•*Drinks* full licence •*Meals* lunch (AC + T d'H), dinner (AC + T d'H), bar food •*Cards* American Express, Visa, Access, Eurocard, Airplus •*Cater for* children

LARAGH

WICKLOW HEATHER
Laragh, Co. Wicklow. (One mile from Glendalough.)
Tel. 0404-5157 £ *Service* nil
Open 09.00-21.00 daily. *Closed* 1 Nov-31 Mar.

This bungalow-style restaurant, on the Glendalough road, caters for tourists in the season. It has ample car-parking space, and is simply but attractively furnished. It provides a welcome compromise between the more expensive hotel meals on the one hand and afternoon tea/morning coffee catering on the other. There is a varied menu available all day — a plus if one's exploration of Glendalough does not finish at a conventional meal time. Adult portions may be divided between children.

Reporters who ate there had soup and fruit juice as starters, with chicken, roast beef, lamb chops, and grilled trout for main dishes, and apple tart, ice cream, and sherry trifle for dessert. Children in one party had chips, eggs and sausages. House wine was satisfactory.

Cooking was excellent, and service good.

•*Drinks* wine licence •*Meals* breakfast, tea, lunch (AC + T d'H), dinner (AC + T d'H), tourist menu 12.00-15.00/18.00-21.00 daily •*Cards* Visa, Diners, American Express •*Cater for* children, wheelchair

NEWTOWNMOUNTKENNEDY

HARVEY'S BISTRO
Newtownmountkennedy, Co. Wicklow.
Tel. 01-819203 ££ *Service* nil
Open 12.30-14.30 Tues-Sun. *Closed* 24 Dec-4 Jan.

Harvey's Bistro, serving lunch only, is located right in Newtownmountkennedy, but it is easy to miss the sign. It is just opposite the sharp right-hand bend at the top of the village as you travel towards Dublin. It is in a courtyard with clothing and gift shops. Its exterior is basic and honest, 'nothing much to look at from the outside'. One reporter said he wondered why he had bothered to stop there in the first place but, having done so, his comment was that the food was 'excellent'.

Salmon with cream cheese pâté, shrimps, scallops and white fish served in shells, and Harvey's fish pie were just a few of the dishes on offer. Desserts included raspberry pavlova, almond slices and plum tart with cream. Calvet Carte D'Or was requested from the wine list and was well cooled. Cooking was extremely good and service excellent.

•*Drinks* wine licence •*Meals* lunch (AC) •*Cards* none •*Cater for* children, wheelchair

RATHNEW

HUNTER'S HOTEL
Rathnew, Co. Wicklow. (On Greystones-Rathnew road;
turn off N.11 at Ashford or Rathnew.)
Tel. 0404-40106   ££   Service nil
Open 13.00-15.00/19.30-21.30 daily. Closed Christmas Day.

Hunter's Hotel is set in beautiful gardens on the banks of the River Vartry. The well-kept gardens provide not only flowers but vegetables and fruit for the hotel. Hunter's is an old coaching inn, and retains an old-world air. As it is a popular venue within easy reach of Dublin, it is advisable to check on reservations at busy times.

Reporters had both lunch and dinner there. At lunch, mushroom soup, smoked mackerel, and game terrine were starters, with fillet of plaice and roast lamb and beef as main dishes. Sliced melon and asparagus, celery soup, seafood cocktail, and smoked trout were starters at dinner; main dishes were pork steak, codling, and spring lamb. There was a good choice of desserts at both meals — vanilla ice cream with blackcurrants, honey and brandy ice cream, apple tart, and profiteroles were some of the choices. House wine was acceptable; as the hotel is licensed, there were other drinks available as one wished.

Cooking was excellent and service competent without being fussy.

•*Drinks* full licence •*Meals* lunch (T d'H), dinner (T d'H), breakfast (to non-residents) •*Cards* all major• *Cater for* children, wheelchair

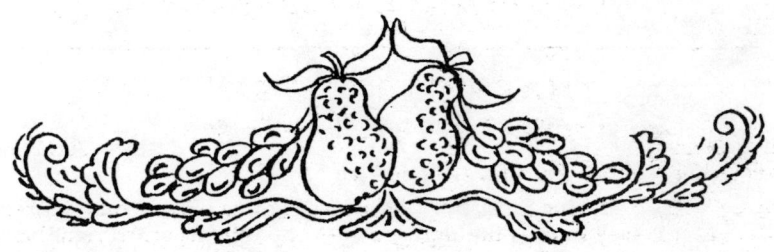

SOUTH EAST

Counties Carlow, Kilkenny, Waterford, Wexford

CARLOW HAS EVERY REASON to resent being thought of as a small agricultural county on the way to Kilkenny, Waterford, or Wexford. Carlow town occupies a pleasant site on the River Barrow, where you may walk along the banks and admire the Anglo-Norman castle. The valley of the Barrow affords some of the best scenery in the county, and there are paths along its banks, or those of the parallel Barrow Canal, in many places. Some of the loveliest spots on the river are at Clashganna, where there is a car park on the main road which allows you to look down at the waters and the old mill, and St. Mullin's, a little village with ancient churches. Borris, in the north of the county, is the ancestral home of the Mc Murrough-Kavanaghs. From there you can find a road which crosses the Blackstairs Mountains by way of Mount Leinster (easily distinguished since it is crowned by a TV mast) to Bunclody in County Wexford. A less spectacular but also less hair-raising road connects the two counties a little to the south through the Scullogue Gap.

It is not far from Borris to Graiguenamanagh, also on the Barrow in Co. Kilkenny. Here is the restored thirteenth-century Duiske Abbey, currently in use as a church again. Looking down on Graiguenamanagh is Brandon Hill; a climb to its 520m summit yields wide views across the Barrow valley to the Blackstairs. Kilkenny city is ancient and full of interest. St. Canice's Cathedral and round tower, Rothe House museum, and the Tholsel (Town Hall) are but some of the sights. On a height above the River Nore stands the historic Butler stronghold of Kilkenny Castle. It has recently been restored, and both the castle and its grounds are open to the public. A few miles from Kilkenny, on the road to Castlecomer, is the large Dunmore Cave, open to visitors, and signposted from the main road.

Waterford is another ancient city, originally settled by the Norsemen. Reginald's Tower, now a museum on the quay, is one of the Norse fortifications. Visitors may inspect the Waterford Crystal factory, which has revived the craft for which the city was famous in the eighteenth-century. Waterford has long had a flourishing shipping trade, the River Suir being tidal and navigable as far up as Fiddown Bridge, which, with its old toll house and wide span over the river, is worth looking at en route to Carrick-on-Suir. Waterford Harbour, the estuary where the waters of the Barrow, the Nore, and the Suir flow out to the sea, is not as well known as it should be for its scenic attractions. Cheekpoint is a picturesque little fishing village at the junction of the Suir and the Barrow. Also in this area, at the mouth of the estuary, is the resort of Dunmore East, and, not far away, the huge strands of Tramore. At the western end of the county is Ardmore with its round tower and strand; further inland is Lismore, with its imposing castle. From there a road leads over the Knockmealdown Mountains, across a gap known as the Vee, near Mount Melleray Monastery, giving sweeping views across Tipperary. The Comeragh Mountains, north of Dungarvan, have hidden 'hanging' valleys and lakes such as Coomshingaun.

From Passage East, on Waterford Harbour, a shuttle car ferry operates to Ballyhack on the Wexford shore. Near here are the ruins of Dunbrody Abbey, and, nearer to New Ross, Sliabh Coillte, with its John F. Kennedy Memorial Park. Duncannon, further down the estuary, has a splendid beach, as has Fethard-on-Sea, where the Normans landed at Baginbun. Kilmore Quay, a little fishing village and the nearest point to the Saltee Islands, has some thatched houses. Some of the best strands in Ireland are on the east coast of Wexford, from Carnsore Point, up through Rosslare, Curracloe, Blackwater, Courtown, and Ballymoney to Clone, just south of Arklow. Wexford town is of Norse origin, with narrow streets and Georgian houses down near the harbour. The Opera Festival, held here annually at the end of October, is internationally known. The wild-fowl reserve of the nearby sloblands on the Slaney estuary is a wintering area for migrant geese. There are fine ridge walks in the Blackstairs Mountains in the west of the county, but, because valuable agricultural land runs right up to the base of the hills, they are not as accessible as the neighbouring Wicklow Mountains.

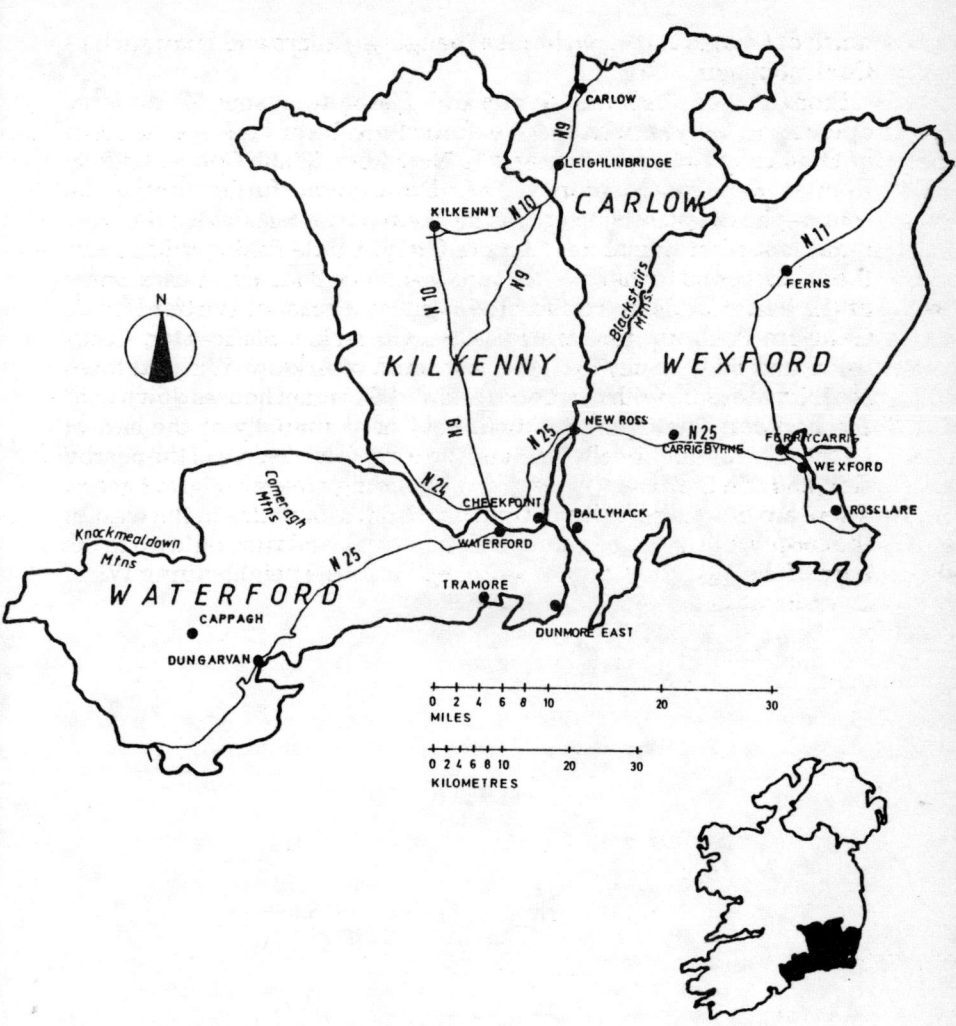

Co. Carlow

CARLOW TOWN

SEVEN OAKS HOTEL
Athy Road, Carlow.
Tel. 0503-31308   ££   Service nil
Open 12.30-14.30/18.00-21.30. *Closed* Christmas Day, Good Friday.

The exterior of this hotel is bright and well-kept. In the restaurant, tables are rather close together, but the place is comfortable. The atmosphere is welcoming and there is a general impression of care for the customer.

Our reporters had lunch and dinner there. Curried eggs, pâté, and prawn cocktail were among the starters; steak chasseur and corned beef were two of the main dishes. There was a good variety of vegetables. Fresh fruit, including strawberries in season, were the favourite desserts. House wine, Carlsberg, and Guinness were all commended.

Cooking was rated very good — 'second to none', 'cooked as requested'. The only reservation was about the curried eggs, considered to be lacking in spice.

•*Drinks* full licence •*Meals* lunch (AC + T d'H), dinner (AC + T d'H) •*Cards* Access, Visa, Diners, American Express •*Cater for* children

LEIGHLINBRIDGE

THE LORD BAGENAL INN
Leighlinbridge, Co.Carlow. (In Leighlinbridge village, just off Dublin-Carlow-Kilkenny road — signposted.)
Tel. 0503-21668   ££   Service nil
Open 12.30-22.30 weekdays, 12.30-21.00 Sun. *Closed* Christmas Day.

This is a substantial building beside the River Barrow, with an ample car park and a children's playground, overlooked from the dining-room. The interior is warm and tastefully decorated in an old-world style. The restaurant uses locally grown vegetables and buys meat from a local butcher. It has a tank for keeping shellfish alive until they are ordered for a meal. Reporters recommended The Lord Bagenal for value in promptly-served good food for lunch. Starters for dinner included French onion soup, mussels, smoked salmon, and egg mayonnaise. Among the main courses on offer were roast duck, tournedos steak, escalopes of pork, and seafood wrapped in tinfoil. Some of the desserts chosen were pavlova, lemon meringue, Black Forest gâteau, and apple tart. There was a good selection of local cheeses. House wine at £6.95 a bottle was very acceptable. Cooking was of a high standard. Service was friendly and prompt, without rushing the customer.

•*Drinks* full licence •*Meals* lunch (bar weekdays, T d'H Sun), dinner (AC + T d'H) •*Cards* Visa, Diners

Co. Kilkenny

KILKENNY CITY

LACKEN HOUSE
Dublin Road, Kilkenny. (In the city, at start of N10 to Carlow.)
Tel. 056-61085/65611 ££ *Service* 10%
Open 19.00-22.30 Tues-Sat. *Closed* one week at Christmas.

This restaurant is in the basement of an old Georgian house on the Carlow road, just under one km from the town centre. It is well decorated and comfortably furnished with well-spaced tables. The atmosphere is very welcoming, both on arrival and throughout meals. It serves evening dinner only, using local produce, including fish caught in the River Nore. Some of the starters were innovative. Nettle and parsley soup was chosen one evening by a reporter who had seen a young trainee chef picking fresh young nettles in a nearby field. Smoked venison was another slightly unusual starter. Main courses included duck and caramel sauce, suprême of fish in chive sauce, steak, and pan-fried, breaded chicken. Terrine of chocolate and gratin of fresh fruit were sampled as desserts. Wine was pronounced good but expensive — 'hard to find a bottle under £15'.

Cooking and presentation were very good. One person said that it was 'obvious that time was spent in preparing fresh food in a creative manner'. Service was at all times attentive without being intrusive.

•*Drinks* full licence •*Meals* dinner (AC + T d'H) •*Cards* American Express, Visa, Diners, Access

LANGTON'S RESTAURANT/BAR
69, John Street, Kilkenny.
Tel. 056-21728 £ *Service* nil
Open 10.30-22.00 weekdays, 12.30-14.00 Sun. *Closed* Christmas Day, Good Friday.

This pub-cum-restaurant is in the city centre. Kilkenny being a mediaeval city, parking can be a problem during the working day. The exterior of Langton's is refurbished in a traditional style. Inside is well decorated, with a 'beautifully designed' dining-room, and a rear extension opening onto a walled garden. Meals taken ranged from a snack through lunch to full evening dinner, and earned general approval. Poached salmon, roast beef, lamb, pork, and chicken Cordon Bleu were among the main courses with home-made ice cream and apple tart for desserts. Coffee was excellent. Despite being in a pub, few of our reporters had alcohol with their meal, but the house wine and beer were judged good by those who did.

Cooking and presentation were good; service friendly, efficient, and well-supervised.

•*Drinks* full licence •*Meals* lunch (AC), dinner (AC + T d'H), **tourist menu 15.30-22.00 throughout the year.**

NEW PARK HOTEL
Castlecomer Road, Kilkenny

Tel. 056-22122 ££ *Service* 10%
Open restaurant 12.30-14.30/18.30-21.30 daily, grill room 12.00-23.00 daily. *Closed* varying periods in January and February.

This is a large hotel in its own grounds, with a large car park, about 1.5km from the city centre on the Castlecomer road. It is well signposted in the city. It has a comfortable, relaxed atmosphere, and is well kept. There is a grill-room and a more expensive dining-room, and snack lunches are also served.

Our reporters ate in the dining-room and in the grill room, and found them both good. Starters in the restaurant included avocado, melon, and home-made mushroom soup; main dishes were roast beef, deep fried prawns, and sole on the bone. Plaice and chips were chosen in the grill room. Among the desserts were lemon cheesecake and fresh fruit salad. House wine was good. Cooking and presentation were excellent; food was served piping hot. The service was attentive from friendly waiters.

•*Drinks* full licence •*Meals* breakfast, lunch (AC + T d'H), dinner (AC + T d'H), tourist menu for tour groups, May-September inclusive (12.30-23.00) •*Cards* Access, Visa, Diners, American Express •*Cater for* children, wheelchair

Co. Waterford

CAPPAGH

WHITECHURCH HOUSE HOTEL
Cappagh, Co. Waterford. (5.5km outside Cappagh, 12km from Dungarvan.)
Tel. 058-68182 ££ *Service* nil
Open 19.00-21.30 Mon-Sat, 12.30-15.30 Sun.

This is a country mansion converted into a hotel. It serves evening dinner on weekdays and lunch on Sundays. It has its own vegetable and fruit gardens. Reports related to lunch and dinner. Tomato soup was a starter at lunch; at dinner, there were pâté, mushroom soup, egg mayonnaise, and melon in port. Roast lamb must be very good at Whitechurch House — it was chosen from six dishes at both lunch and dinner by all reporters. A wide selection of desserts, included meringue, lemon mousse, and apple tart. Red and white wines were both pleasant. Cooking was excellent, service professional and friendly. In spite of two sittings for lunch, people did not feel rushed. 'Good value for money' was the general verdict.

•*Drinks* full licence •*Meals* Sunday lunch (AC + T d'H), dinner (AC + T d'H) •*Cards* Visa •*Cater for* children

CHEEKPOINT

THE JOLLY SAILOR
West End, Cheekpoint, Co. Waterford.
Tel. 051-82227 ££ *Service* nil
Open 12.00-23.00 daily (May-Sept); 18.00-23.00 daily (Oct-Apr). *Closed* January and February, Christmas Day.

Its surroundings alone would sell this restaurant. It is a two-storey Georgian house with a verandah, on the banks of the Suir near where it joins the Barrow to flow out to the sea. Dinner is served all year round, lunch from May to September inclusive. Seafood is, naturally, a speciality; and at dinner a comprehensive salad bar is included in the price of the meal. There is a special-price meal available every evening. In addition to salads, our reporters, who all had dinner, had smoked salmon and prawn cocktail as starters, with fillet steak and baked fresh salmon as main dishes. Desserts included Black Forest gâteau and strawberry mousse. House white wine was very good. Cooking was highly praised and service good. All considered, the Jolly Sailor has more to offer than the view.

•*Drinks* full licence •*Meals* lunch (AC), dinner (AC), tourist menu 18.00-23.00 •*Cards* Visa, Access •*Cater for* children over 10, wheelchair (not to toilets)

DUNGARVAN

MERRY'S
Lower Main Street, Dungarvan, Co. Waterford.
Tel. 058-41974/42818 ££ *Service* nil
Open 12.00-15.00/18.00-22.00, bar food 10.00-22.00 daily. *Closed* Good Friday, two days at Christmas.

This restaurant is in an old merchant's premises, and is quite small inside, where one can still see the drawers where loose tea and coffee were formerly kept. One person remarked that the 'very quaint and homely' impression left her 'totally unprepared for an elaborate menu'. A man who has often eaten there says that there is always an excellent menu.

All our reporters had lunch there. Home-made potato and leek soup was rich in flavour, roast beef and crab Newburg very good. Vegetables were 'just right'. Black Forest gâteau, and strawberries, were two of the sweets chosen. Although Merry's is fully licensed, coffee and iced water were the only drinks chosen.

The cooking was 'top class'. Service was excellent. One reporter mentioned specially the kind consideration shown to her elderly father and children.

•*Drinks* full licence •*Meals* lunch (AC), dinner (AC), bar food •*Cards* Access, Visa, Diners •*Cater for* children, wheelchair (not to toilets)

DUNMORE EAST

CANDLELIGHT INN
Dunmore East, Co. Waterford.

Tel. 051-83215/83239 ££ Service nil
Open 13.00-14.00 1 Apr-30 Sept, 18.00-22.00 1 Feb-31 Dec. *Closed* Christmas Day, month of January.

This restaurant is part of a small hotel, one of the attractions of which (in season) is an outdoor heated swimming pool. It is in the village, and its surroundings are pleasant. The dining room gives a welcoming impression, with a lighted candle on each table.

All our reporters had dinner there. As befits its location in the long-established fishing port of Dunmore East, the restaurant specialises in seafood; starters were crabs' claws and lobster bisque. Main dishes were sole, turbot, and salmon. Portions were not too large, more being provided on request. 'Light, home-made desserts with flavour' included pavlova, orange jelly, and lemon cheesecake. The house wine was good; there was also a full range of drinks available from the bar. Cooking and presentation were excellent, service friendly and attentive.

•*Drinks* full licence •*Meals* lunch (T d'H), dinner (AC + T d'H), tourist menu 13.00-14.00/18.00-19.30, 1 Apr-30 Sept •*Cards* Access, Visa, American Express

THE SHIP
Dunmore East, Co. Waterford.

Tel. 051-83141/83144 ££ Service nil
Open 12.30-14.30 daily, Jun-Aug, 18.00-23.00 daily throughout year. *Closed* five days at Christmas.

This pub-cum-restaurant in upper Dunmore overlooks the bay. The decor has a pleasant flavour of ships and fishing. Meals are taken at pub tables, a drawback being that seating may become uncomfortable after a while. The atmosphere is relaxed and friendly. As appropriate to its situation, the restaurant specialises in seafood. Fish, therefore, predominates in reports on both lunch and dinner. John Dory, French fries, and home-made ice cream were chosen for lunch. At dinner, starters were garlic mushrooms, and smoked salmon in pastry; main dishes were sole, monkfish, turbot, brill, and roast lamb. There were, of course, desserts available, but not sampled by our reporters. House wine was 'decent', and there was a wide range of drinks in the pub. Cooking and presentation were excellent, and service satisfactory.

•*Drinks* full licence•*Meals* lunch(AC), dinner (AC) •*Cards* Visa, Access •*Cater for* children

STRAND INN

Dunmore East, Co. Waterford. (In the lower village, overlooking the bay.)
Tel. 051-83174 ££ Service nil
Open 13.00-14.30 bar food, 19.00-22.00. Closed October to Easter.

This bistro-type restaurant serves a bar lunch and an evening dinner. It is near the boat slip in the lower village. Some of our reporters thought the outside unimpressive, but inside it has been recently redecorated, and a bay window commands a lovely view across the sea to the Wexford coast. One reporter, who otherwise obviously enjoyed her visit, thought the tables too small and close together. The atmosphere is very pleasant. Emphasis is on home produce; herbs and vegetables are grown in the garden, fish landed on the local pier.

All reporters had dinner there. A good range of starters offered potato and sorrel soup, prawn cocktail and mushrooms. Steak, salmon, and turbot figured among the main dishes. Almond cream meringue was an unusual dessert.

The house wine at £7.50 a bottle was satisfactory, Gaelic coffee was good. Our reporters were pleased with the service.

•*Drinks* full licence •*Meals* lunch (bar food), dinner (AC), tourist menu 18.45-20.00 •*Cards* Access, Visa •*Cater for* children (up to 20.00), wheelchair

TRAMORE

PINE ROOMS

Turkey Road, Tramore, Co. Waterford. (Main Waterford-Tramore road.)
Tel. 051-81686 ££ Service nil
Open 12.00-14.30 tourist season, 17.30-22.30 year round. Closed week at Christmas, month of February, Sun-Tues in January.

This restaurant is in a converted two-storey-over-basement house not far from the central car park, promenade, and tourist office. The interior is nicely decorated with pine furniture and sanded floors. There is no reception area — one goes straight to a table, if there is one free. Our reporters felt that the proprietor and staff took pleasure in pleasing customers. The restaurant serves dinner all year round, lunch in summer.

All our reporters had dinner. For starters, they chose garlic mushrooms, 'Molly Malone' cockles and mussels, melon, and smoked salmon platter. Steak (peppered, in garlic butter) was by far the most popular main dish, but roast pheasant and poached salmon were also chosen. There was a good selection of vegetables — broccoli, carrots, cauliflower, and turnips. Side salads were also served. Desserts included chocolate mousse, trifle, and fresh fruit salad. The house wine was sound. Cooking was highly commended; steaks were cooked to the degree ordered, vegetables *al dente*; the meals were well presented, tasty, and appetising. Service was pleasant, efficient, and personally supervised by the proprietor.

•*Drinks* wine licence •*Meals* lunch (AC + T d'H Sun), dinner (AC) •*Cards* Visa

WATERFORD CITY

GRANVILLE HOTEL
Meagher's Quay, Waterford.

Tel. 051-55111 ££ *Service* nil
Open 07.30-22.30. *Closed* two days at Christmas.

The Tapestry Room Restaurant in this hotel is, as its name implies, attractively decorated with tapestries on the wall. Food is also served in the Bianconi Grill.

Reports dealt with both lunch and dinner. Seafood pancakes as a starter were very substantial. Stuffed lamb ('nicely cooked'), roast beef and sirloin steak were some of the main dishes selected. The absence of fresh fruit from the desserts in the month of July was lamented, but pavlova and Black Forest gâteau were chosen.

House wine was average, and coffee very good. Cooking was good, service helpful and friendly.

•*Drinks* full licence •*Meals* breakfast, lunch (AC + T d'H), dinner (AC + T d'H), tourist menu 12.30- 14.30 (1 Apr-31 Oct) •*Cards* all major

HAPPY GARDEN CHINESE RESTAURANT
53, High Street, Waterford.

Tel. 051-55640 ££ *Service* 10%
Open 12.30-14.30/17.30-24.00 weekdays, 17.00-24.00 Sun. *Closed* Christmas Day, Chinese New Year (6-8 February).

This is a Chinese restaurant, small and unassuming on the outside; inside, it is newly refurbished, open plan with alcoves, with Chinese decor. In addition to a wide range of Chinese food, it serves a selection of European dishes. Fish is obtained daily from nearby Dunmore East.

All our reporters were there for an evening meal, and as usual in a Chinese restaurant, the number of courses varied with the number in a party. Chicken and corn soup, spring rolls, and spare ribs were some of the starters. Sweet and sour pork, duck in blackbean sauce, beef in chili sauce, and chicken Maryland were among the main dishes. Desserts chosen were all based on ice cream, but apple tart and fritters were also on offer. Piesporter wine was good; coffee and Chinese tea were also chosen.

Cooking was excellent; service efficient and courteous.

•*Drink* wine licence •*Meals* lunch (AC), dinner (AC + T d'H) •*Cards* Visa, Access •*Cater for* children, wheelchair

THE JADE PALACE
3, The Mall, Waterford.
Tel. 051-55611/55612 ££ Service 10% (dinner only)
Open 12.30-14.30 Mon-Fri, 17.30-24.00 daily.

This is a Chinese restaurant, offering Cantonese and Sichuan cuisine, situated near the Reginald Tower. It is decorated in delicate Chinese style, and is clean and comfortable, with a friendly relaxed atmosphere. Our reporters had dinner there. Starters chosen were prawns and spare ribs, with sweet and sour chicken, and steak 'with an array of sauces' as main dishes. The desserts were fruit cocktail, and banana fritters with ice cream. Wine chosen from the wine list was very good, but two people thought that the prices were high; one man was charged £27 for a bottle of Chablis. Cooking was good, service efficient and friendly. The only reservation that reporters had about this restaurant was that for standard Chinese meals it was somewhat dear.

•*Drinks* full licence •*Meals* lunch (AC + T d'H), dinner (AC + T d'H) •*Cards* all major

Co. Wexford

BALLYHACK

NEPTUNE RESTAURANT
Ballyhack, Co. Wexford. (In Ballyhack village, on Waterford estuary, 19km from New Ross.)
Tel. 051-89284 ££ Service nil
Open 12.30-15.00/18.00-21.30 Tues-Sat. Closed 1-16 Oct, 23 Dec-17 Mar.

This is a renovated old two-storey school house overlooking the quay and terminus of the car-ferry from Passage East. It has a conservatory in which coffee and snacks are served on a limited basis. The restaurant, nicely refurbished, commands a view of the water. Home-grown herbs and local salmon and shell-fish, especially hot crab dishes, are specialities. Reports dealt with dinner: hot crab and fish soup for starters, with poached salmon and monkfish for main dishes. The selection of vegetables was excellent. Apple tart and home-made ice cream were among the desserts

Cooking received praise — 'an excellent meal throughout'. House wine at around £7.50 a bottle was satisfactory; Sancerre was £17 a bottle. Service was competent.

•*Drinks* wine licence •*Meals* lunch (AC + T d'H), dinner (AC + T d'H), tourist menu (evenings only), vegetarian salads available •*Cards* all major

FERNS

BUTTLE ARMS
Ferns, Co. Wexford.
Tel. 054-66490 ££ Service 10%
Open 12.00-14.00 daily, 18.00-21.30 weekdays.

This is a renovated pub-cum-restaurant serving lunch and dinner. Its old-world interior has a warm and homely air. The restaurant serves home-grown vegetables only.

Reports covered both lunch and dinner. Thick vegetable soup and egg mayonnaise were starters, and turkey and ham, and roast beef — 'a very large helping' — the main courses. Banana split was chosen for dessert. None of our reporters had a drink with their meal, but the establishment is, of course, fully licensed. Cooking was very good, service helpful.

•*Drinks* full licence •*Meals* lunch (T d'H), dinner (T d'H) •*Cards* Access, Visa •*Cater for* children, wheelchair

FERRYCARRIG

FERRYCARRIG HOTEL
Ferrycarrig, Co. Wexford. (On Wexford-Dublin road, 5km north of Wexford town.)
Tel. 053-22999 £££ Service nil
Open 12.30-14.30/19.00-21.30.

Ferrycarrig Hotel commands a view of the Slaney estuary. Apart from the landscaped ground, the outside is not very beautiful, but the interior, with a newly-added conservatory, gives 'a feeling of spaciousness and opulence'. The restaurant uses home produce, fresh seafood, and Irish cheeses. All reports concerned dinner, and a wide variety of food was sampled. 'Outstanding' sea-food chowder, sea-food pâté, and melon in port, were some of the starters. Wiener schnitzel, entrecôte steak, roast duck, and chicken Kiev were among the main dishes. Some of the desserts were profiteroles, Irish Mist soufflé, and Bailey's mousse. The only criticism of cooking, otherwise judged very good indeed, was that the vegetables were 'disappointing'. House wine was thought to be good at £8.50 a bottle.

All our reporters were satisfied with value, their meals costing just over £16 a head.

•*Drinks* full licence •*Meals* breakfast, lunch (AC + T d'H), dinner (AC + T d'H), snacks in bar all day •*Cards* all major •*Cater for* wheelchair (not to toilets)

OAK TAVERN
Ferrycarrig, Co. Wexford.

Tel. 053-22138　　　　　　££　　　　　　　　　Service 10%
Open 10.30-23.30

This bar-cum-restaurant has an old-world exterior and an attractive setting on the banks of the Slaney.

Reporters had both lunch and dinner there. Home-made pâté and garlic mussels were chosen as starters. Fish bake (a nicely arranged variety of prawns and other shellfish), lobster, salmon, and peppered steak were some of the main courses; burgers and chips were provided for children at lunch.

Crêpes with ice cream and chocolate sauce was one dessert at dinner; at lunch, the choice of desserts was deemed 'unexciting'. The house wine was good. There was a small but excellent selection of wines; other drinks were selected from the bar. Cooking was excellent and imaginative, service friendly and attentive.

•*Drinks* full licence •*Meals* lunch (AC + T d'H), dinner (AC + T d'H), tourist menu 12.30-14.30/19.00-20.00 throughout the year •*Cards* Access, Visa, Diners •*Cater for* children

NEWBAWN

CEDAR LODGE
Carrigbyrne, Newbawn, Co. Wexford. (19km west of Wexford, on Wexford-Waterford N25 road.)

Tel. 051-28386/28436　　　　£££　　　　　　　Service nil
Open 12.30-14.00/18.30-21.00. Closed 23 December-1 February.

This restaurant is a large dormer-type bungalow with adequate parking space. Inside, it is very pleasant and comfortable; there is an enormous fireplace in the dining-room, and a soft background of light music. 'One has the impression of arriving at a friendly house.' Organically grown vegetables, Slaney salmon, and Carrigbyrne cheese are used.

Our reporters, who all had dinner, chose avocado with prawns and crab chowder among their starters. Roast duck with orange sauce, roast pheasant, and bass with Pernod sauce were some of the main dishes. Peppermint ice cream and cranberry mousse were two of the desserts.

The cooking was in general highly praised — 'first class', 'every choice is freshly cooked'. The house wine was considered very good value at £7.90 a bottle.

A similarity in the names might lead to the confusion of this hotel with Casey's Cedars Hotel, Rosslare. They are not the same place.

•*Drinks* full licence •*Meals* lunch (AC + T d'H), dinner (AC + T d'H), salads in lounge 11.00-18.00 •*Cards* Access, Visa •*Cater for* children (up to 20.00), wheelchair

NEW ROSS

THE OLD RECTORY
Rosbercon, New Ross, Co. Wexford.

Tel. 051-21719   ££   *Service* nil
Open 12.30-14.00/18.30-21.45 daily. *Closed* four days at Christmas.

This old country house is just over the bridge from the main part of the town, overlooking the River Barrow. (There are other restaurants with the same name throughout the country, these old rectories having had to be sold off as they were too large for a modern clergyman's residence.) This one is set in scenic grounds, and is very well maintained. It is tastefully decorated, with antique furniture. It has 'a friendly, warm atmosphere'. It specialises in home-made bread and pastry, and buys fresh fish daily; herbs are grown in the garden.

Both lunch and dinner were sampled here. Stuffed mushrooms, home-made pâté, and seafood chowder were some starters chosen; roast lamb with home-made mint sauce, sirloin steak, veal à l'orange, and grilled Dover sole among the main dishes. At dinner, there was a dessert trolley, from which cheesecake, fresh fruit salad, and profiteroles were chosen.

Cooking was generally highly commended, apart from the sole, which tasted as if it had been fried, not grilled. Coffee was 'genuine', and the Sauvignon Blanc 'fine for house wine'.

Service was 'a bit slow to start', otherwise good. One reporter summed up her experience as 'nice for a meal in that price range'.

•*Drinks* full licence •*Meals* breakfast, lunch (AC), dinner (AC), snacks in lounge all day, tourist menu •*Cards* Access, Visa, Diners •*Cater for* children up until 20.00, wheelchair, non-smokers

ROSSLARE HARBOUR

HARBOUR LODGE
Wexford Road, Rosslare Harbour, Co. Wexford.

Tel. 053-33216   £   *Service* nil
Open 06.00-23.00. *Closed* three days at Christmas.

This is one of the buildings on the clifftop above Rosslare Harbour. It deserves mention for providing welcome facilities for ferry passengers who might not wish to patronise any of the 'plusher' hotels near by. It is a self-service restaurant in an unpretentious building, and as it has well-spaced tables it can accommodate car passengers' small children and back packers' rucksacks alike. Added to that, it is open almost round the clock. The proximity of a Bureau de Change and petrol station add to its advantages for the traveller.

Our reporters found that full hot meals were available, as well as a variety of salads and desserts. Food was good and well flavoured. Service was friendly and efficient.

•*Drinks* wine licence •*Meals* breakfast, lunch (AC), dinner (AC), tourist menu 12.30-21.00 (1 June-30 Sept) •*Cards* Access, Visa •*Cater for* children

WEXFORD TOWN

CHAN'S CHINESE RESTAURANT
90, North Main Street, Wexford.
Tel. 053-22356   ££   *Service* 10%
Open 12.30-14.15/17.30-24.00 weekdays, 13.00- 15.00/17.30-24.00 Sun.

This Chinese restaurant is well maintained, with a relaxing atmosphere. It has a tropical fish aquarium, and soft music is played. Szechuan and Cantonese cooking are on offer.

Reports featured dinner. Vegetable soup, well flavoured chicken Maryland, and sweet and sour pork were among the selections, with fruit cocktail as a dessert. The restaurant has a wine licence, but our reporters did not have any. Cooking was good in the main, although pork was rather tough. Service was satisfactory.

•*Drinks* wine licence •*Meals* lunch (T d'H), dinner (AC + T d'H) •*Cards* Access, Visa

THE GRANARY
West Gate, Wexford. (On the edge of Wexford town, on Waterford N25 road, five minutes' walk from main street.)
Tel. 053-23935   ££   *Service* 10%
Open 12.30-14.30 Mon-Fri, 17.30-22.30 Mon-Sat. *Closed* Immediate Christmas period.

This is an old converted corn store, near the County Council offices. It has a cosy and inviting interior, with wooden beams on the ceilings, and a display of old agricultural tools. The dining area is good for intimate dining. The restaurant specialises in seafood, home-made pâté, and a wide choice of home-made desserts.

Melon wedges, prawn cocktail, corn on the cob, and mussels in garlic were chosen by our reporters, who all took dinner there. Main courses included lobster and chicken flambé, beef Wellington, sirloin steak. Five various desserts from the sweet trolley were voted excellent by one party.

Both red and white house wine met with approval. The cooking was good, especially of main course dishes and vegetables. Service was prompt and pleasant.

•*Drinks* full licence •*Meals* lunch (AC in bar), dinner (AC), pub snacks •*Cards* Access, Visa •*Cater for* children

ROBERTINO'S
19, South Main Street, Wexford.

Tel. 053-23334 £ *Service* nil
Open 10.00-18.00 weekdays, 19.00-00.30 daily. *Closed* two days at Christmas, New Year's Eve.

With its Opera, Wexford has to have an Italian restaurant. Robertino's is near Dunnes' Stores, and, with an aluminium frontage, could be mistaken for a fast-food outlet. Inside it is pleasantly lit, clean, with well-placed seating to ensure privacy, and, usually, soft classical music playing.

Pizzas and lasagne predominated in our reporters' choices, with hot garlic bread as a starter and various ice creams as desserts. The garlic bread was fresh, well seasoned, and piping hot. Chips were available. House wine at £4 for a half bottle was very good. Service was 'mannerly, and genuinely interested in customers' needs'.

•*Drinks* wine licence •*Meals* lunch (AC), dinner (AC) •*Cards* Access, Visa •*Cater for* children, wheelchair

CORK CITY
AND
COUNTY

CORK CITY CAN BE CONFUSING to the stranger, largely because of the way in which the River Lee divides into two channels, so that you seem to be constantly crossing and re-crossing water. The Lee, however, adds greatly to the city, with its promenades such as the Mardyke along its banks. Among the many striking buildings in Cork are the imposing Court House, St. Finbarr's Cathedral, and University College. An outstanding example of modern church architecture is the Church of Christ the King at Turner's Cross. The Bells of Shandon may be heard from St. Ann's Church. Nearby Blarney Street was the scene of Frank O'Connor's childhood, vividly described in his book *An Only Child*. In Emmet Place, not far from Patrick Street, is the Crawford Municipal Art Gallery, and near there, too, is the Cork Opera House.

Within easy reach of Cork is the Fota Island Wildlife Park, on the way out to Cobh, where the tall elegant buildings on the waterfront recall its days of glory as port of call for transatlantic liners, and its importance as a naval base on Cork Harbour. Crosshaven, on the western side of the harbour, is a well-known seaside resort and yachting base.

South-west of Cork are a series of bays and inlets, each one worth exploring. Kinsale, with its narrow streets, ancient buildings, and ruined Charles Fort looking down on the town, is remembered as the scene of the Battle of Kinsale in 1601, when the surrender of the Spanish invading forces finally turned the tide against the Irish whom they had come to help. Today's Kinsale is well known as a pleasure port, particularly for deep-sea fishing, and for its restaurants, some of which feature in this Guide. Further west again, on the shores of Courtmacsherry Bay, are the ruins of Timoleague Abbey. Clonakilty with its sheltered Inchydoney strand, the picturesque little village of Glandore, Baltimore with its boat service to Sherkin and Clear Islands, should not be missed. Mizen Head, Ireland's most southerly point, is at the tip of a peninsula reached by way of Ballydehob and Schull. Bantry Bay is beautiful, with its backdrop of mountains, and the Italian gardens of Garnish Island near Glengarriff. It is well worth your while penetrating to the extreme western limit of the county by going out from Glengarriff through Castletownbere to where the novel transport of a cable car links Dursey Island to the mainland. The scenic route around the Bere Peninsula, the Ring of Béara, embraces some of the loveliest scenery in Ireland. The long disused copper-mines near Allihies and Eyeries inspired Daphne du Maurier's *Hungry Hill*.

Inland from the Bantry-Glengarriff road, through the stern Pass of Keimaneigh, the subject of the early nineteenth-century Irish song, 'Cath Chéim an Fhéidh', you reach the Forest Park of Gougane Barra, with its picnic sites, waterfall, and tiny lake with its ancient oratory. Lough Allua, close by, is within the Cork Gaeltacht area of Ballingeary; between there and Ballyvourney is the small village of Cúil Aodha (Coolea), where Séan O Riada did so much for the revival of Irish music, and where the work is now carried on by his son Peadar.

East Cork is a much gentler region (geographically) than the western part of the county. Youghal, with its long sandy beach, retains part of the old town walls, and has a large clock-tower arching across one of the main streets. Sir Walter Raleigh lived here at Myrtle Grove, where he allegedly planted Ireland's first potatoes. Youghal is on the estuary of the Blackwater; all the Blackwater valley is lovely, but access to the river is not very easy because in many parts it flows through private land. Fermoy and Mallow are both on the river. Thomas Davis, the founder of the Young Ireland movement, was born at Mallow, and the novelist Anthony Trollope was stationed there as a postal surveyor. Doneraile, near Mallow, was the home of Canon Sheehan, whose novels such as *Glenanaar* and *My New Curate* enjoyed great popularity earlier in this century.

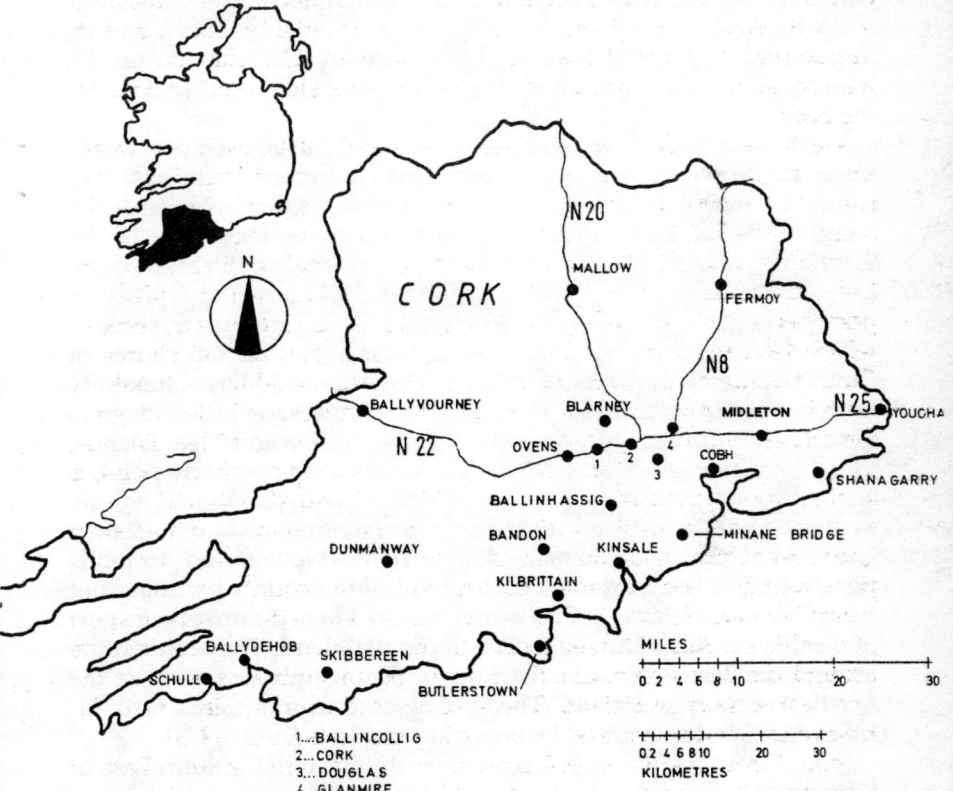

Cork City

AMBASSADOR RESTAURANT
3, Cook Street, Cork.
Tel. 021-273261 ££ Service 10%
Open 17.30-00.30 daily. Closed two days at Christmas, Good Friday.

This is a Chinese restaurant serving dinner only. It has a wooden front, not specifically Chinese; inside it is a well-appointed restaurant, with very clean tablecloths. The cooking is Cantonese.

In the manner of Chinese restaurants, the number of dishes sampled varied with the size of the party. Starters included crab and sweetcorn soup, barbecued spare ribs, prawns with ginger and spring onions, and corn on the cob soup with prawn crackers. Among the main dishes were a combination of roast duck, king prawns and beef, sweet and sour pork, chicken in orange sauce, and beef with green peppers in blackbean sauce. Only one party had dessert, banana splits and fresh fruit salad — 'nothing exceptional'. Niersteiner and Muscadet were the wines, deemed satisfactory, but in the case of one party who had Muscadet, thought expensive at over £8 a bottle.

All reporters were pleased with the cooking, but one (who otherwise had high praise for it) made the reservation that the roast duck in a combination meal for four was fatty and greasy.

Service was friendly and helpful.

•*Drinks* wine licence •*Meals* dinner (AC), •*Cards* Visa, Access, Diners, American Express

ARBUTUS LODGE RESTAURANT
Montenotte, Cork. (Near St. Luke's Cross.)
Tel. 021-501237 £££ Service nil
Open breakfast 08.00-10.00, lunch 13.00-14.00, dinner 19.00-21.30. Closed 24-29 December.

This assessment and details relate to the main hotel restaurant; food is also available in the bar, 12.30- 15.00.

Arbutus Lodge, one of Ireland's leading restaurants, is set in lovely grounds on a height overlooking the River Lee. The house is a solid Victorian building. Inside, it is furnished with period furniture and displays many modern Irish paintings. The table-ware is monogrammed, and linen table-cloths and napkins have the words Arbutus Lodge woven into their design. This elegance, which one might imagine as daunting, goes hand in hand with a welcoming, "non-stuffy" atmosphere — 'unmistakeably Irish', one reporter put it. Ninety per cent of produce used in the restaurant is specially raised for it, or grown or caught locally.

Reporters had both lunch and dinner there, from an à la carte menu. Starters were melon and Muscat, and mushroom soup served hot in a heated bowl, with brown bread. For lunch, bacon and cabbage was one dish chosen; this consisted of thick pieces of bacon served on a bed of crisply-cooked cabbage. Another was bass flavoured with basil and tomato. For dinner, roast pheasant was selected. All these dishes were accompanied by an assortment of nicely cooked vegetables. Desserts included fresh pineapple, home-made ice cream — 'lovely texture and flavour' — and Hawaian cake (sponge topped with passion fruit).

Muscadet wine — 'very high quality from an enormous wine list' — was drunk with dinner. Cooking was rated as excellent and 'superb' and service was very good. Of interest is a 'tasting menu', not sampled by any of our reporters, but available for groups of people. It consisted of eight or nine courses at £25 a head.

It is expensive to eat at Arbutus Lodge but one is paying for 'old world luxury with superb food', as somebody who had dinner there described it. One reporter, struck by 'the friendly atmosphere in a hotel with such a prestigious reputation', said that 'one would like to go back, especially if entertaining people from other countries.'

•*Drinks* full licence •*Meals* breakfast, lunch (AC + T d'H), dinner(AC + T d'H) •*Cards* Visa, Access, American Express, Diners, Airplus •*Cater for* children

THE BARN RESTAURANT

Lotamore, Glanmire, Co. Cork. (Address may be also given as Mayfield.)
Tel. 021-866211 £££ *Service* nil
Open 19.00-24.00 Mon-Sat,12.30-15.00/19.00-24.00 Sun. *Closed* Good Friday.

This is a bungalow-style building with a spacious car park, and it looks inviting inside, with an open fire and a warm welcome.

All our reporters had dinner there. From the number of reports received, The Barn seems to be a very popular venue for Cork people. Starters included carrot and apple soup, stuffed mushrooms, smoked salmon, avocado, and cream of vegetable soup. The favourite main dish was fillet (or Gaelic) steak; chicken, veal, plaice, and trout were also selected. Helpings were generous. Mille-feuille, pavlova, and profiteroles were among the desserts. The house wine was found to be satisfactory, and the Blue Nun good. Two people, however, lamented the lack of draught beer.

Cooking was rated excellent — 'everything done to the correct requirement'. Service was prompt and pleasant; there was no undue delay between courses, but nobody felt rushed. One reporter wistfully remarked: 'If we could go there every week, we would.'

•*Drinks* full licence •*Meals* dinner (AC + T d'H), Sunday lunch (T d'H)

BULLY'S
40, Paul Street, Cork

Tel. 021-27355 £ *Service* nil
Open 12.00-23.30 (not lunch-time Sun). *Closed* Christmas and New Year's Day, Good Friday.

This city centre restaurant serves mainly Italian food, specialising in pizzas, pasta, and grills. It has a simple white-painted shop-front; inside, it is a long narrow room, with white walls and a tiled floor, very clean. It is bright and cheerful, with a 'buzz', but some people might find the music a bit loud.

Pizzas, lasagne, and Sicilian chicken were reporters' selections, at an evening meal. Cooking was good, but the quality of pizzas could vary from night to night. House red wine was acceptable. Service was fast and efficient
•*Drinks* wine licence •*Meals* lunch (AC only), dinner (AC only), tourist menu in summer 17.00-19.30 •*Cater for* children

CRAWFORD GALLERY CAFE
Emmet Place, Cork.

Tel. 021-274415 ££ *Service* nil
Open 12.00-14.30 except Sun/18.30-21.30 Wed-Fri. *Closed* one week at Christmas.

This restaurant, in the Cork Municipal Art Gallery, is operated by the well-known Ballymaloe House, who use fresh home-made food. It is located in a spacious room; the widely-spaced tables are decorated with fresh flowers and candles, and there are paintings and sculptures on show. Some reporters regarded the decor as rather clinical. Harp music is often played here.

Although lunch is served as well, reporters all had dinner. Many dispensed with a starter, but others had soup and fondue. Main dishes included roast lamb, fillet of pork en croûte, chicken breasts, and ham cooked in mushrooms and Chablis. Almond tart, chocolate layer cake, and blackcurrant pie were among the desserts. Coffee was excellent, with unlimited refills. The house wine was considered good value at £8 a bottle.

Cooking was praised by all reporters — 'meat dishes just cooked to perfection' — but was rated by one as 'not quite up to the standard of the parent restaurant' (Ballymaloe House, Shanagarry, also featured in this guide).

Service was friendly and, in the main, efficient. In one case, where there was a long delay between the starters and the main course, a complimentary glass of wine was served to each of the party, with apologies.
•*Drinks* wine licence •*Meals* lunch (AC), dinner (AC), tea, coffee all day •*Cater for* wheelchair

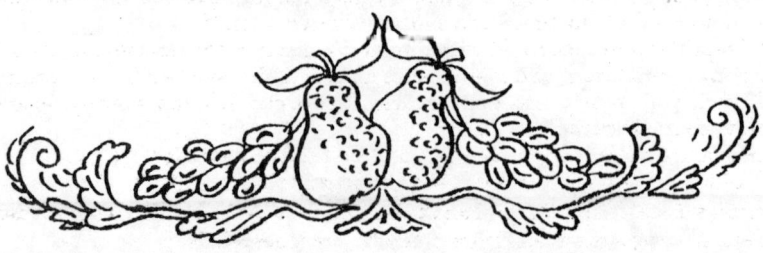

HALPIN'S RESTAURANT
Cook Street, Cork.

Tel. 021-277853 ££ *Service* nil
Open 08.00-24.00 weekdays, 12.15-15.15/17.30-23.30 Sun. *Closed* two days at Christmas, Good Friday.

With a shopfront, this is a cellar-type restaurant, quite large, but broken up into sections. There is adequate space between the tables, and one section is entirely devoted to tables for two. It serves Continental breakfast and during the daytime has both self service and table service.

Both lunch and dinner figured in reports. Starters included vegetable soup, mushrooms in garlic sauce, egg mayonnaise, and prawn cocktail. Some of the main dishes were pork steak, chicken in a whiskey and cream sauce, fillet of plaice, roast beef, and Indian-style beef curry. One of the desserts was crushed biscuits steeped in sherry and served with fresh cream — 'delicious but very filling!'; others were apple crumble, and fresh fruit salad. Calypso coffee was served with real Tia Maria liqueur. The white house wine was 'pleasant'.

Cooking was considered very good — 'everything cooked to perfection', 'cannot be faulted' — except in the case of one reporter who thought roast beef too underdone. Service was attentive; when one party asked for a delay of ten minutes or so between their main course and dessert, their dessert order was taken exactly ten minutes later.

•*Drinks* wine licence •*Meals* breakfast, lunch (AC + T d'H), dinner (AC + Td'H), tourist menu all day weekdays •*Cards* Access, Visa

HUGUENOT RESTAURANT
Frenchchurch Street, Cork.

Tel. 021-273357 ££ *Service* 10%
Open 12.30-14.30/18.30-22.30 Mon-Sat, 23.00 Thur-Sat. *Closed* bank holidays.

This restaurant is housed in an old converted building with mahogany fittings, decorated in period style, with antique furniture. Its name and that of the street are reminders of the French Protestant refugees who sought sanctuary in Ireland from the end of the seventeenth century onwards. Appropriately, the restaurant specialises in French cuisine, as well as seafood. It uses local produce, bought fresh. Vegetarians can be catered for, as can coeliac and other diets if notice is given. Stock and sauces do not contain flour.

All reports were concerned with dinner. Veal and bacon terrine and gravlax (salmon) were starters, and main dishes included pheasant, scallops in pastry, and duck with honey and peppercorns. Raspberries, nutty meringue, and pavlova were desserts.

Rioja and Sancerre wine, chosen from the list, were satisfactory.

Cooking was excellent. Service was informal but efficient.

•*Drinks* wine licence •*Meals* lunch (AC), dinner (AC + T d'H) •*Cards* Visa, Diners, Access, American Express •*Cater for* wheelchair

IMPERIAL HOTEL (CLOUDS GRILL)
South Mall, Cork.
Tel. 021-274040 ££ Service 10%
Open 12.30-14.30/18.00-22.00 daily. *Closed* ten days at Christmas.

This is the grill room of the Imperial Hotel on the South Mall. It is pleasantly decorated in soft pastel shades, but some of the tables are 'sandwiched' uncomfortably between high-backed seats. There is piano music during meals.

Reporters had both lunch and dinner. For lunch, starters were seafood parfait (a type of seafood pâté), leek and potato soup, and fruit juice. There was a salad bar at dinner, and, as well, one reporter a hot starter of deep-fried cod with garlic mayonnaise. Main dishes at lunch were plaice, salmon, and steak; at dinner, veal, and beef kebabs. Sweets included brandy torte (with very little brandy), peach melba, apple tart, and rice pudding.

Red and white house wine were 'drinkable'; service was pleasant and prompt.

The cooking was good, but reporters were somewhat critical of prices here, holding it to be expensive when vegetables and potatoes were charged separately in addition to the main dish.

•*Drinks* full licence •*Meals* breakfast, lunch (AC + T d'H), dinner (AC + T d'H) •*Cards* all major •*Cater for* children, wheelchair

JACQUES' RESTAURANT
9, Phoenix Street, Cork. (Near G.P.O.)
Tel. 021-277387 ££ Service nil
Open 09.00-16.00 Mon, 09.00-16.00/18.00-22.30 Tues-Sat. *Closed* one week from Christmas Day.

The outer appearance of this restaurant is plain and unobtrusive. Inside, it is small but comfortable, with well spaced tables, and glass divisions partitioning some cubicles. The general atmosphere is relaxed and pleasant.

It is advisable to book for dinner. Lunch is self-service and the minimum charge is only £2. Organically grown vegetables are used. While the restaurant specialises in seafood, items such as duck and quail appear on the menu throughout the year, and game from November to February. There is a vegetarian dish available daily.

All reports dealt with dinner. Some of the starters were scallops in cream sauce and herbs, crab, and onion soup. Main dishes included fillet steak, roast lamb, roast pork, sole on the bone, and stuffed trout with orange and herbs. Desserts were home-made ice cream, and almond and coffee meringue with raspberry and cream sauce. Only one party had wine, a bottle of Sancerre and a glass of house wine; both well rated.

Cooking met with approval in all reports; one said that Jacques' was 'the sort of place where you could take any person and be sure of a good meal'. Service by a very friendly staff was good but unobtrusive.

•*Drinks* wine licence •*Meals* lunch (AC + T d'H), dinner (AC + T d'H) •*Cards* Visa, Access, Diners, American Express •*Cater for* children, wheelchair (not to toilets)

OYSTER TAVERN
Market Lane, Cork. (Off Patrick Street.)
Tel. 021-272716   £££   Service nil
Open 12.30-14.30/18.00-22.00 Mon-Sat. Closed Sundays and bank holidays.

The approach to and exterior of this bar-restaurant are not very impressive; it is down a 'pedestrians only' laneway. Inside, it is 'old world' and pleasant, with timber panelling, and comfortable seating in the waiting area.

It serves local produce, and specialises in char-grilled steak, roast beef, and seafood.

Lunch and dinner both featured in reports. The only lunch starters mentioned were soup, tomato and mushroom. The main dishes were grilled salmon steak, grilled plaice, roast pork, and roast chicken, with cheesecake, gooseberry crumble, and rhubarb fool for desserts. No wine was ordered; reporters drank Guinness and whiskey.

Cooking was in the main good — 'food was hot, tasty, and well presented' — but one reporter thought that the vegetables were 'indifferent'. Service was helpful and friendly..

•*Drinks* full licence •*Meals* lunch (AC+ T d'H), dinner (AC+ T d' H), tourist menu 18.00-19.00 daily •*Cater for* children, wheelchair (not to toilets)

PADDY GARIBALDI'S
Carey's Lane, Cork.
Tel. 021-277915   £   Service nil
Open 09.00-00.30 daily. Closed one week at Christmas, Good Friday.

This pizza restaurant is in a pedestrianised lane connecting Paul Street Shopping Centre with Patrick Street. It is in a new building with an old-fashioned front. Inside, it is bright and airy, with seating both up and downstairs. One reporter described it as a casual restaurant, with a very friendly staff but somewhat limited menu. Burgers and steaks are available as well as pizzas and lasagne.

Pizzas, naturally, were the order of the day, but deep-fried scampi and lasagne also appeared in reports, and one reporter had stuffed mushrooms in garlic — 'somewhat tasteless' — as a starter. Home-made apple pie, described as 'excellent' and cheesecake — 'average only' — were the only desserts sampled. House wine, considered 'quite good for the price', and a bottle of white Chianti, 'fresh and light', were the drinks.

Pizzas were described as good, very large, and with a lovely home-made base. In general, cooking was held to be excellent. Service was prompt, organised, and friendly.

•*Drinks* wine licence• *Meals* lunch(AC), dinner (AC) •*Cards* Visa, Access, American Express, Luncheon vouchers •*Cater for* children (encouraged)

TRISKEL ARTS CAFE
Triskel Arts Centre, 15, Tobin Street, Cork.
Tel. 021-272022 £ *Service* nil
Open 11.00-18.00 Mon-Sat.

This is on the first floor in an old building and somewhat hard to find, as from the street one would not guess that there was anything other than an Arts Centre there. The restaurant is modern inside, and has a stained glass window. It is open during the day only, specialising in self-service lunches. Items chosen by our reporters were salad and tuna sandwiches, home-made leek and potato soup, salads, sweet and sour pork, with strawberry gâteau as a dessert. Drinks were tea and coffee.

Cooking was good, home-made soup being particularly commended, and the staff friendly and helpful. 'Very unpretentious and moderately priced' was one person's verdict; 'a great place for lunch and meeting people' was another's.

•*Drinks* wine licence •*Meals* lunch (AC) •*Cards* none •*Cater for* vegetarians

TUNG SING CHINESE RESTAURANT
23A, Patrick Street, Cork.
Tel. 021-274616/273793 ££ *Service* nil
Open 12.30-00.45 Mon-Thur, 12.30-01.00 Fri-Sun. *Closed* two days at Christmas, Chinese New Year.

This is a Chinese restaurant upstairs over H. Samuel's shop on the south side of Patrick Street. There is a narrow ground-floor doorway. Inside, it has oriental decor, and the atmosphere is welcoming — 'the people who work there make you feel as if you were the only one in the place.' It serves European and Chinese cuisine, sizzling steaks being a speciality. Set price lunch and dinner are available.

Reporters ate there at lunch and dinner. Starters were chicken and corn soup, and spring rolls. Main dishes included chicken and bean sprouts, sweet and sour pork, and beef curry. The only dessert chosen was ice cream.

The house wine was 'reasonable'. Cooking was 'properly done', and service was good.

•*Drinks* wine licence •*Meals* lunch (AC + T d'H), dinner (AC + T d'H)
•*Cards* Access, Visa, Diners, American Express, and Luncheon Vouchers

County Cork

BALLINHASSIG

BILLY MACKESY'S (BAWNLEIGH HOUSE)

Ballinhassig, Co. Cork. (On 'back' Kinsale road.)
Tel. 021-771333 ££ Service nil
Open 19.30-23.00 Tues-Sat. Closed 22 Dec-31 Jan, last two weeks in August.

This restaurant is in a ranch-style, newly renovated building with well laid out grounds and good parking space. Inside, it is spacious, with tasteful decor, and has a pleasant atmosphere. It serves evening dinner only, using home-grown produce, including fruit and a wide range of herbs.

Starters chosen by our reporters included seafood pancakes, sweetbreads, melon Parisienne, and potato and leek soup. Among the main dishes were lamb cutlets en croûte, sole with crab stuffing, and fillet of beef mignon. Desserts were strawberry shortcake, mille-feuille with home-made ice cream, and fresh fruit. Australian white wine and Côtes du Rhône Pascal were satisfactory.

Cooking was pronounced 'superb'. Service was efficient without being obtrusive.

•*Drinks* full licence •*Meals* dinner (AC) •*Cards* none

BALLYDEHOB

ANNIE'S

Ballydehob, Co. Cork. (In the village, which is on the road to Mizen Head.)
Tel. 028-37292 ££ Service nil
Open 12.30-14.30/19.00-21.30 Tues-Sat. Closed 1-21 Oct, 15-28 Feb, two days at Christmas.

Annie's is a bistro-type restaurant in a small converted shop. One of its interesting features is that while it has only a wine licence, patrons may go across the road to a pub; the restaurant staff come across with menus and then summon the guests when their meals are ready. The whole atmosphere is easy-going and friendly. The restaurant uses organically grown vegetables, and everything is home-made.

All reports dealt with dinner. Lemon sorbet, baked avocado with crab, melon in port, and mussels in garlic were some of the starters. Among the main dishes were poached salmon, monkfish (this last described as 'mediocre'), fillet steak ('beautifully flavoured and cooked'), scallops, veal and lamb cutlets. Hot chocolate fudge cake and Bailey's ice cream figured among the desserts. House wine was judged pleasing.

Cooking was rated very good, with emphasis on fresh produce and home-made food, mostly cooked to order. Service was friendly, informal, and competent.
•*Drinks* wine licence •*Meals* lunch (AC + T d'H), dinner (AC + T d'H), snack lunches •*Cards* Access, Visa

TEACH DEARG
Ballydehob, Co. Cork. (Scarteenakillen, off Bantry-Ballydehob road — signposted.)
Tel. 028-37282 ££ Service 10%
Open 12.30-14.30/19.30-21.45. *Closed* Mondays in season, early Oct-17 Mar.

This name, meaning 'red house' is pronounced — more or less — as 'Tchock Djarreg'. It refers to a restaurant in a red- painted farm house. Inside, it is nicely set out, with good space between the tables, and a gallery bar above the dining area. There is a very friendly atmosphere. The restaurant specialises in wild venison, fillet steak, and salmon, and always has vegetarian dishes on the menu.

Reporters had both lunch and dinner there. Smoked mackerel and chicken liver pâté were starters at lunch, melon with port and home-made pea soup for dinner. Main dishes included moussaka, roast pheasant, and black-peppered steak. Chestnut and Kiwi ice cream, chocolate cake, and baked bread and raisin pudding were some of the desserts. House wine was pleasant, and good value at £7.75 a bottle.

Cooking was excellent, and service friendly and efficient.
•*Drinks* wine licence •*Meals* lunch (AC), dinner (AC) •*Cards* Access, Visa, Diners •*Cater for* children, vegetarians

BALLYVOURNEY (BAILE MHUIRNE)

THE MILLS INN
Ballyvourney, Co. Cork.
Tel. 026-45014 ££ Service nil
Open 12.30-14.00/16.00-21.30 daily. *Closed* Christmas Day, Good Friday.

This inn, at the foot of the Derrynasaggart mountains, provides a suitable halting place on the main Cork-Macroom-Killarney road. It has a nice lawn outside, and an old-fashioned interior with antiques. It provides 'good country home cooking'.

All reports were concerned with dinner. Seafood cocktail, stuffed mushrooms, smoked salmon, and mulligatawny soup were among the starters; black sole, sirloin steak, roast pork and chicken were some of the main dishes. Desserts were Black Forest gâteau and strawberries.

Bulgarian house wine at £9 a bottle was highly commended.

Cooking was rated very good and service excellent, with personal attention by the proprietor.
•*Drinks* full licence •*Meals* lunch (AC only), dinner (AC only), bar food, tourist menu 18.00-21.30 Tues- Sat •*Cards* all major •*Cater for* children, wheelchair

BANDON

MUNSTER ARMS HOTEL
Bandon, Co. Cork.

Tel. 023-41562 ££ Service nil
Open 12.30-14.30/18.00-21.30 daily, 17.30-21.00 Sun, breakfast from 07.30, coffee corner open all day. *Closed* Christmas Day.

This hotel has been renovated, and the busy restaurant is pleasant.
Dinner was the meal dealt with in all reports. Mussels in garlic butter and chicken liver pâté were starters, with poached salmon, fillet of beef, and prawns as main dishes. The dessert menu was limited, chocolate gâteau and pear Belle Hélène being two of the choices. House wine was good, at £6.25 a bottle.
Cooking was 'good, solid, plain cooking, consistently up to a high standard'. Service was very satisfactory from a well-trained, friendly staff.
•*Drinks* full licence •*Meals* breakfast, lunch (AC + T d'H), dinner (AC + T d'H) •*Cater for* children, wheelchair (restaurant only)

BUTLERSTOWN

DUNWORLEY COTTAGE RESTAURANT
Dunworley, Butlerstown, Co. Cork. (Near Dunworley beach, 24km south of Bandon.)

Tel. 023-40310 ££ Service nil
Open 13.00-23.00 Wed-Sun, reservations only. *Closed* November, January, February.

According to the reports which reached us, many people are surprised 'to find a good restaurant in the middle of nowhere', as one person expressed it. It is a renovated cottage, with a very friendly atmosphere. The German chef-proprietor, Herr Otto Kunze, uses organically grown vegetables and locally caught seafood. His style of cooking is based on traditional recipes, and one-third of his dishes cater for vegetarians.
Reports dealt with both dinner and a fixed-priced lunch. The latter consisted of vegetable soup, poached cod with cauliflower cheese, and apfel strudel. Starters for dinner included dunkel soup (a German recipe using beetroot and roasted buckwheat), lemon sorbet, rabbit pâté, crabmeat in garlic, and nettle soup. Some of the main dishes were sea trout, pan-fried duck in a honey, raisin and brandy sauce, poached cod (tourist menu), fillet steak, and —a vegetarian dish — celeriac deep-fried in butter, with blue cheese sauce. Desserts included an array of fruit purées, home-made ice cream, and apfel strudel —this last on the tourist menu. There was 'a bottomless coffee pot'.

The cellar was well-stocked, the dry white French house wine good value. Customers could bring their own wine, the corkage charge being £2.

Cooking was, in the main, excellent, but three people who had duck found it tough. Service was well-timed rather than rapid; the proprietor took an interest in discussing dishes personally with clients.

Meals at Dunworley Cottage were obviously considered very good value; one reporter said that it was 'a little restaurant in the wilds of West Cork that could teach many restaurateurs in many cities to dispense with pretension and concentrate on the culinary art.'

•*Drinks* full licence •*Meals* lunch (AC + T d'H), dinner (AC + T d'H) •*Cards* Visa, Access, Diners, American Express

COBH

RINN RONAIN HOTEL
Rushbrooke, Cobh, Co. Cork.

Tel. 021-811407/812242   ££   *Service* nil
Open 12.30-14.30/17.00-22.30.

Two reports on this hotel-restaurant, just outside Cobh and near Fota Wildlife Park, will be of interest to the holiday or business traveller. One report is from a party who arrived there looking for a main meal at the unusual hour of 3.45 p.m., the other from a family on holiday (non-residents at the hotel) who enjoyed evening meals for two adults and two children.

The first party were given the dinner menu and were able to choose sirloin steak with a bottle of St. Emilion, and peach Melba to follow. The reporter who brought children there on two consecutive evenings was favourably impressed by the restaurant's readiness to serve half-size portions from the standard menu to children rather than offering them sausage or chicken with chips.

This party had melon, and vegetable soup, followed by turkey and ham and salmon steaks, with fresh fruit salad and cheesecake for dessert. Wine was good.

Service was attentive and pleasant, and the cooking was good. The people who had an early meal said it was 'excellent, especially taking the time of day into account', the family found theirs 'beautiful, good flavour, nicely presented'.

Drinks full licence •*Meals* breakfast, lunch (AC + T d'H), dinner (AC + T d'H) *Cards* Access, Visa

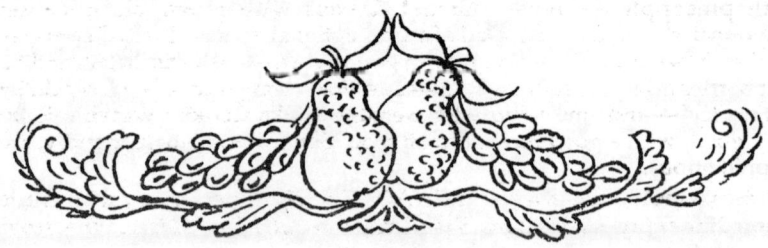

DOUGLAS

O'DRISCOLL'S BAR AND RESTAURANT
Douglas, Cork.

Tel. 021-893927   ££   *Service* nil
Open 12.15-14.30 daily, 17.45-22.30 Mon-Sat.

This pub-cum-restaurant is in Douglas village, which is really a suburb of Cork city. The restaurant is upstairs, over the pub. Its exterior is modern, but not flashy; inside, it is bright, with wood panelling. Although it is quite small, it does not give the impression of being cramped.

Dinner was the subject of all reports. Starters were mushroom soup, home-made quiche, egg mayonnaise, and melon in port wine. Two main dishes were plaice and prawns in butter, and sirloin steak. Lemon meringue pie, ice cream, and pavlova were desserts.

White house wine was pronounced excellent.

The cooking was very good, and the service efficient and 'caring'.

•*Drinks* full licence •*Meals* lunch (AC + T d'H), dinner (AC), tourist menu Mon-Sat 17.45-19.30 •*Cards* Access, Visa, Diners

DUNMANWAY

BRIDGEMOUNT HOUSE
Bandon Road, Dunmanway, Co. Cork.

Tel. 023-45260   ££   *Service* nil
Open 12.30-14.00 Tues-Sun, 19.00-21.30 Thur-Sun, (also Tues and Wed Jun-Aug). *Closed* February.

The restaurant is in a large period house, in its own grounds, on the outskirts of Dunmanway town. It is very comfortably furnished, with a three-piece suite in front of the dining-room fire where one may sit for drinks. Organically grown vegetables and free range poultry and pork are used in the restaurant.

Reporters had both lunch and dinner there. Starters included prawn cocktail with pineapple — 'most unusual flavour with pineapple juice and mayonnaise' — and mixed salad of an 'exceptional variety'. Main dishes were chicken in wine sauce, and steak with peppercorns. Fresh fruit salad, and hot raspberries in brandy sauce were desserts. Fresh orange juice — 'nicely chilled but not icy' — and 'fine' white wine were the drinks. Cooking was simple, but very good, with a good flavour to all food. Service was quick, friendly, and unpretentious.

•*Drinks* wine licence •*Meals* lunch (AC + T d'H), dinner (AC + T d'H) tourist menu dinner Jun-Aug •*Cards* Visa, Diners. •*Cater for* children, wheelchair (not to toilets)

FERMOY

ROYAL RESTAURANT
Pearse Square, Fermoy, Co. Cork.
Tel. 025-32428 ££ Service nil
Open 12.30-15.30/18.00-21.30 Tues-Sun. *Closed* one week at Christmas.

This is on the first floor, over the Royal Bar, in the centre of the town. The restaurant is not conspicuous, and a stranger would hardly know it was there; it needs a prominent sign. Inside, it has been completely renovated. It was opened only towards the end of 1987 and is attractively decorated. Food is also available in the bar.

Both lunch and dinner were the subject of reports. Soup, chicken pâté, and avocado with seafood were some of the starters. Poached salmon, roast duckling, and beef Stroganoff were main dishes, with fresh fruit salad, apple pie, and Black Forest gâteau for desserts.

Both Beaujolais and house wine, at dinner, were considered very good. The cooking was described as 'top class'. One reporter, however, thought that as there were a lot of sauces the menu could do with more explanation.

Everyone was pleased with the service. One person was impressed by what he thought was a nice touch — at a Silver Wedding celebration meal the management supplied a cake as a surprise.

•*Drinks* full licence •*Meals* lunch (AC +T d'H),dinner (AC + T d'H) •*Cards* Access, Visa, Diners •*Cater for* children

KILBRITTAIN

PINK ELEPHANT
Harbour View, Kilbrittain, Co. Cork. (3km south of Kilbrittain.)
Tel. 023-49608/49760 ££ Service nil
Open 17.00-21.45 weekdays, 12.30-14.30/17.00-20.45 Sun all year.

This is a medium-sized restaurant-cum-lounge in the Harbour View district, overlooking Courtmacsherry Bay. It is decorated in pink inside and out. It is a family-run establishment, very clean, and well heated in cold weather. It has a restful, friendly atmosphere. A novel feature is the boat-shaped counter in the bar, bearing the legend: 'I am the captain of this ship, when my wife is absent.'

Reporters had both Sunday lunch and dinner, the menus for which seemed to be much the same. Starters included egg mayonnaise, fish pâté, quiche, and soup with home-made brown bread. Some of the main dishes were grilled salmon, grilled trout, roast lamb, plaice, and lamb cutlets. For dessert, there was a selection from a trolley; apple pie, fruit salad, crème caramel, and brandy gâteau were some of the choices. One reporter, there for lunch, criticised the brandy gâteau as having no taste of brandy.

The house wine was said to be 'drinkable'.
Cooking was excellent— 'could not ask for better' — although one person thought that the vegetables, carrot and turnip, were rather soggy. Service was rated good by most reporters, friendly and efficient, but one said that it could have been better for a party of eight booked almost a week previously.
•*Drinks* full licence •*Meals* lunch (T d'H Sun.), dinner (AC + T d'H), bar food 11.00 onwards •*Cards* Visa •*Cater for* wheelchair

KINSALE

Kinsale, a pleasure port town, is noted for its restaurants, and might be described as a gourmet centre for the south of Ireland. The three restaurants on which we report are all fairly expensive, with the exception of a lunch and tourist menu available in the Blue Haven Hotel. They are not, therefore, in general, the type of restaurant to which an ordinary holiday maker in the area would repair each evening for his dinner, unless he were very rich. It will be understood that they are recommended mainly as restaurants for an occasion.

BLUE HAVEN HOTEL
Pearse Street, Kinsale, Co. Cork.

Tel. 021-772209   £££   *Service* 10%
Open 12.30-14.30/18.30-24.00 daily, limited menu 07.30-24.00 daily. Closed Christmas Day.

This hotel in the centre of Kinsale is an old town house, redecorated inside and out. Window boxes and canopies make for an attractive appearance outside. It is pleasant inside, and from the dining-room one can look out at a small garden. It has a busy, efficient, but relaxed atmosphere. It serves local produce and freshly caught local fish. There is a tourist menu for lunch and early evening.
 Reporters had both lunch and dinner there. At lunch,mushroom soup, seafood vol-au-vent, and melon slices were starters,with salmon Hollandaise, roast beef, and quiche with mixed salad as main courses, and profiteroles and apple pie for dessert.
 Most reporters had dinner. Oysters, stuffed mussels, sorbet, and Senegalese and cream of broccoli soups were chosen as starters. Some of the main dishes were duckling, sole, rack of lamb, lobster Thermidor, beef en croûte, and monkfish, with highly commended home-made ice cream and cheese to follow. Wines — Muscadet, Australian Cabernet Sauvignon, Côtes du Rhône — were pronounced very good, and dry white house wine was very satisfactory. The wine list was very comprehensive, with many bottles at £10 or £12.
 Cooking was judged 'excellent', 'consistently top class', with the reservation by one reporter that a starter, mussels in breadcrumbs, was not so good, as it had been kept hot in an oven. Service was pleasant, friendly, and competent, although somewhat slow at times.
•*Drinks* full licence •*Meals* lunch (AC only), dinner (AC + T d'H), tourist menu 12.30-14.30/18.30-20.00 •*Cards* Access, Visa, Diners, American Express •*Cater for* children (before 20.00), wheelchair (not to toilets)

JIM EDWARDS
Market Quay, Kinsale, Co. Cork.
Tel. 021-772541 ££ Service nil
Open 12.30-15.00/18.00-22.30 weekdays, 12.30-15.00/18.00-21.30 Sun. *Closed Christmas Day, Good Friday, three weeks in January.*

This bar-restaurant, run by a husband-and-wife team, has ample car-parking facilities, old-style windows, and a clock over the door. There is good seating and table accommodation in a warm atmosphere with a gas fire of coal-flame effect. The restaurant specialises in steaks and seafood.

All reports dealt with dinner. Starters were French onion soup, garlic stuffed mushrooms, and prawn cocktail, with fillet steak and sole on the bone as main dishes, accompanied by a good selection of vegetables. Desserts were cream gâteau, and fresh strawberries and cream. White house wine was good.

Cooking was highly rated — 'steak cooked exactly to order' — fish and starters just right. One reporter said that she would recommend this restaurant (which she has patronised on several occasions) mainly as a steak house. Courses were served at well spaced intervals, and the staff were friendly and courteous.

•*Drinks* full licence •*Meals* lunch (AC + T d'H Sun), dinner (AC) •*Cards* Access, Visa, American Express •*Cater for* children, wheelchair

MAN FRIDAY
Scilly, Kinsale, Co. Cork.
Tel. 021-772260 ££ Service nil
Open 19.00-22.30.

This restaurant, serving evening dinner only, overlooks the harbour. Ambience and decor are very attractive, but a word of warning has been sounded about the approach to the restaurant — a pleasant way down steps through a shrubbery, not too easy to find on a dark night. It is cosy inside, with wood panelling, and adorned by antiques. The atmosphere is warm and relaxing.

Menus had a heavy accent on seafood, both as starters and main course, but roast duck, steak, and lamb were also offered, and very favourably regarded. A good selection of desserts included Bailey's cream soufflé and a popular Man Friday coupé. There was an adequate choice of wines. The fact that patrons were welcome to linger after their meal, with frequently replenished coffee cups, was an added attraction.

Cooking was 'superb', and service competent and pleasant. Man Friday, while not cheap, is obviously regarded in Cork as giving value for money — we received many enthusiastic reports about it.

•*Drinks* wine licence •*Meals* dinner (AC) •*Cards* Access, Visa

MALLOW

KEPPLER'S RESTAURANT AND BAR
26, Bank Place, Mallow, Co. Cork.
Tel. 022-21946   ££   *Service* nil
*Open*12.00-23.30 daily, 12.00-22.00 Sun. *Closed* two days at Christmas, Good Friday.

This is in the basement of an old Georgian house, in the centre of the town. It is comforting and inviting, with high-backed wooden partitions for cubicles, and an open fire in winter. It was described by one person as unpretentious and informal.

Reporters had both lunch and dinner there, dealt with together here. Egg mayonnaise, cream of vegetable soup, and prawn cocktail were starters. Main dishes were scampi, roast beef, and peppered steak, with Black Forest gâteau, hazelnut meringue, and ice cream for dessert. White house wine was pleasant, and Gaelic coffee very good. Cooking was 'reliable but basic'; vegetables were cooked to the right degree, and steaks as ordered. Service was adequate.

•*Drinks* full licence •*Meals* lunch (AC), dinner (AC) •*Cards* Visa, Access •*Cater for* children

SPRINGFORT HALL HOTEL
Mallow, Co. Cork. (Limerick road from Mallow; turn right onto Doneraile road, for 0.5km.)
Tel. 022-21278   ££   *Service* nil
Open 19.00-23.00 Mon-Sat. *Closed* three days at Christmas.

Springfort Hall serves evening dinner only, using local cheese, vegetables, and Blackwater salmon, among other produce. It is an old manor house in a woodland setting, with a warm, pleasant lounge, a bright fire, and two dining-rooms suitable for either large or small parties. The bar area is somewhat small. The atmosphere is very welcoming, made more so by two friendly St. Bernard dogs that sit at the hall door greeting visitors. Some of the starters chosen by our reporters were prawn cocktail, soup, and garlic mushrooms. Among the main dishes were chicken Kiev, steak, and sea bass. There was Bailey's ice cream (home-made), cheesecake, and pavlova for dessert. Red house wine was 'good value' at £8.25 a bottle. The cooking was unanimously praised by our reporters — 'every dish was freshly cooked ... the vegetables were crispy and delicious', 'steak cooked exactly as requested'. Service was 'skilled and friendly', 'prompt or leisurely, at the diner's choice'.

•*Drinks* full licence •*Meals* dinner (AC) •*Cards* Visa, Access •*Cater for* children, wheelchair

MIDLETON

THE FARM GATE
The Coolbawn, Midleton, Co. Cork.

Tel. 021-632771 ££ *Service* nil
Open 09.30-17.00 Mon-Sat, 19.00-21.30 Fri-Sat. •*Closed* Christmas Day, Good Friday, August Monday.

This is at the rear of the proprietor's vegetable and delicatessen shop and the entrance is through the shop. It is simply furnished in country-kitchen style. One reporter said that 'money obviously has been invested in kitchens and food rather than cosmetic trappings'. Locally grown produce of the East Cork area is used in the restaurant.

All our reporters had dinner there. Mushroom soup, mussels in garlic, pancakes with mussels were starters; poached salmon, chicken á la crême, pork Provençale, and curry were main dishes. Desserts included strawberries, choux rings, kiwi cheesecake, and pavlova.

House white wine (Muscadet) at £7.50 a bottle was 'pleasant'. The cooking was 'excellent', and vegetables were 'crunchy fresh'. One reporter thought the desserts an exception to this; 'too much cream and too little meringue in pavlova; tough pastry, and fruit very scarce in choux rings.' Service was efficient and pleasant.

•*Drinks* wine licence •*Meals* lunch (AC + T d'H), dinner (AC + T d'H) •*Cards* Access, Visa •*Cater for* children, wheelchair (not to toilets), non-smokers

FININ'S
75, Main Street, Midleton, Co. Cork.

Tel. 021-631878/632382 ££ *Service* 10% à la carte menus only
Open 12.00-15.00/19.00-22.00 weekdays, bar food 10.30-23.00. *Closed* two days at Christmas.

This pub-cum-restaurant is in the Main Street. There is an area downstairs where one may eat bar food, and the main dining-room is upstairs. The surroundings are pleasant and the tables not too crowded. The owner is a chef.

Both lunch and dinner were the subject of reports. For lunch there was an excellent salmon salad. Seafood cocktail, 'plenty of fish ... in a tangy sauce', was a starter at dinner; medallions of fillet steak followed, each cooked exactly as variously requested. There was a selection of desserts: 'Finin's,' said the reporter, 'caters for people like myself, who like to taste different desserts.' These included home-made lemon mousse, coffee and rum gâteau, home-made apple pie, and fresh fruit salad. House wine was satisfactory.

Cooking was, without exception, considered excellent, and service was prompt.

•*Drinks* full licence •*Meals* lunch (AC + T d'H), dinner (AC + T d'H), tourist menu daily, lunch and dinner, Apr-Sept •*Cards* all major •*Cater for* children

MINANE BRIDGE

THE OVERDRAUGHT
Tracton, Minane Bridge, Co. Cork.
Tel. 021-887136/887177 ££ Service nil
Open 10.30-24.30. Closed Christmas Day, Good Friday.

This is a bar/bistro in an old country house. A monetary note is struck by an outside sign depicting an old Irish pound note, and by the bar counter which was originally part of the Provincial Bank on the South Mall in Cork. One reporter remarked on the warm welcome which greeted his arrival. Food is served all day in the bar.

Dinner was the subject of all our reports. Prawn cocktail was a starter, with fillet steak the favourite main dish; there was also poached salmon. Apple tart and cream was a dessert.

Red and white house wine were good, and both were served at the correct temperature. Cooking was highly approved. One reporter said: 'They have a particularly good way of cooking fillet steak,' and another, 'the apple tart was just as I would like to be able to bake it.' There were conflicting reports on the service from people who use the restaurant regularly. One said that it was very efficient, the other that 'it is always slow but one accepts it.'

•Drinks full licence •Meals barfood, dinner (AC) •Cards Access, Visa

MONKSTOWN

THE BOSUN
Monkstown, Co. Cork. (On the seafront — main road, 9km from Cork City.)
Tel. 021-842172 ££ Service nil
Open 12.15-14.30 Mon-Sat, 19.00-21.30 Tues-Fri. Closed Christmas Day, Good Friday.

This bar-cum-restaurant is on the outside an ordinary, well- kept pub; inside, it is well-appointed and very clean, with a nice friendly atmosphere. It specialises in seafood, home-made pâté, and home-made ice cream, using home grown vegetables and herbs.

Both lunch and dinner were taken there. For lunch, our reporter's party had mushroom soup as a starter, with sea bass and roast lamb as main dishes, and apple crumble and ice cream for dessert. Coffee was good. For dinner, the main dishes were scallops, steak, and sole on the bone, with a selection of desserts. The wine chosen was Sancerre, thought 'a bit expensive' at £17.50 a bottle.

Cooking, particularly of vegetables, was very good. Service was efficient and friendly. One reporter said that 'although the place was full they made you feel that you were the only customer.'

•Drinks full licence •Meals lunch (AC + T d'H), dinner (AC + T d'H), bar food •Cards Visa, Access •Cater for children, wheelchair

OVENS

TATLER JAC'S
Ovens Co. Cork. (14.5km west of Cork City on main Killarney road.)
Tel. 021-331659 £££ Service nil
Open 18.00-22.00 Mon-Sat, bar food 11.00-22.00 Mon-Sat, 12.00-14.00/16.00-21.00 Sun. ClosedGood Friday, Christmas Day, one week in spring, two in October (variable).

This is a combination of an à la carte restaurant serving dinner only and a pub serving food. Reports here relate to the restaurant, which offers a wide menu with emphasis on fish dishes and fresh vegetables, locally caught and grown. It is an old building, mock Tudor, well maintained, with an ample car park. The restaurant is attractively decorated, with flowers and candles on the tables, and an open fire. Our reporters chose as starters garlic mushrooms, home-made soup, scallops, and home-made chicken liver pâté. The main courses were roast duckling and fillet steak, with pear pavlova as dessert. Wine was very good—particularly the Murietta recommended by the proprietor.

Cooking was excellent and service very attentive.

•Drinks full licence •Meals dinner (AC) •Cards Access, Visa, Diners, American Express •Cater for children 18.00-20.00, wheelchair (not to toilets)

SCHULL

THE ALTAR RESTAURANT
Toormore, Schull, Co. Cork. (8km west of Schull on road to Mizen Head.)
Tel. 028-35254 ££ Service 10%
Open 19.30-24.00 daily. Closed 26 December.

Advance booking is required for this restaurant, which is in a converted school house. The name derives from an altar rock nearby, where, according to tradition, Mass was celebrated in penal times. For the twentieth-century visitor parking space is limited. Inside, the two dining-rooms have fresh, bright tablecloths and lights on each table. There is a warm atmosphere: 'You feel you are really welcome — like going to a friend's house,' one reporter said. An interesting feature of this restaurant is that you bring your own wine.

Reports related solely to dinner as it is an evening restaurant. Melon stuffed with crabmeat was a starter — 'unusual, and very good'. Lamb chops, T-bone steak, dolmades (meat balls wrapped in vine leaves) and plaice were main dishes. Desserts included knickerbocker glory, chocolate gâteau, (thought 'somewhat dry'), and home-made ice cream.

Cooking was, in general, very good, with the exception of the plaice, described as 'not as good as it sounds'. Service was excellent; this is a family-run business and, at the time of reporting, the daughters of the house acted as waitresses.

•Drinks full licence •Meals dinner (AC) •Cards Access, Visa

THE COURTYARD
Main Street, Schull, Co. Cork.

Tel. 028-28209 £££ Service 10%
Open 19.30 Mon-Sat in summer, weekends in winter ex. Jan, Feb. Bar food and coffee shop 11.00-17.00.

This restaurant, serving evening dinners only is in a converted stable at the back of an old building leading to an open courtyard. It is part of a complex with a bar, (which serves pub food) delicatessen, bakery, and craft shop. There is adequate space in the restaurant, which has original paintings on display and flowers and candles on the tables. Locally grown shellfish and local farmhouse cheeses are used, as is hand-made bread. Guests were particularly impressed by the friendly and helpful attitude of the staff— particularly when, on request, leftover fish was 'cheerfully wrapped up for the cat'.

Our reporters' starters included chicken livers flamed in brandy, curried avocado with prawns, and gravlax (grilled, cured salmon) with dill sauce. Main dishes were chicken supréme, peppered steak, monkfish, and sole on the bone with crab and saffron sauce. There was a wide selection of vegetables. Crêpes with brandy sauce, and strawberries in an almond basket, were the only desserts reporters could manage.

Muscadet and Côtes du Rhône were chosen from a wide selection of wines. Cooking was excellent, service was very good — 'no hurry and no delay'.

•*Drinks* full licence •*Meals* dinner (AC), bar food •*Cards* Visa, Access, Eurocard

SHANAGARRY

BALLYMALOE HOUSE
Shanagarry, Midleton, Co. Cork. (On L.35, 3km outside Cloyne on the Ballycotton Road.)

Tel. 021-652531 £££ Service 10%
Open 13.00-13.30/19.00-21.30 daily. *Closed* three days at Christmas.

This internationally-known restaurant is in a large country house, in extensive grounds up a long avenue. Despite the fact that it is 'in the luxury class in every way' and would have been a Big House in the days of *The Irish R.M.*, nearly all reporters stressed its restful and natural atmosphere. One man said that his party 'went for a walk between courses; we'd feel inhibited in this regard in most other establishments.' The restaurant serves a buffet lunch and an evening dinner, specialising in typical Irish country house food with some new dishes as well, and using home-grown produce and fresh seafood caught locally.

Dinner was featured in all reports. One person described the food as 'fresh from nearby farm and sea'. Seafood predominated in a beautifully laid out buffet of starters. Soups were seafood bisque, mushroom, and watercress. Roast duckling, monkfish, leg of lamb, fillet steak, and steak and oyster pie were among the main dishes, with a varied selection of fresh home-cooked sweets and fresh fruit from a trolley for dessert.

Bordeaux, Châteauneuf du Pape, and Coronas Black Label (a dry, full-bodied red Spanish wine) were chosen from an extensive wine list. All reporters were enthusiastic about the cooking, with one reservation, that garlic lamb and rosemary did not taste of either garlic or rosemary. One man thought his meal 'lacking in volume'. Service was friendly and competent. While Ballymaloe is not cheap, it is definitely recommended for an occasion. That our reporters thought it value for money may be judged from the simple comment of a Dublin man visiting the area: 'We went back two nights later'.

•*Drinks* full licence •*Meals* lunch (T d'H), dinner (T d'H) •*Cards* all major •*Cater for* children, wheelchair

SKIBBEREEN

WEST CORK HOTEL
Skibbereen, Co. Cork.

Tel. 028-21277　　　　　　££　　　　　　Service 10%
Open 12.30-14.30/18.00-21.00 daily. *Closed* six days at Christmas.

This hotel, near the River Ilen, faces out on to one of the town's streets. It is tastefully decorated and well maintained, and is popular both as a local venue and with foreign tourists. One reporter says that 'it shows signs of obviously dedicated and efficient management.'

Reporters had both lunch and dinner there. Soup — 'delicious home-made vegetable' — fried plaice, and 'too generous portions' of jelly trifle, and ice cream were the lunch dishes. For dinner, fresh lobster mayonnaise with 'unlimited vegetables' and salad, with a mixed cheese board — 'as good as any in Ireland' — was the chosen menu. Red house wine and Gewürztraminer wines were both good.

Cooking was excellent — ' simple local produce prepared and cooked on the premises'. Service was 'informal — extremely friendly, thoughtful, and efficient'.

•*Drinks* full licence •*Meals* lunch (AC + T d'H), dinner (AC + T d'H) •*Cards* Access, Visa, Diners, American Express •*Cater for* children, wheelchair

YOUGHAL

AHERNE'S
163, North Main Street, Youghal, Co. Cork.
Tel. 024-92424/92533   ££   Service 10%
Open 12.30-14.15/18.30-21.30 Tues-Sun, bar food 11.30-22.30 Tues-Sun.

This pub-cum-restaurant has a Georgian, latticed front, and — a great advantage in a town that goes back to the time of Sir Walter Raleigh — ample parking. It is comfortable, with wooden fixtures, and crisp white tablecloths and napkins.

Both lunch and dinner were sampled. For lunch, there was 'creamy, generous' mussel chowder, pan-fried cod fillet — 'from that morning's trawler' — and orange mousse. Dinner starters included prawns in garlic butter, smoked salmon, mussels in wine, and potato and leek soup. Chicken Kiev, sirloin steak, and prawns Mornay were some of the main dishes, with chocolate roulade, ice cream, lemon cheesecake and fresh fruit salad as desserts.

House wine was 'O.K.'. Service was very attentive — 'competent yet conversational'. Cooking was dubbed 'first rate'.

•*Drinks* **full licence** •*Meals* **lunch (AC + T d'H), dinner (AC + T d'H), bar food** •*Cards* **Access, Visa, Diners, American Express** •*Cater for* **children (over 8 years), wheelchair**

SOUTH WEST

Counties Kerry, Limerick and Tipperary

TIPPERARY IS THE ONLY COUNTY IN IRELAND to have the distinction of being divided into two administrative regions—the North and the South Ridings, with offices in Nenagh and Clonmel respectively. Near Clonmel is one of the best-known points in the south of the county, Slievenamon. Because of its relatively isolated position this mountain gives unrivalled views in clear weather. There is a fairly easy approach to the summit through the village of Kilcash, just off the Kilkenny-Clonmel road. This is the Cill Chais of the Irish song lamenting the felling of the woods and the disappearance of the Irish nobility.

The road from Carrick-on-Suir to Clonmel follows the River Suir, with the Comeragh Mountains to the south. There are roads into the Comeraghs from Clonmel. Part of the old town walls remain in this town, and the West Gate has been reconstructed across one of the main streets. Laurence Sterne, the author of *Tristram Shandy*, was born here. It was from Clonmel that Bianconi founded his car service in the first half of the last century as a cheap means of public transport. The large castle at Cahir, west of Clonmel on the Dublin-Cork road, is a National Monument open to the public. From Cahir you can reach the Glen of Aherlow and the Galtee Mountains.

The Rock of Cashel, one of Ireland's best-known landmarks, is in the heart of the county, and not far to the north of it lies the restored Abbey of Holy Cross. The River Shannon and Lough Derg form the western boundary of Tipperary. From Nenagh, a large town at the foot of Keeper Hill, you can move on to the lake shore at Dromineer, a favourite sailing centre. To enjoy the best views of the lake, it is worth going to Ballina (the other 'half' of Killaloe on the Tipperary side of the Shannon) and taking the scenic route north along the edge of the lake to Portroe, as several look-out points have been provided along this road. At the northern end of the lake is Terryglass, another port of call for people boating on the Shannon.

Limerick city is remembered for the historic siege in 1691, after which Patrick Sarsfield signed the Treaty commemorated by the Treaty Stone near Thomond Bridge. Some of the many impressive buildings in the city are the Georgian houses, two cathedrals, and King John's Castle near the river. With the National Institute of Higher Education (soon to be a university) at Castletroy, as well as Thomond College of Physical Education and a teacher training college, Limerick is full of young people during term times. At Lough Gur, twenty kilometres from the city, archaeological excavations have uncovered settlements of various eras, including crannógs (lake dwellings), stone circles, and Early Bronze Age tombs. Kilfinane, not far from Lough Gur, has an enormous rath encircled by a ring fort.

West of Limerick city, a road leads along the Shannon estuary through Foynes (a flying-boat base in the 1930s and 1940s) and Glin. Inland, on the main road leading to Killarney, is Adare; it is charming but not typically Irish, for it belonged to the estate of the Earls of Dunraven and is in appearance like an English village.

From Adare the road south-west leads to County Kerry. Known to its proud natives as 'The Kingdom', Kerry is one of the most popular tourist areas in the country. It has superb mountain and lake scenery on its two peninsulas, Iveragh and Dingle. The mountain ranges on Iveragh include the highest peaks in Ireland, the MacGillycuddy Reeks. The scenic route of The Ring of Kerry encompasses the entire coastline of the Iveragh peninsula. Killarney, the usual starting and finishing point for The Ring is, of course, a world-known beauty spot, but such places as Kenmare, Sneem, Waterville, and Glenbeigh have very much to offer, too. Derrynane, near Waterville, was the home of Daniel O'Connell, and his house — beside a very pleasant beach — is open to the public. There are several excellent beaches on both peninsulas.

The Dingle peninsula also has spectacular mountain scenery, particularly in the remote west. The unique attraction of this peninsula is, however, the number of reminders of early Christian and Celtic times in its standing stones, ancient graves, and early churches such as Gallarus Oratory, near Smerwick Harbour. The western tip of the Dingle peninsula is the Irish-speaking area of the Kerry Gaeltacht. The Blasket Islands are no longer inhabited, the islanders having transferred to the nearby mainland. The islands produced an extraordinary number of writers and poets, some of whose works are available in English translations, Muiris O Súilleabháin's *Twenty Years A-Growing* being one of the best known.

Outdoor activities in Kerry, as well as fishing, boating, and swimming, include mountain climbing, walking, and golf. Tralee, in the north of the county, is a busy, friendly town, with splendid beaches in the vicinity at Banna and Ballyheigue. The Rose of Tralee contest, which is staged there every September, brings a large number of visitors to the district. Another annual event is Writers' Week in Listowel, a town associated with the writers John B. Keane and Bryan MacMahon. From Tarbert, on the Shannon estuary, a frequent car-ferry operates to Kilrush in County Clare, providing a link-up with the main Limerick-Shannon Airport-Ennis-Galway road without the need to follow the estuary into Limerick.

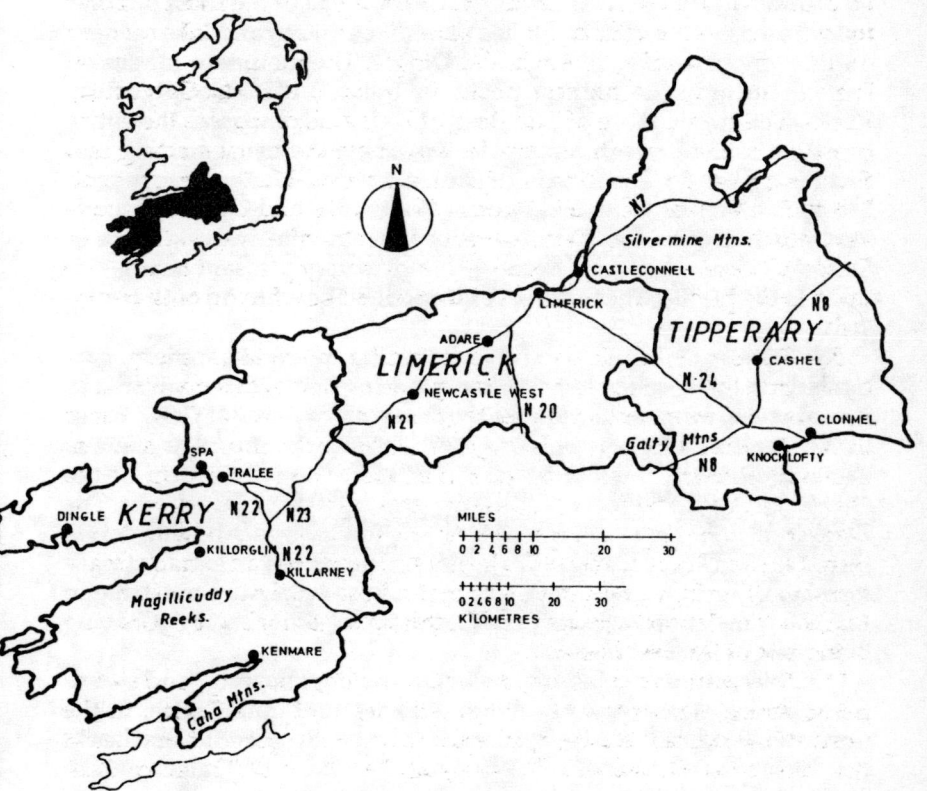

Co. Kerry

DINGLE

DOYLE'S SEAFOOD RESTAURANT
John Street, Dingle, Co. Kerry.
Tel. 066-51174 ££ Service nil
Open 12.30-14.15/18.00-21.00 Mon-Sat. Closed mid-November to early March.

Situated in the middle of the town, Doyle's is painted red and white on the outside and is well signposted. The owner is in attendance, and all reports stressed the friendly atmosphere of this restaurant. Dingle being the gateway to one of Kerry's most scenic peninsulas, the restaurant is well patronised and the only reservation expressed in one of the reports was that, because of the numbers, the seating was a trifle close so that one could maybe overhear other people's conversations. All seafood served is caught locally, organically grown vegetables are used, and the knowledgeable enthusiasm of the owner for the food he was serving made a meal memorable for some of our reporters.

All reports related to dinner. Nettle soup figured on the menu, and was enjoyed. Main fish dishes included sole stuffed with crabmeat, crabs' claws, turbot. There was also rack of lamb. One reporter waxed enthusiastic over a white wine sauce with garlic and tarragon — 'writing about it ... makes my taste buds hark back to Dingle.' A wide range of desserts was on offer — one person found the meringue with raspberry purée rather dry and was supplied with ice cream to go with it at no extra cost. Strawberry soufflé, home-made ice cream, and raspberries and cream were enjoyed. Cooking was first-class.

All our reporters agreed on the excellence of service and presentation; it was friendly and efficient. Wines were declared to be of good quality.

While this restaurant is not in the cheapest bracket food here seems to be good value.

•*Drinks* full licence •*Meals* lunch (AC), dinner (AC) •*Cards* all major •*Cater for* children, wheelchair

THE HALF DOOR
John Street, Dingle, Co. Kerry.
Tel. 066-51600 ££ Service nil
Open 12.30-14.00/18.00-22.00 daily. Closed 15 Nov-15 Mar.

This seasonal restaurant, specialising in seafood, is a standard terrace house; it is well-maintained, with an indoor plant garden at the rere of the restaurant. All reports related to dinner. Mussels in garlic, seafood chowder, and salmon pâté were starters, with medallions of monkfish, fillets of John Dory and steak in mushroom sauce as main dishes. Desserts included pavlova, hot apple pie,

and chocolate mousse with Bailey's cream. The house wine — Muscadet — was good. Cooking was excellent. Service was helpful and obliging and the staff were 'above all, humourous, which added a lot to the meal'.
•*Drinks* full licence •*Meals* lunch (AC), dinner (AC) •*Cards* all major

KENMARE

THE OLD DUTCH
Henry Street, Kenmare, Co. Kerry.
Tel. 064-41449   ££   *Service* nil
Open 12.30-21.45.

The comfortable surroundings of this restaurant enhance the enjoyment of a meal.

Reporters had dinner there. Home-made vegetable soup was 'beautiful'. Steak, pork steak, trout and monkfish were some of the main dishes. Fresh pineapple dressed with grapes and cream was among the more unusual sweets. There was also apple tart, and ice cream with raspberry sauce.

House wine was good, but Irish coffee, in one case, 'rather on the cool side'. Cooking was good except for the pork steak, which was somewhat dry. Service was friendly and efficient.
•*Drinks* wine licence •*Meals* lunch (T d'H), dinner (T d'H), tourist menu 12.30-16.00/18.00-21.45 (1 Feb-31 Dec) •*Cards* Visa

KILLARNEY

BRIAN MAC'S
11, High Street, Killarney, Co. Kerry.
Tel. 064-33398   £   *Service* nil
Open 11.00-22.00 daily (dinner after 19.00). *Closed* four days at Christmas.

This restaurant, with a clean and pleasant dining-room, is upstairs over Eager's newsagent's shop. It is patronised by both tourists and local people for lunch and for an evening out, and can often be crowded. The atmosphere is friendly and homely. The owner is a chef, and the restaurant is family-run. Reporters had lunch and dinner there. Side salad, breast of chicken, quiche, and home-made apple tart were lunch-time choices. For dinner, starters included salmon mousse and prawn cocktail; main dishes were roast lamb, and sirloin steak.

Desserts were pears in chocolate sauce, also a popular home-made apple tart. Red and white house wines were very pleasant. Cooking was highly commended. Service was excellent, from a friendly staff.
•*Drinks* wine licence •*Meals* lunch (AC + T d'H), dinner (AC + T d'H) •*Cards* Visa, Access •*Cater for* children

FOLEY'S SEAFOOD AND STEAK RESTAURANT
23, High Street, Killarney, Co. Kerry.
Tel. 064-31217 ££ *Service* nil
Open 12.30-15.00/17.00-23.00 daily, bar food 12.30-17.00 daily. *Closed* two days at Christmas.

This is a pub-cum-restaurant, entered through a traditional shop-style front. The atmosphere is very friendly and the staff welcoming. There are flowers on the restaurant tables, and soft music is played in the background. All reporters had dinner there, except one who appreciated a snack of piping hot mussel soup with home-made brown scones. At dinner starters were prawn cocktail, melon, and salads. Steaks were very popular as a main course, and trout in mushroom sauce was also enjoyed. Nobody had room for dessert — as one person put it, 'The portions [of the main dish] are ample.' Drinks were chosen from the bar. Cooking was excellent, service friendly and competent. One couple who went there at night with a baby said that the head waiter was kind, courteous, and helpful in accommodating them.

• *Drinks* full licence • *Meals* lunch (AC + T d'H), dinner (AC + T d'H) • *Cards* all major • *Cater for* children, wheelchair

KILLORGLIN

NICK'S RESTAURANT
Main Street, Killorglin, Co. Kerry.
Tel. 066-61219 ££ *Service* nil
Open 11.00-15.00 bar food Easter-Nov, 18.30-22.30 daily. *Closed* three days at Christmas.

This old stone house on the main street of the well known Puck Fair town has a bar-cum-dining-room with a second dining-room at a higher level. One reporter thought that the lighting was not good, and that as there were a number of steps in the restaurant this could be dangerous for older — or intoxicated! — people. The restaurant serves evening dinner only (see data above for availability of bar food at other times). All vegetables used in the restaurant are grown locally. Game, Kerry mountain lamb, and locally caught fish are other specialities.

All our reporters who ate dinner there praised the food. Cockle and mussel soup earned special commendation — 'a meal in itself'. Steaks and seafood — sole, scallops, lobster — were the most popular choices for the main course; portions were generous, and there was 'a sinful dessert choice', including rum and raisin ice cream, éclairs and fresh pineapple. The cooking met with full approval, food was 'cooked to bring out its full tenderness and flavour'. Presentation was excellent.

The house wine was pleasing. One man, whose party had red house wine and vinho verde, claimed that the wine list was as fine as he had encountered outside France.

Unfortunately there seems to be a problem on occasions with service in this otherwise highly commended restaurant. While some people found it quick, efficient and friendly, others complained of the delay in being seated (in spite of having booked a table for a specific time) and in having initial orders delivered.

•*Drinks* full licence •*Meals* dinner (AC) •*Cards* Visa, Access, Diners •*Cater for* children

TRALEE

BROGUE INN
Rock Street, Tralee, Co. Kerry.
Tel. 066-23357/22126   ££   *Service* nil
Open 10.30-22.30 weekdays. *Closed* Christmas Day, Good Friday, and advertised holidays.

This restaurant was commended by our reporters for both lunch and dinner. They liked the privacy afforded by the cubicle arrangements for tables, and the atmosphere appealed to them, one person summing it up as 'a place where an ordinary person would feel at home'.

It specialises in home-made pasta and desserts, and serves local seafood.

The quality of the food was good, helpings very generous, and the cooking excellent, dishes (e.g. steak) being cooked as requested. Steak, in fact, was one of the favourite main courses, and Baked Alaska was a popular dessert. One reporter who brought two children for lunch was very pleased with the generous children's portions, and with the attention paid to the children by the manager. Drinks were selected at the bar.

All our reporters found the service very good.

•*Drinks* full licence •*Meals* lunch (AC + T d'H), dinner (AC + T d'H) •*Cards* Access, Visa •*Cater for* children (up to 20.00 hours), wheelchair

MOUNT BRANDON HOTEL
Princess Street, Tralee, Co. Kerry.
Tel. 066-23333/213111   £££   *Service* nil
Open 12.30-14.30/19.00-21.30.

The Brandon is an expensive restaurant, suited rather to a meal for a special occasion than to a hurried repast en route to the Dingle peninsula.

Our reporters had both lunch and dinner there, choosing for starters mushroom soup, egg mayonnaise, and corn on the cob. 'Beautiful' roast beef, and sole on the bone were the main-course dishes selected, with fresh fruit salad and rum and raisin ice cream for dessert. The hotel, of course, has a full licence, but our reporters confined themselves to water with their meals. Cooking came in for high praise, and service was good.

•*Drinks* full licence •*Meals* lunch (T d'H), dinner (AC + T d'H) •*Cards* all major

OYSTER TAVERN
The Spa, Tralee, Co. Kerry. (5km from Tralee on Fenit road.)
Tel. 066-36102 ££ *Service* nil
Open 18.30-22.30 daily Easter to Nov, weekdays Nov to Easter. Lunch served Jun-Sept.

This is is a renovated pub and restaurant, with a large car park. It specialises in seafood, with some meat dishes. It is comfortable, with a friendly, relaxed atmosphere. There is Irish music, and a resident pianist on certain evenings of the week in summer. Dinner was the subject of all reports. Since it is a seafood restaurant, most people chose fish in some form, with seafood chowder as a starter, and sole on the bone, scampi, and salmon as main dishes. Mushrooms as a starter, and sirloin steak, were also popular. Desserts did not figure among their choices. Drinks were selected from the bar. Cooking and presentation were acclaimed in all cases, particularly in the case of fish. Service was efficient but not intrusive.

• *Drinks* full licence • *Meals* lunch (AC), dinner (AC) • *Cards* Visa, Access
• *Cater for* children, wheelchair

Co. Limerick

ADARE

DUNRAVEN ARMS HOTEL
Adare, Co. Limerick.
Tel. 061-86209 £££ *Service* 12.5%
Open 08.00-10.00/12.30-14.15/19.30-21.30 daily. *Closed* Christmas Day, Good Friday.

This is an old hotel in Adare village, its old-world character carried through to the interior, maintained like a country house.

Our reporters had lunch and dinner, dealt with here together. Some of the starters chosen were mussels, egg mayonnaise, seafood cocktail, avocado, and pâté. Main dishes included eels in white wine sauce, roast beef, stuffed pork steak, duckling, and poached salmon. Chocolate gâteau, fresh fruit salad, apple pie, strawberry mousse, and home-made ice cream were chosen from a well-stocked dessert trolley. The house wine was good. Cooking and presentation were highly praised, and there was a high standard of courteous and efficient service.

• *Drinks* full licence • *Meals* breakfast, lunch (AC + T d'H), dinner (AC + T d'H) • *Cards* all major

THE MUSTARD SEED
Adare, Co. Limerick.

Tel. 061-86451 £££ Service nil
Open 19.00-22.00 Tues-Sat.*Closed* month of February.

This restaurant has accommodation for just 30 diners, in a small old-style terraced house which blends in with the old estate village of Adare. It caters only for evening dinner and is mainly used as a dining-out venue rather than by passing trade. Prices are relatively high, but all our reporters were pleased with their evening.

The interior decor, flowers, and table appointments received favourable comment. As it is a small establishment, patrons feel that they are treated more as personal guests than as customers. One person, however, complained of having to give his order in a 'waiting room' within earshot of other people.

Food, cooking and presentation were unanimously praised. Green and red seaweed with French dressing was an unusual starter appreciated by one of our reporters. Some of the main dishes on offer on different dates were free-range duck, veal stuffed with blue cheese, roast lamb, and shark steaks about which the only complaint was that the serving was 'over enthusiastic'. Bananas baked in rum, home-made praline ice cream, and rich chocolate gâteau were among the desserts. In some cases the proprietor was asked to suggest the wine to go with the meal, and this was very good. Other reporters praised the Bulgarian wine available.

•*Drinks* wine licence •*Meals* dinner (T d'H) •*Cards* Visa, Access, Diners •*Cater for* wheelchair (not to toilets), non-smokers

WOODLANDS GUESTHOUSE
Knockanes, Adare, Co. Limerick. (On a side road on the Limerick side of Adare.)

Tel. 061-86118/86511 £ Service nil
Open 18.30-22.00 daily, 13.00-15.00 Sun, bar food 10.30-23.30. *Closed* two days at Christmas.

This country-house restaurant has been the subject of enthusiastic reports citing it as giving very good value. 'Excellent food for extraordinarily low prices,' one home economics teacher summed it up. It serves evening dinner, and Sunday lunch, while bar food is available all day.

Nearly all our reporters had dinner. Starters included seafood cocktail, home-made soup, deep-fried garlic mushrooms, chicken vol-au-vent, and melon. Main dishes were sole, trout, sirloin steak, chicken Maryland, roast pork. Pavlova, fresh fruit salad, apple tart, cheesecake, and chocolate mousse were chosen from a very ample dessert trolley. Wine was satisfactory.

Cooking was highly commended. This restaurant caters for over 70 people at a sitting, and there can be three sittings in an evening. Nonetheless, our reporters remarked on the well-supervised, attentive level of the service and felt that there was no pressure placed on them to vacate their tables for the next customers.

•*Drinks* full licence •*Meals* Sunday lunch (T d'H), dinner (T d'H) •*Cards* all major

CASTLECONNELL

CASTLE OAKS HOUSE HOTEL
Castleconnell, Co. Limerick.
Tel. 061-377666 ££ Service nil
Open 12.30-14.30/19.00-21.45 daily, bar food 12.00- 20.00. *Closed* Christmas Day.

This hotel, an old Georgian house overlooking the River Shannon, was formerly a convent, and the main function room retains stained glass windows. The interior decor is elegant. It is some two miles off the main Dublin-Limerick road and has spacious parking facilities. One of our reporters recommends that the main entrance to the hotel should be better signposted, as it is at the opposite end of the building from the road entrance to the car park.

All reports dealt with dinner. Starters were mainly seafood crêpes, and chicken liver pâté. Veal, fillet steak, beef medallions, and grilled salmon were among the main dishes. At dinner, there was a wide choice from the sweet trolley, but one person found fault with the cheesecake because it did not appear to be home-made. Wine was good except that the house wine supplied as part of an all-in Dinner for Two was, in one case, somewhat watery.

Cooking was generally excellent; one reporter described his meal as having 'nouvelle cuisine lightness without nouvelle cuisine meanness in regard to portions'. Service 'gave first class attention'.

•*Drinks* full licence •*Meals* breakfast, bar food, lunch (AC + T d'H), dinner (AC + T d'H) •*Cards* Access, Visa, Diners, American Express •*Cater for* children, wheelchair

LIMERICK CITY

DE LA FONTAINE RESTAURANT
10-12, Upper Gerald Griffin Street, Limerick.
Tel. 061-44461 ££ Service nil
Open 12.30-14.30/19.00-22.30 Mon-Sat. *Closed* 25 Dec-16 Jan.

This is a French restaurant in the old heart of the city, and the outside is not very impressive. Inside — it is upstairs — it is nicely decorated. Home grown produce is used in the cooking, as well as ingredients imported from France.

The menu was described by one of the reporters as 'somewhat limited', but hot salad of kidney and liver, spinach and potato soup, sole with prawns, fish platter, and veal with bananas and rum, were well received. The cooking, including the cooking of vegetables, was good; in particular, the sauces complemented the food. A variety of desserts included pears in red wine and French apple tart.

Special mention was made of the proprietor's knowledge of wines and his readiness to impart it.

Service was friendly and efficient, and the staff well informed about the various dishes.

•*Drinks* wine licence •*Meals* lunch (T d'H), dinner (T d'H) •*Cards* none •*Cater for* children, non-smokers

JASMINE PALACE
O' Connell Mall, O' Connell Street, Limerick.
Tel. 061-42484 ££ Service 10%
Open 12.30-14.30/17.00-24.00. Closed Christmas, Good Friday.

This Chinese restaurant, using Cantonese cuisine, is not remarkable on the outside, but is very pleasant inside, beautifully clean, nicely decorated in Chinese style, warm and relaxing. In addition to a wide variety of Cantonese dishes served à la carte, it provides some European food, a set-price lunch, and a set-price dinner with the number of courses varying according to the number in the party ordering the meal. All our reporters had dinner there. Sweet corn and crabmeat soup, barbecue spare ribs, roast duck in lemon sauce, garlic chicken, and beef in blackbean sauce were some of their choices. Main desserts were fresh fruit salad, lychees, and ice cream. The house wine met with approval. Cooking was good; the food was well flavoured. Service was attentive; there was a pause between courses, but this was acceptable.
•*Drinks* wine licence •*Meals* lunch (AC + T d'H) dinner (AC + T d'H) •*Cards* Visa, Access, American Express, Diners, Luncheon Vouchers •*Cater for* children

NEWCASTLE WEST

THE MALLARD
3, North Quay, Newcastle West, Co. Limerick.
Tel. 069-62825 ££ Service 10% dinner only
Open 12.30-15.00/19.00-22.30 Tues-Sat,12.30- 15.00 Sun.

The restaurant is on the ground floor of a large three-storey house, overlooking the River Laune. It is well kept with well maintained interior decor, but one of our reporters lamented that there was no area available where one could sit before or after the meal, all the space being given over to the dining-room area.

All our reporters had dinner. Starters were pâté, mushrooms, and 'the best cream of chicken soup I've tasted ... for years'. Duckling and fresh grilled salmon were the main dishes, with a good selection of desserts which included crème caramel. Reasonably priced house wine was very good. The cooking was excellent, service friendly but a little slow.
•*Drinks* wine licence •*Meals* lunch (AC + T d'H), dinner (AC + T d'H) •*Cards* Access, Visa, Diners •*Cater for* children

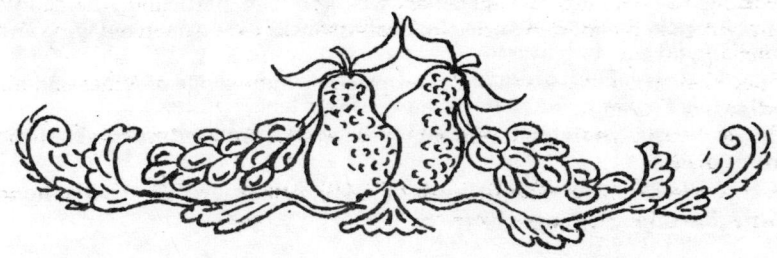

Co. Tipperary

CASHEL

BAILEY'S OF CASHEL
Main Street, Cashel, Co. Tipperary.
Tel. 062-61937   ££   Service nil
Open 12.00-23.00 daily. Closed Christmas Day.

This is a basement restaurant in a renovated Georgian house, set back from the main street of Cashel opposite the Post Office. The restaurant is well laid out, and our reporters found the atmosphere homely and welcoming.

Sirloin, minute and garlic steaks predominated in our reporters' choices of a main dish. Smoked salmon and mussels (the latter 'could have been anything') were among the starters chosen. Cheesecake was the main dessert. The house wine was good.

Cooking of minute and sirloin steaks was criticised as not quite right, but the cooking of vegetables was praised. One reporter said that there seemed to be some difficulty in serving food hot enough, particularly the consommé which was the soup chosen by one of his party. Service was otherwise satisfactory.

•Drinks wine licence •Meals lunch (AC + T d'H), dinner (AC + T d'H), tourist menu 15.00-19.00 daily •Cards Access, Visa, Diners •Cater for children (before 19.00 hrs), non-smokers

CHEZ HANS
Rockside, Cashel, Co. Tipperary.
Tel. 062-61177   £££   Service nil
Open 18.00-23.00 Tues-Sat. Closed three days at Christmas, first three weeks of January.

This is a small converted church at the foot of the Rock of Cashel. Naturally, the national monument adds to the ambience of the restaurant when it is floodlit at night. The interior of the old church has been made very comfortable, but as it is a stone building it demands a high degree of heat in cold weather. Table linen and arrangements are tasteful and appealing, but one reporter deprecated the lack of linen napkins in a restaurant of its price range. The proprietor is the chef.

Our reporters found a wide range of food on offer. Roast pheasant featured as the main dish choice of several people; brill, fillet of lamb, and salmon in sorrel sauce were others. Two reporters felt that the helpings of various starters were too large, and if eaten completely left little room for the equally generous portions of the main dish. Other starters were mussels with garlic, pâté, and mushroom soup. Home-made Irish Mist and walnut ice creams were chosen as desserts when the diners had room for them. Wine was very pleasant or, in one case, 'very good but expensive'.

Service was rated friendly and in the main, efficient, although some people found it slow. Cooking was highly acclaimed.

•*Drinks* full licence •*Meals* dinner (AC) •*Cards* none •*Cater for* children, wheelchair

CLONMEL

CLONMEL ARMS HOTEL
Sarsfield Street, Clonmel, Co. Tipperary.
Tel. 052-21233 ££ *Service* nil
Open 12.30-14.30/18.00-22.00 daily. *Closed* three days at Christmas.

A substantial, solid hotel in the town centre, it is unimpressive outside but well lit up at night. The dining-room and lounge have been renovated. The environment was described by one of our reporters as high-class — there was live piano music, and women were presented with roses. There is, however, no question of grandeur; one party who were delighted to dine there after climbing Slievenamon felt quite at home with the minimum of change to their tramping gear. All our reporters rated it good value, as a five course meal was available for £10 at weekends.

Starters included mushrooms in garlic sauce and egg mayonnaise. Venison was a main dish choice for one reporter, who pronounced it 'delightful'. Fillet of beef was another popular choice. Fresh fruit salad and pavlova were among the desserts — the pavlova in one case did not live up to expectations as there was no real taste of meringue. Assessments of the cooking ranged from 'good for the price range' to 'superb'. Venison, beef, and salmon served are specially supplied locally. There was a good value wine list, the house wine (red and white) being judged as 'very acceptable'.

Service was 'first class' — fast, courteous, and good humoured.

•*Drinks* full licence •*Meals* all served to non-residents, lunch (AC + T d'H), dinner (AC + T d'H) •*Cater for* children

THE EMERALD GARDEN
O'Connell St., Clonmel, Co. Tipperary.
Tel. 052-24270 ££ *Service* 10%
Open 12.30-14.00/17.30-24.00 Mon-Fri, 13.00-14.30/17.30-24.00 Sat-Sun. *Closed* Christmas Day, Good Friday.

This is a well-known Chinese restaurant in the centre of Clonmel. It has an unusual black façade, and a pleasant interior with (naturally) Chinese decor, very clean and well-kept. The tables, however, are slightly cramped.

Chow Mein and sizzling steak with black bean sauce were main dishes chosen at lunch-time. For dinner, sliced beef and green pepper and beansprout sauce, and roast duck with fried rice were among the chief courses. The dessert menu was limited, the apple pie available being dubbed 'poor'. Mateus Rosé was chosen from the wine list.

Presentation and cooking were good, the only criticism, apart from that of the apple pie, being that 'the beansprout sauce was too salty'.
Service was attentive but not intrusive.

•*Drinks* wine licence •*Meals* lunch (AC), dinner (AC) •*Cards* Access, Visa, Diners •*Cater for* children (special menu), wheelchair

KNOCKLOFTY HOUSE HOTEL
Clonmel, Co. Tipperary. (Off Clonmel-Ardfinnan road.)
Tel. 052-38222   ££   *Service* nil
Open 12.30-14.30/19.00-22.30 daily.

This is a large country house overlooking the River Suir. The wood-panelled library is used for reception and pre-dinner drinks. Our reporters did not feel overawed by the stately home surroundings, remarking on the friendly, personal attention received. One Dublin man commented wistfully, 'I could get used to this style all too easily.'

Reporters had dinner there. Oysters and avocado cocktail were selected for starters. Turbot and filet mignon steak in pepper sauce were main courses, with fresh fruit and Black Forest gâteau among the desserts. Presentation was excellent, as was the cooking in general. Wine, selected from the wine list, met with approval.

•*Drinks* full licence •*Meals* lunch (T d'H), dinner (T d'H) •*Cards* Access, Visa

WEST

Counties Clare, Galway, Mayo

OUR WEST REGION INCLUDES County Clare, as well as Galway and Mayo. We hope that we may be forgiven for filching it from Munster in this arbitrary fashion.

The coast of Clare has long been regarded as a playground for Limerick city, and with its fine strands such as Kilkee and Lahinch and further north at Fanore, you can understand its popularity. Atlantic rollers make an impressive sight in rough weather, while the Cliffs of Moher, one of Ireland's main tourist attractions, can be awe-inspiring even in a mist.

Clare is bounded on the east by Lough Derg, and in recent years the development of cruising on the Shannon waterway has opened up this part to many people. Even for people not into boating, the marinas at Mountshannon and Killaloe are interesting, with the constant coming and going of yachts and cruisers and the sound of Continental tongues. The Burren, in the north-west of the county, is an area of terraced limestone hills unique in western Europe. The alpine vegetation is best seen when the blue gentian and red bloody cranesbill are in bloom in early summer. The caves in the limestone, notably at Slieve Elva, attract pot-holers. One of them, Aillwee, not far from Ballyvaughan, has been opened to the public, and is unspoiled despite the frequent visits of tour buses and school trips.

The poet Brian Merriman is connected with the Feakle and Lough Graney district, and the Merriman Summer School, held at various venues annually in August, discusses many issues far removed from the poet's *Midnight Court*. For those interested in antiquities, these range from prehistoric burial places such as the Poulnabrone dolmen in the Burren, seen to advantage against the limestone pavement and a clear sky, to remains of abbeys such as Corcomroe and Quin. There are round towers on Inish Caltra (Holy Island) near Scariff and Scattery Island near Kilrush. The castles of Knappogue and Bunratty are used in the tourist season for mediaeval banquets. The Folk Park at Bunratty and the reconstructed early settlement at Cregganowen give a glimpse of life in Clare in long-vanished times. Doolin, north of Lisdoonvarna, is a centre for Irish music, well-known even outside Ireland.

East and south County Galway are quite different from the western part, namely Connemara. The limestone of east Galway is responsible for the wide plains dotted with sheep and broken up by stone walls. Portumna in the south is on the upper end of Lough Derg, and as well as a forest park on the shores of the lake, has a large marina. If you happen to be held up by the opening of the Shannon Bridge at Portumna, it is a compensation to watch the craft passing upstream and downstream. South-west County Galway is the countryside of Yeats and Lady Gregory. Thoor Ballylee, near Gort, is a Yeats Museum. Lady Gregory's house at Coole has crumbled, but the grounds are now part of an open forest and the gardens are well maintained, with pleasant walks.

Galway city is arguably the most interesting city in Ireland. Small enough to explore completely on foot, it contains many old buildings connected with the merchant families who were the 'Tribes of Galway' and developed its trade with the Continent. The Spanish Arch near the docks is a fragment of the old city walls. In contrast to this, across the Corrib, the huge new Catholic Cathedral dominates the skyline. Its interior is ornately decorated and worth viewing. The main Galway races meeting at the end of July is one of Ireland's foremost sporting events; the city is thronged with visitors, and business comes almost to a standstill as most people take to the racecourse at Ballybrit. Taibhdhearc na Gaillimhe, the small theatre which has launched many internationally known actors and actresses, regularly puts on plays in Irish, and plays in English are staged at the Druid Theatre. Also, there are Irish music sessions in many pubs. Apart from its intrinsic interest, Galway is the gateway to Connemara. From the rocky coast of Cois Fharraige which extends along the north side of Galway Bay, you can see the Aran Islands, which may be visited by boat from Rossaveal, about forty kilometres out on that road. This is the Gaeltacht (Irish speaking) area, and in summer the roads are alive with teenagers from the many Irish language colleges. Inland is a region of mountains and lakes. Going up by Lough Corrib and Oughterard towards Clifden you approach the ranges of both the Maamturk and Beanna Beola (Twelve Bens) Mountains. These may be seen more fully by going up Glen Inagh, which divides them, towards Letterfrack National Park and Kylemore Abbey. Clifden and Roundstone are popular venues in summer; the coast there has not only magnificent rocky inlets but beautiful strands, such as that at Dog's Bay near Roundstone. Killary Harbour, which is a fjiord, is the northern limit of Connemara. The mountains slope steeply down on both sides; crossing at Leenane, the head of the inlet, you can travel to Westport and Louisburgh in Mayo by Aasleagh Falls and the long narrow lake of Doolough.

Near Westport is Croagh Patrick, the scene of a pilgrimage at the end of July. Pilgrimage apart, its slopes afford a sweeping view of Clew Bay and its many islands. Achill Island is easily reached from Westport. Its white houses, golden sands, and imposing scenery of the Minaun Cliffs and the Atlantic Drive, are only some of the things which draw holidaymakers back to Achill year after year. The blanket bog of North Mayo terminates in the cliffs of the North Mayo coast. Inland from Belderrig the remains of a neolithic farm settlement have been excavated from the bog, and you may still see where people cooked and worked thousands of years ago. Killala and the surrounding coast is where the French invasion force landed in 1798. The Humbert Summer School, held in August in Ballina, deals generally with topics of European interest. Ballina, on the River Moy, and the neighbouring Loughs Conn and Cullin, are noted fishing areas, as is Lough Mask in the west of the county. In the north-east of Mayo is Knock Shrine, a place of frequent pilgrimage. Connacht Regional

Airport, near there, has defied all gloomy commercial prophecies by providing facilities for people from the West working in England to come home at week-ends.

Ballintubber Abbey, not far from Castlebar, and Cong Abbey are just two of the county's National Monuments which will repay a visit. Ballintubber is not far from Lough Carra and Moore Hall, the ruined home of George Moore, the novelist.

Cong, a picturesque village between Lough Mask and Lough Corrib, is still remembered for its connections with the film *The Quiet Man*.

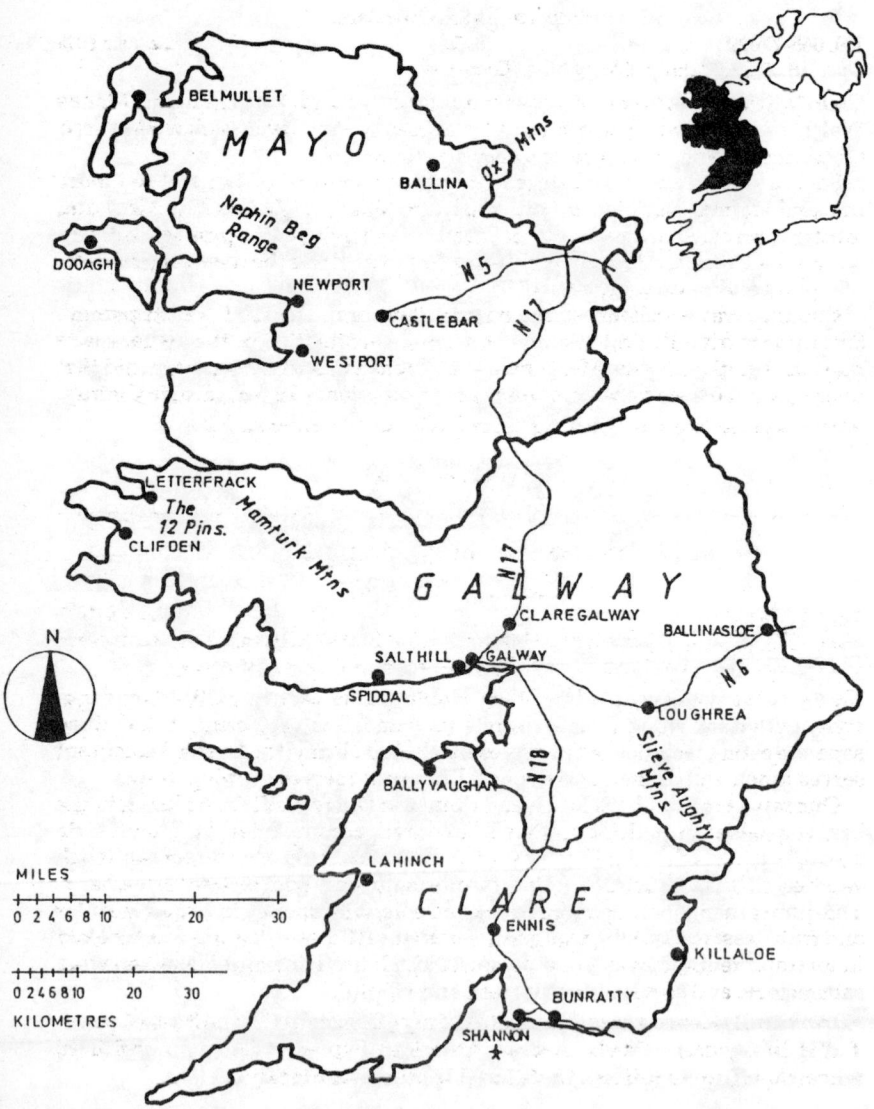

Co. Clare

BALLYVAUGHAN

CLAIRE'S RESTAURANT
Ballyvaughan, Co. Clare.
Tel. 065-77029   £££   Service 10%
Open 18.30-22.00 daily. *Closed* Nov- Easter.

Claire's Restaurant is part of a craft shop and art gallery, with the name 'Manus Walsh' over the door. The restaurant itself is at ground level, with well-spaced tables and an open fire. It serves evening dinner only.

Savoury profiteroles and carrot and orange soup were some of the more unusual starters sampled by our reporters. Baked crab, chicken Kiev, and lobster were chosen as main dishes; strawberry pavlova and praline ice cream were some desserts. House wine met with approval and the wine list generally was good and reasonably priced.

Cooking was excellent — 'the natural flavour of the food was apparent'. Service was friendly and attentive; the personal attention of the owner made patrons feel like friends. Meals here are expensive, but one reporter said that over a period of twelve years she has never experienced a bad meal in Claire's.

•*Drinks* wine licence •*Meals* dinner (AC) •*Cards* Access, Visa

BUNRATTY

DURTY NELLIE'S
Bunratty, Co Clare.
Tel. 061-364861   ££   Service 10%
Open Oyster Restaurant 10.30-23.30 weekdays, 12.00-23.00 Sun; Loft Restaurant 18.00-23.00 daily, bar food all day. *Closed* Christmas Day, Good Friday.

The building now occupied by Durty Nellie's dates back to 1620. It is cottage-style, with dark wood inside; despite its name, it is very clean. It has three separate eating facilities. A bar serves snack food all day; the Oyster Restaurant serves lunch and dinner; and the Loft Restaurant serves evening dinner.

Our reporters had both lunch and dinner in Durty Nellie's. At lunch in the bar, vegetable soup, thick and well-flavoured, accompanied by brown soda bread, was considered good value at £1, and a toasted corned-beef sandwich was described as 'much better than the normal greasy ham on offer elsewhere'. The dinner menu included roast duck and sole, with sponge in Grand Marnier and fruit dessert. Cooking was good at both meal times — 'simple food cooked in an unpretentious way', one person said. House wine and Heineken were satisfactory, and service friendly, fast, and helpful.

•*Drinks* full licence •*Meals* lunch (AC only), dinner (AC in Loft and Oyster, T d'H in Oyster) •*Cards* Access, American Express •*Cater for* children, wheelchair (not to toilets), traditional Irish music nightly

MC CLOSKEY'S

Bunratty House Mews, Bunratty, Co. Clare. (Near Bunratty Castle.)
Tel. 061-364082   £££   Service 10%
Open 19.00 hours Tues-Sat. Closed 20 Dec-25 Jan.

This restaurant, serving evening dinner, is in the converted cellars of an old Georgian house, near Bunratty Folk Park. The reception area, for drinks, is somewhat cramped, but the dining-room is nicely broken up into small divisions of three or four tables. The tables have fresh, real linen napkins and tablecloths.

Dinner was the subject of all reports. Crab and pepper crêpes, cheese soufflé, and veal terrine with blackcurrant and orange were some of the starters. Noisettes of lamb, stir-fried beef, sole, brill, and veal with fresh lime sauce were among the main dishes. Two of the desserts were Irish liqueur ice cream and fruit salad with ginger sauce. House wine was good, but most diners chose from the wine list.

Cooking was very good. In one case where the customer thought the roast beef did not come up to standard — not having been 'hung' for long enough — the dish was immediately replaced and the item removed from the menu for the evening.

The general opinion of our reporters was that service was rather slow.

•*Drinks* wine licence •*Meals* dinner (T d'H) •*Cards* Visa, Diners, American Express

CRATLOE

LIMERICK INN
(RENDEZVOUS RESTAURANT)

Ennis Road, Limerick. (This is actually in Co. Clare, on main Limerick-Shannon-Galway road.)
Tel. 061-26920   ££   Service nil
Open 07.30-10.00/12.30-14.30/18.00-21.30.

The Rendezvous Restaurant is part of the Limerick Inn, with a warm and comfortable atmosphere. Lunch and dinner were featured in our reports. Lunch starters included consommé and fruit cup. The main course for adults was pork steak; a half-portion of roast beef was sufficient to divide between two children, chips being offered to accompany it. Sherry trifle and cheesecake were desserts. Tournedos Rossini, with a seafood starter and a selection from the sweet trolley, was the dinner. Muscadet and Côtes du Rhône were the wines, deemed very good.

Cooking and presentation were highly commended. Vegetables were crisp, and the food was served piping hot on piping hot plates.
Service was attentive.

•*Drinks* full licence •*Meals* breakfast, lunch (AC + T d'H), dinner (AC + T d'H), tourist menu 12.30-14.30 daily except Sundays and Christmas •*Cards* all major •*Cater for* children

ENNIS

THE CLOISTER
Abbey Street, Ennis, Co. Clare.
Tel. 065-29521 ££ Service 10%
Open 10.30-22.00 weekdays, 18.00-22.00 Sun.

The Cloister is near the old Franciscan Abbey. It has a well-kept exterior, with attractive flower boxes, and its rear patio is actually part of the abbey ruins. Inside, it is comfortable and well appointed; the tables are rather close together, so one might overhear other people's conversations.

Lunch and dinner were the subject of our reports in almost equal proportions. Lunches included sandwiches, crab salad, and Fergus salmon. One of the starters at dinner was stir-fried duck; there was also pasta and lobster bisque. Veal cutlets, roast lamb, and grilled salmon were some of the main courses. Blackberry pie and summer fruits in white wine were among the desserts. The house wine earned approval; other drinks were selected from the bar.

Cooking was very good. One reporter was very pleased that food did not come in large quantities but was very tasty with 'superb' sauces. Service was friendly, and, in the main, prompt, but some people who had lunch there thought that, with the number of staff available, it could have been quicker.

•*Drinks* full licence •*Meals* lunch (AC + T d'H), dinner (AC + T d'H), tourist menu 12.15-16.00 except Sun •*Cards* all major

SHERWOOD INN
Ennis Shopping Centre, Ennis, Co. Clare.
Tel. 065-20255 £ Service nil
Open 08.30-18.00 Mon-Wed, Sat, 08.30-21.00 Thur- Fri.

This is in the Ennis shopping centre, with good parking facilities. It has a carved wooden exterior; inside, there is a self-service counter, with comfortable seating around the walls and small tables in the middle. It is popular, and tends to be crowded at lunchtime. As it is part of the shopping centre it is restricted to shopping hours, so all our reports dealt with lunch.

Roast chicken and lasagne were chosen, with fresh fruit salad, apple tart, and cheesecake as sweets. Cooking was 'not exotic, but not boring either'. Staff were pleasant and helpful.

All reports showed enthusiasm for the value for money offered here.

•*Drinks* soft•*Meals* breakfast, lunch (AC) •*Cards* none •*Cater for* children

WEST COUNTY INN HOTEL
Ennis, Co. Clare. (On the outskirts of town on Limerick road.)
Tel. 065-28421   ££   Service 10%
Open Pine Room 12.30-14.30/19.00-21.00 daily, Grill Room 14.30-22.00 daily.

This purpose-built modern hotel has ample parking facilities. It is nicely decorated and furnished in functional style. It has both a grill-room and a dining-room; one reporter recommended it specially because it is nearly always possible to get a meal in one of them — important to the traveller.

Reports covered both lunch in the grill-room and dinner in the Pine Room.

Grilled plaice, grilled salmon, and roast lamb were choices for lunch. One party had no room for dessert, but apple pie and fresh fruit were chosen by others. At dinner, there was chicken bouchée, pâté, cream of asparagus and Stilton soup, then entrecôte chasseur and veal steak stuffed with cheese and ham. Fruit trifle and fresh fruit salad were desserts.

The only wine drunk at either meal was the house wine, judged 'acceptable'. Cooking was excellent for both meals — 'steak perfectly cooked to order, vegetables firm and crisp'. Service was good — 'always somebody available to help'.

•*Drinks* full licence •*Meals* lunch (AC + T d'H), dinner (AC + T d'H), tourist menu 18.00-21.00 •*Cards* all major •*Cater for* children, wheelchair

KILLALOE

LAKESIDE HOTEL
Killaloe, Co. Clare.
Tel. 061-76122   ££   Service nil
Open 12.30-14.30/19.00-22.00 weekdays, 12.30-14.30/18.00-21.00 Sun. *Closed* three days at Christmas.

This hotel is situated at the water's edge, on the banks of the Shannon just at the southern end of Lough Derg, and in good summer weather the boat traffic makes an animated scene. The hotel was renovated in recent years and has an attractive decor. There are two sittings for Sunday lunch, and booking is necessary for that meal.

Our reporters had both lunch and dinner there. Dinner earned high approval from somebody who had eaten there five times in twelve months, but lunch called forth less enthusiasm from a reporter who described it as 'typical Sunday lunch fare in an Irish hotel'. Main lunch courses — chicken, lamb, and roast beef — were well flavoured and tender, but a coleslaw salad as a starter was limp and the vegetables were not good. Dessert was ice cream. Beaujolais was a satisfactory wine.

A much more favourable picture of dinner emerged. Avocado salad and pâté were starters, and lobster bisque was a welcome soup. Entrecôte chasseur was cooked to taste, vegetables were just right, and there was a choice of six

good desserts on the trolley. House wine was reasonably priced at £7.75 a bottle. Cooking was 'above average' and service good.
•*Drinks* full licence •*Meals* breakfast, lunch (AC + T d'H), dinner (AC + T d'H) •*Cards* Access, Visa, Diners, American Express •*Cater for* children, wheelchair

LAHINCH

ATLANTIC HOTEL
Lahinch, Co. Clare.

Tel. 065-81049 ££ *Service* 10%
Open 12.30-14.30 bar food and Sunday lunch, 18.00-19.15 tourist menu daily/19.30-21.00 dinner only. *Closed* October-Easter.

This is a town house in the main street of this holiday resort town. Inside, it is plainly furnished, with a friendly atmosphere.

All our reporters had dinner. A very welcome feature of this hotel is that there is a special early dinner at a cheaper rate, with a wide menu selection. This is very suitable to the holiday-maker who has to eat out every evening.

A reporter who had the early menu in a party of three listed pâté maison, smoked mackerel, and mushroom soup as first courses, with chicken, baked ham, and plaice to follow, and strawberry parfait and apple pie as dessert. The cooking was of 'good Irish standard'.

At the later dinner, there were mussels in garlic butter, curried mushrooms en croûte, and mulligatawny soup, with main dishes of beef Wellington and fillet of trout. There was a choice of five desserts, including walnut meringue and mint ice with hot chocolate. 'Each dish was carefully and tastefully prepared.'

Wines were 'fine' with both menus, and service friendly and efficient.
•*Drinks* full licence •*Meals* bar lunch, Sunday lunch, dinner (AC + T d'H), tourist menu •*Cards* Visa, Access •*Cater for* children, wheelchair

Co. Galway

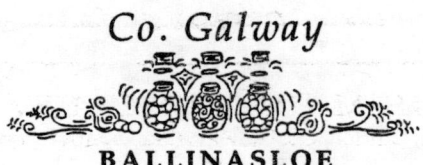

BALLINASLOE

HAYDEN'S HOTEL
Dunlo Street, Ballinasloe, Co. Galway.

Tel. 0905-42347   ££   Service nil

Open restaurant 12.30-14.30/18.00-22.00 daily, buffet 10.00-20.00 daily. *Closed* two days at Christmas.

This hotel is a nicely kept small town hotel, with an attractively decorated interior, and seating available in an enclosed garden in good weather. As well as a restaurant, it has a buffet serving food all day, and the hotel is well patronised by travellers between Dublin and Galway.

Reporters had both lunch — at the buffet — and dinner there, and all our reporters were very favourably impressed. For lunch, there was seafood — salmon and prawns — with unlimited amounts of various salads.

Starters at dinner were seafood cocktail and prawns, with roast lamb and grilled salmon as main dishes. Fresh fruit salad and home-made ice cream were the desserts. House wine (good) was the only alcohol mentioned in reports. Robert Roberts' coffee was served at the buffet.

Cooking was rated excellent, and service very efficient.

•*Drinks* full licence •*Meals* lunch (AC + T d'H), dinner (AC + T d'H), buffet food •*Cards* Access, Visa, American Express, Diners •*Cater for* children, wheelchair

CLAREGALWAY

THE ABBEY RESTAURANT
Claregalway, Co. Galway. (On main Galway-Tuam-Sligo road.)

Tel. 091-98244   ££   Service nil

Open 19.00-22.30 Mon-Sat. *Closed* one week at Christmas, Good Friday.

The exterior of this restaurant is not impressive, but it is warm and comfortable, if rather small, inside. It serves evening dinner only.

Some of the starters chosen by our reporters were scampi, prawns in avocado, crab claws and barbecued ribs. Main dishes included rack of lamb, veal, fillet of beef, and roast duck. Among the desserts were Bailey's Cream mousse and crème de menthe caramel. One reporter stressed that 'the table d'hôte dinner menu is very plain, so one would certainly choose the à la carte', which would, of course, be more expensive. House wine was good — 'properly chilled'.

The cooking was very good — 'food very tasty, and easy to identify individual tastes'. Service varied somewhat; on some occasions it was fast, but on others there was a wait for a pre- booked table and for initial service.

•*Drinks* full licence •*Meals* dinner (AC + T d'H) •*Cards* Visa, Access, American Express

CLIFDEN

HIGH MOORS RESTAURANT
Dooneen, Clifden, Co. Galway. (1km south from Clifden.)
Tel. 095-21342 ££ *Service* 10%
*Open*19.00-21.00 Wed-Sun.*Closed* Oct-May.

This summer restaurant, serving evening dinner, is in a stone-built single storey house, on a hill with views of sea and mountains. It has adequate parking. Connemara lamb, locally caught fish, and home produce, with organically grown vegetables, are its specialities.

Starters for our reporters included tomato and lovage soup, smoked trout, smoked salmon stuffed with crab meat, and Stilton pâté. Among the main dishes were roast lamb with apricot sauce, monkfish with garlic and pine nuts, poached John Dory, and salmon in pastry. A variety of desserts included chocolate marquise, gooseberry fool, and meringue with kiwi fruit. Both red and white house wine were very acceptable.

Food and cooking were in the main highly commended, but one person claimed that the roast lamb (a dish which called forth much praise from others) 'should have been better in Connemara'. Vegetables were perfectly cooked. Service was unobtrusive and helpful.

•*Drinks* wine licence •*Meals* dinner (T d'H) •*Cards* Visa, Access •*Cater for* children, wheelchair

O'GRADY'S SEAFOOD RESTAURANT
Market Street, Clifden, Co. Galway.
Tel. 095-21450 ££ *Service* nil
Open 12.30-15.00/18.30-22.00 Mon-Sat, Sun 1 Jun-30 Sept. *Closed* one week at Christmas, 20 Jan-15 Mar.

This is in the town of Clifden, which is a mecca for tourists in the summer, and, despite broad streets, can be very crowded. The outside of the restaurant is not very impressive; inside, it has nice decor and is small and inviting, with well divided tables.

The restaurant serves à la carte only, and provides home-grown vegetables, as well as fish caught in its own boat.

Reporters had both lunch and dinner there. Naturally, seafood was prominent on the menu, but there were other choices. Starters included seafood chowder, mussels in garlic butter, and avocado with citrus fruits. Some main dishes were turbot, steak, black sole, and Connemara lamb. Sweets were profiteroles, lemon soufflé, and home-made ice cream.

House wine (white Burgundy) was accounted good value at £7.50 a bottle.

Cooking was deemed 'excellent use of fresh local ingredients, especially sea food'. Service was 'first class'. 'Very good value' was the general verdict on O'Grady's.

•*Drinks* wine licence •*Meals* lunch (AC only), dinner (AC only), tourist menu 12.30-14.30 •*Cards* Access, Visa, Diners •*Cater for* children (lunch only), wheelchair (not to toilets)

ROCK GLEN HOTEL

Clifden, Co. Galway. (On the Ballyconneely road, 1.5km south of Clifden.)
Tel. 095-21035 £££ Service 12.5%
Open 19.00-21.00 daily, snack lunches 12.00-17.00. Closed 1 November-mid-March.

This is an old country house, with a friendly, relaxed atmosphere, serving snack lunches and evening dinners. It uses home-grown vegetables, and local fish and meat. Starters chosen by our reporters were liver pâté, smoked salmon, gazpacho, and celery and Stilton soup — this last criticised as having no taste of Stilton. Trout, sole, roast lamb, and chicken Maryland, were among the main courses, with chocolate rum gâteau, fresh fruit, and Bailey's ice cream as the desserts. The white house wine was adequate.

Cooking was good, and service excellent.

•*Drinks* full licence •*Meals* snack lunch (AC), dinner (T d'H) •*Cards* all major •*Cater for* children, wheelchair

SHADES RESTAURANT
The Square, Clifden, Co. Galway.
Tel. 095-21215 ££ 10%
Open 12.30-15.00/18.30-22.30. Closed 1 Nov-1 May.

This restaurant is on the first floor. It has an ante-room with a turf fire, and the dining-room is decorated in matching colours. It has a pleasant and peaceful atmosphere.

Dinner was the subject of all reports. Starters included vegetable strudel, oysters and salad, scallops, and cheese baked in pastry. Main dishes were wild trout, salmon, roast lamb ('classic Connemara — beautiful!') and roast duckling. The vegetable selection was described by one reporter as nice, but dull. There was a good cheese board, mostly Irish. Desserts included Irish Mist ice cream. Drinks were selected from the bar; there was a good wine list.

Food presentation here was 'studied and artistic'. Cooking was very good — 'not afraid to try new dishes and sauces, very nice subtle use of herbs'. Service was pleasant and efficient. Shades was described in one report as 'a serious restaurant where one can look forward to very interesting and well presented food'.

•*Drinks* full licence •*Meals* lunch (T d'H), dinner (AC + T d'H) •*Cards* all major

GALWAY CITY

CASEY'S WESTWOOD RESTAURANT
Dangan, Newcastle, Galway. (On main Galway-Oughterard-Clifden road, about 2.5km from city centre.)
Tel. 091-21442/21645 ££ Service 10%
Open 11.30-23.30. Closed three days at Christmas, Good Friday.

The address of this restaurant is most confusing for a stranger, being attributed variously to Dangan, Bushy Park, Oughterard Road, Moycullen Road, Clifden Road, and Newcastle. There is no difficulty in locating it once one grasps that these are all one and the same place. The restaurant is clearly visible from the road, near a corner on the left-hand side going out from the city. It is a dormer bungalow with a large extension and ample car parking. The dining-room is spacious, and attractively furnished and decorated.

Our reporters had both lunch and dinner there. For lunch, they had mushroom soup, melon, trout, roast beef, and plaice, with fruit salad and cheesecake for desserts. There was a special children's menu at the Sunday lunch which provided roast chicken and chips, and apple tart.

At dinner, avocado salad, apple sorbet, pan-fried scallops, home-made soup, and crabs' claws with avocado were some of the starters. Roast lamb, sirloin steak, and fillet of veal were some of the main dishes; profiteroles and fresh pears among the desserts. Petit-fours were served with freshly brewed coffee.

House wine was of good average quality.

Cooking was very good — 'each course cooked to perfection'. Service was prompt and attentive.

A special dinner offer in July which included a free bottle of wine was thought to be very good value.

•*Drinks* full licence •*Meals* lunch (T d'H), dinner (AC + T d'H) •*Cards* Access, Visa, American Express •*Cater for* children

THE CHESTNUT RESTAURANT
Bushy Park, Moycullen Road, Galway. (Rear of Keleghan's Bar.)
Tel. 091-25888 £££ *Service* nil
Open 12.30-14.30/18.45-22.00 Wed-Sun. *Closed* four days at Christmas, Good Friday.

The address of this restaurant, as in the case of Casey's Westwood Restaurant, may be given as Dangan, Oughterard Road, Clifden Road, Newcastle. When this confusion is sorted out, The Chestnut is easily found, in a location which commands a view over Lough Corrib. It is a new building attached to a bar and lounge. The dining-room is pleasantly decorated and the tables well appointed; they are, however, somewhat close together. All reports dealt with dinner. Seafood bouchées, lobster bisque, salmon mayonnaise, home-made pâté, and stuffed mushrooms were some of the starters. Rack of lamb, Wiener schnitzel, sole on the bone, noisettes of beef, duckling, and monkfish were some main dishes from a wide variety available on various evenings. Strawberry flan and lemon cheesecake were among the desserts.

German, French, and Italian wines all received praise.

The cooking was highly commended in all reports. Vegetables were fresh and crisp, and the flavour of food retained. Service was courteous, attentive, and efficient.

•*Drinks* full licence •*Meals* lunch (AC + T d'H), dinner (AC + T d'H), tourist menu 18.45-19.30 •*Cards* all major •*Cater for* children, wheelchair (not to toilets)

EYRE HOUSE
10, Eyre Square, Galway.
Tel. 091-62396 ££ *Service* nil
Open 12.00-22.30 daily. *Closed* one week at Christmas.

Eyre House is a restaurant with a pleasant facade looking out on Eyre Square. The interior is warm, clean and cosy, but the tables are rather too close together.

Reports covered both lunch and dinner. Starters included hot orange and grapefruit segments and a 'very tasty' cream of vegetable soup. Among the main courses chosen were trout with almonds, Wiener schnitzel with fresh vegetables, fresh prawns in cream sauce, and grilled salmon. Pavlova, strawberry cheesecake with fresh strawberries and cream, and Bailey's soufflé featured on the dessert menu. Those reporters who explored the wine list appeared satisfied; the Niersteiner in particular, at £7.50 a bottle, was felt to be good value. There was a uniformly high standard of cooking and presentation, but one lunch-time customer expressed disappointment that there was no choice in the vegetables served with the midday meal.

Service was friendly and efficient. All our reporters felt that they had got value for money.

•*Drinks* wine licence •*Meals* lunch (AC + T d'H), dinner (AC + T d'H), tourist menu 12.00-15.00, 18 Apr-31 Oct •*Cards* Access, Visa •*Cater for* children

LYDON HOUSE RESTAURANT
Shop Street, Galway.
Tel. 091-64051/61131 £ *Service* nil
Open 11.00-21.00 daily/22.30 in summer. *Closed* three days at Christmas.

Lydon House restaurant is on the first floor above Lydon's bakery shop and coffee/salad bar. It is pleasantly decorated and furnished, the walls bearing pictures and plaques relating to the history of the city. Dinner was the meal eaten there by all our reporters. There are two dinner menus, the less elaborate priced at under £10. Choices are adequate on that menu, including terrine of smoked salmon, melon and mandarin cocktail, and home-made soup. Beef Stroganoff, pork chops, and lasagne were chosen as main courses, with items from a children's menu for the youngsters. Crème caramel, hot apple tart, and soufflé Grand Marnier were some of the desserts. Wine was available but our reporters confined themselves to coffee, milk and iced water — this last served with a slice of lemon. Cooking was good, and service very friendly and efficient. The restaurant offered very good value in its price range.

•*Drinks* wine licence •*Meals* lunch (AC + T d' H), dinner (AC + T d'H), tourist menu available for lunch Jun-Sept •*Cards* Visa, Access, American Express •*Cater for* children (special menu)

MALT HOUSE RESTAURANT
Olde Malt Mall, High Street, Galway.
Tel. 091-63993/67866   ££ (restaurant)   Service 10% (not in bar)
Open 12.30-14.30/19.00-22.00 Mon-Sat. *Closed* one week at Christmas, Good Friday.

The Malt House comprises a bar and restaurant. A relatively new building designed to look old, it has an attractive exterior and is clean and comfortable inside, with a pleasant atmosphere.

Most of our reporters ate dinner in the bar, which they felt represented good value. Starters chosen included egg mayonnaise, seafood chowder (actually a thick vegetable soup with pieces of seafood, but judged 'very pleasant' nonetheless), and shrimp and prawn Thermidor in 'an unusually good sauce'. Beef Stroganoff and veal Viennoise featured prominently on the main course menu, and apple pie and cheesecake proved the most popular desserts. Those who had dinner in the restaurant found it 'most enjoyable but a little expensive'. Pâté, avocado with prawns, and chowder were starters, with scampi and turbot in a herb crust — 'far too heavily herbed' — were the dishes chosen. House wine was satisfactory.

The quality of the cooking was in general good, sauces and vegetables being singled out for special praise. Service was friendly and attentive.

•*Drinks* full licence •*Meals* lunch (AC + T d'H), dinner (AC + T d'H) •*Cards* Access, Visa, American Express •*Cater for* children, wheelchair

NORA CRUB'S
8, Quay Street, Galway.
Tel. 091-68376   £   Service nil
Open 09.00-21.00 weekdays. *Closed* bank holidays.

The outside of this restaurant, which is entered through a delicatessen, is unimpressive, but the interior is described as cosy, with a relaxed and friendly atmosphere.

The dinner menu featured soup of the day, chowder (both 'very good'), chicken Kiev, described as excellent, and cod concassé. Lasagne was a popular choice. There was a good choice of desserts, including home-made ice cream, which was well received.

All reporters opted for the house wine, which met with general approval, the white being labelled 'superb' by one customer.

Cooking was very good and food appetisingly served. Service was good and helpful. Extra touches such as the nibbles provided before the meal and the water served iced with lemon were also appreciated.

•*Drinks* wine licence •*Meals* lunch (AC), dinner (AC) •*Cards* none •*Cater for* children, vegetarians

PARK HOUSE
Forster Street, Galway. (Just off Eyre Square.)
Tel. 091-64924/68293 ££ *Service* nil
Open 12.00-15.00/18.00-22.00 weekdays. *Closed* one week at Christmas.

Park House restaurant is located beside a large public car park. Its appearance, both outside and in, is attractive. There is a fully-licensed bar on the premises, 'tastefully' divided from the restaurant proper. The decor of both was the subject of several favourable comments.

Reports related to both lunch and dinner. Starters included cream of mushroom soup, seafood cocktail, melon in port, and crème de menthe sorbet. Grilled salmon steak, chicken chasseur and beef Madagascar all featured on the main course menu, served in each case with a selection of vegetables. The dessert trolley offered at dinner provided a very wide selection, from which profiteroles, fresh fruit salad, and ice cream with hot chocolate sauce were sampled. Drinks were selected from the bar before or after the meal.

Cooking was of very high standard for both meals. Soups were home-made and vegetables perfectly cooked. Service was friendly and professional, and customers were not hurried to finish their meal.

•*Drinks* full licence •*Meals* lunch (AC + T d'H), dinner (AC + T d' H) •*Cards* Access, Visa, American Express, Diners •*Cater for* children (up until 19.30, half portions provided)

SACRE COEUR HOTEL
Salthill, Galway.
Tel. 093-23355 ££ *Service* 10%
Open 13.00-14.15/18.00-20.15 daily. *Closed* 23-31 December.

The dining-room of this seafront hotel is described by one reporter as a 'typical hotel dining-room', remarkable only in being larger than the average.

Our reports all related to dinner. Starters were pancakes and pâté; main dishes included mixed grill and roast turkey and ham with carrots and sprouts. The portions were very generous and the cooking good, although one reporter found it a little greasy. Pineapple soufflé and cheesecake to finish the meal excited little comment. Red house wine was deemed mediocre.

Service was good.

•*Drinks* full licence •*Meals* lunch (T d'H), dinner (T d'H) •*Cards* Access, Visa •*Cater for* children, wheelchair

LETTERFRACK

ROSLEAGUE MANOR HOTEL
Letterfrack, Co. Galway. (Off main Clifden-Westport road, 11km from Clifden.)
Tel. 095-41101 £££ *Service* nil
Open 13.00-14.30/20.00-21.30 daily in season. *Closed* Nov-Easter.

This lovely old manor house is a small hotel, serving dinner, and afternoon tea in the tourist season. The dining-room is a recent addition, with fine views. The hotel and restaurant have a friendly ambience; it has been described by one reporter as a 'comfortable, top-class, country house hotel, but not at all intimidating — a very relaxing place'. Home-grown produce and local seafood and lamb are specialities.

All reports dealt with dinner. Starters included smoked salmon salad, baked crab, pasta in garlic, and iced curry soup. Some of the main dishes were rack of lamb, salmon in hollandaise sauce, medallions of beef, and sea trout; among these — all thought good — one party felt that 'the lamb stole the show.' Helpings were generous. Vegetables (spinach, red cabbage, parsnips, and potatoes) were all tasty and well cooked. Sweets were chocolate mousse, lemon meringue pie, home-made ice cream, and strawberry tart.

Cooking was highly rated — 'one place I would try dishes that I would never attempt anywhere else.' Service was prompt, friendly, and unobtrusive.

Prices were quite high, but deemed good value by all our reporters.

•*Drinks* full licence •*Meals* lunch (AC+T d'H), dinner (AC + T d'H) •*Cards* Visa, Access•*Cater for* children (over 12 at dinner),wheelchair, non-smokers

LOUGHREA

MEADOW COURT RESTAURANT
Loughrea, Co. Galway. (3km west of Loughrea on Galway road.)
Tel. 091-41051/41633 ££ *Service* 10%
Open bar food 12.30-14.30/18.00-22.30 weekdays,18.00-21.30 Sun, dinner 19.00-22.00 weekdays, 19.00- 21.15 Sun. *Closed* three days at Christmas, Good Friday.

This hotel, approached by a short drive-way, has ample parking (a plus for anybody who has tried to park in the town of Loughrea), and is plain and well kept outside. Inside, it is comfortable, if a bit dark, with a relaxed atmosphere.

Reporters had both bar food and full dinner. Bar food included kebabs and rice, steak, lasagne, and chicken, with apple pie and cheesecake as desserts. The full dinner menu was, of course, more elaborate. Seafood cocktail — 'too much lettuce, too little seafood' — melon melba, and mussels in garlic were some of the starters. Main dishes included sirloin steak, roast duck, roast beef, and pan-fried chicken. Among the desserts were Irish Mist fruit cocktail, Bailey's mousse, and profiteroles. House wine was rated good. Cooking of both the bar menu and the full dinner was adjudged very good, although one reporter, there for dinner, thought some items a little overcooked. Service was friendly and attentive, with adequate time between courses.

•*Drinks* full licence •*Meals* dinner, bar lunch •*Cards* Visa, Access, American Express

SPIDDAL (AN SPIDEAL)

BOLUISCE BAR AND RESTAURANT
Spiddal, Co. Galway (In main street of the village.)
Tel. 091-83286 ££ Service 10%
Open 12.00-14.30 Mon-Fri, 17.30-23.30 Mon-Sat, 16.00-22.00 Sun. *Closed* three days at Christmas, 1 Jan-11 Mar.

For anybody unfamiliar with Irish this name is pronounced, roughly, 'Bowl Ishka'; it is the name of a little lake up in the nearby hills. The restaurant is over the pub; it is quite small, but comfortable, with an open fire in winter. One special point made by reporters about this establishment is its adaptability — for example a readiness to provide any size portion, or to divide one serving between two people. It is a seafood restaurant, and all fish used is caught locally.

All our reporters had an evening meal there. Starters were chowder, mussels in garlic, and fresh vegetable soup. Main courses were sole, salmon, lobster, and scallops. Children in one party had lasagne, the helping of which was thought to be somewhat sparse for a main dish. The most popular dessert was Irish coffee gâteau, highly praised.

House wine was considered good value. Cooking was excellent — 'beautiful meal', 'all perfectly cooked and presented'. Service was friendly and efficient. Even when the restaurant was busy, there was no attempt to rush people.

•*Drinks* full licence •*Meals* lunch (AC), dinner (AC) •*Cards* Access, Visa, American Express, Diners •*Cater for* children (high chairs)

Co. Mayo

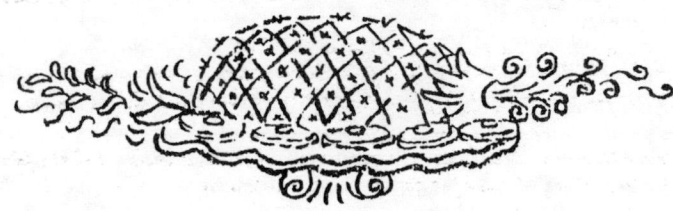

ACHILL ISLAND

ATLANTIC HOTEL
Dooagh, Achill Island, Co. Mayo.
Tel. 098-43113 ££ Service 10%
Open 19.00-23.00. *Closed* 1 Oct-30 Apr.

This hotel is just off the main road across the island and is signposted in the village of Dooagh. Its outer appearance is attractive, on a height, with car parking space. The dining-room is light and airy, with views of the sea and plenty of space between the tables, which have spotless table linen.

Our reporters all had dinner there. Starters, all good, were garlic mushrooms, smoked mackerel salad, and melon and pineapple. Among the main courses were roast pork, roast beef, and lamb cutlets. Chocolate biscuit cake with cream, pavlova, and apple tart were some of the desserts. The house wine was pronounced 'all right'.

Cooking was good; meat was both tender and tasty, and portions very generous. The competence of the service was a noteworthy point for one reporter; two young waitresses kept a busy dining-room going with pleasant efficiency. During the tourist season the restaurant is well patronised by Continental visitors, and recommended by local guesthouse owners on the basis of their visitors' account of it.

•*Drinks* full licence •*Meals* dinner (T d'H) •*Cards* none •*Cater for* children

BALLINA

PADRAIC'S RESTAURANT AND WINE BAR
Tone Street, Ballina, Co. Mayo.

Tel. 096-22383 £ *Service* nil
Open 12.30-15.00/15.30-23.30 (summer) 15.30-20.00 (winter). *Closed* three days at Christmas.

Parking immediately near this restaurant could be a problem in daytime, the narrow street having been there in the 'year of the French', but there is a large car park not far away.

The restaurant has an ordinary shop-front appearance. It is quite spacious inside, with nicely set-out tables. All our reporters had dinner there; it is an alternative to a more expensive meal in one of the large hotels. Vegetable soup was home-made. A mixed grill as a main dish was good, but grilled salmon was somewhat lacking in flavour. Apple tart met with approval for dessert. Coffee was instant.

Cooking was adequate, and house wine acceptable.

Service was the subject of very favourable comment. The constant vigilance of the owner, without 'nagging', ensured that his staff did not neglect any customer.

•*Drinks* wine licence •*Meals* breakfast from 7.30, lunch (AC + T d'H), dinner (T d'H) •*Cards* Visa •*Cater for* children, wheelchair

BELMULLET

WESTERN STRANDS HOTEL
Belmullet, Co. Mayo.

Tel. 097-81096 £ *Service* nil
Open 12.30-14.30/19.00-21.00 daily, pub grub all day. *Closed* one week at Christmas.

This hotel is of undistinguished outer appearance, and the entrance is not attractive — 'off-putting' one of our reporters said, if one used the way in through the public bar. But the dining-room, once located, is well laid out, with space between the nicely-set tables.

Reports all dealt with dinner. Our reporters were impressed because the menu seemed to vary from day to day, and a good selection was available.

Soup of the day was consistently good. Roast pork, lamb, and beef were all tender and well-flavoured. Vegetables, however, — onion rings, cauliflower, and sprouts — were rather insipid. Apple tart, chocolate and strawberry gâteau were good desserts. Coffee was excellent, and generously supplied.

Overall, the cooking was good, and service pleasant and prompt. Prices were extremely reasonable. One of our reporters makes a point that this is the only place to eat in the evening (or, come to that, at any other time for a full meal) other than a fast food outlet, for the whole Mullet peninsula. It has no competition either on the mainland nearer than Ostán Synge in Geesala, some 17.5km away over the Erris bogs. The Western Strands could therefore exploit its position by charging high prices, and it is considered to its credit that it does not.

•*Drinks* full licence •*Meals* breakfast from 8.30, lunch (AC), dinner (AC), snacks •*Cards* none yet •*Cater for* children

CASTLEBAR

DAVITT RESTAURANT
Rush Street, Castlebar, Co. Mayo.

Tel. 094-222333 ££ *Service* nil
Open 12.30-14.30/18.00-22.15 daily, snacks 14.30-18.00. *Closed* three days at Christmas.

The exterior of this restaurant is attractive, with leaded windows. The inside arrangement ensures privacy, and there is a warm, welcoming atmosphere.

Reporters had both lunch and dinner there. At lunch, there was home-made vegetable soup. Roast beef and chicken and ham were served with well-cooked vegetables. There was a good selection of desserts on the menu. For dinner, baked avocado and mussels in white wine were starters. Carpetbagger steak and Mexican beef kebabs were main dishes, with fresh fruit salad and lemon meringue pie for dessert. No wine appeared in reports, but the restaurant has a full bar licence.

Cooking for both meals was very good, and service fast, very friendly and helpful.

•*Drinks* full licence •*Meals* lunch (AC + T d'H), dinner (AC + T d'H) •*Cards* Access, Visa, American Express •*Cater for* children (high chairs), wheelchair, Macra na Feirme discount

WESTPORT

ARDMORE HOUSE
The Quay, Westport, Co. Mayo.
Tel. 098-25994   ££   Service 10%
Open 18.00-22.00 Mon-Sat. Closed three days at Christmas, Good Friday.

This is a large white split-level house, with well-landscaped grounds, on a height overlooking Clew Bay. It specialises in evening dinner.

Seafood au gratin, sorbets with champagne and Benedictine, and chicken and sweetcorn soup were some of the starters chosen by our reporters. Steak — fillet and sirloin — was by far the most popular choice as a main dish. Strawberries in pastry, and apple tart were among the desserts. The red house wine and Liebfraumilch were rated very good.

Cooking was 'top class', 'steak perfectly cooked and very tender'. There was just one reservation — that the chicken and sweetcorn soup was rather tasteless. Service was 'superb', 'the staff are extremely courteous and efficient'. One reporter regards this restaurant as 'one of the best in the West, but not cheap'.

Drinks wine licence •*Meals* dinner (AC + T d'H) •*Cards* all major

THE ASGARD RESTAURANT
The Quay, Westport, Co. Mayo.
Tel. 098-25319   ££   Service 10%
Open bar food 12.00-21.00 daily, restaurant 18.30-22.00 Tues-Sat, Sun in summer. Closed three days at Christmas.

This pub-cum-restaurant is in the small cluster of houses known as the Quay (it is near the actual Westport quay where formerly small coastal vessels used to load and discharge). In keeping with its situation, the Asgard has nautical decorations on its walls inside and out. It is clean and bright, with a cosy atmosphere. It serves bar food daily up to 21.00 hours, and restaurant dinner in the evenings; seafood from Clew Bay is a speciality.

Reporters had both a bar lunch and a full dinner. Seafood chowder, vegetable soup, and quiche Lorraine were chosen at lunch time. At dinner, barbecued spare ribs, mushrooms, and smoked salmon were some of the starters. Garlic steak, chicken, and fillet of beef were main course choices, with cheesecake and chocolate mousse for desserts.

The dinner wine, Bernkastel, was good; water was served with ice at lunch. Cooking for both lunch and dinner was excellent. Soup was piping hot, and of correct consistency. Service was prompt and friendly.

•*Drinks* full licence •*Meals* bar lunch and dinner (AC), restaurant dinner (AC + T d'H) •*Cards* Access, Visa, American Express, Diners •*Cater for children, wheelchair (not to toilets)*

NORTH & NORTH WEST

*Counties Cavan, Donegal, Leitrim,
Louth, Monaghan, Sligo*

North & North West: 149

FOR THE PURPOSES of this Guide, this region stretches across the northern part of the Republic from Carlingford Lough on the east coast and the River Boyne to Donegal and Sligo Bay on the west.

County Louth contains a great deal of interest in its small area. The Boyne forms its southern boundary, flowing into the sea from Drogheda. The well-known Baltray golf links are on the bank of the estuary; further north on the coast is the fishing port and seaside resort of Clogherhead. North again, just outside Dundalk, is the little resort of Blackrock. To be borne in mind by all who aspire to use this coast for swimming and boating is that there are great variations in the tide, which recedes into the far distance on the ebb. Carlingford Lough is a fjord-like inlet between the Mourne Mountains and the Cooley peninsula (signposted for Greenore and Carlingford just north of Dundalk). The Cooley Hills, culminating in Slieve Foy, are well served by motor roads and a way-marked walkers' path; the view across to the Mournes rewards any effort in getting up there. The round tower and high crosses of Monasterboice are just off the main Drogheda-Dundalk road; further inland are the ruins of Mellifont Abbey, which may be reached by travelling up King William's Glen from Oldbridge, the site of the Battle of the Boyne almost three hundred years ago. (Old Mellifont should not be confused with the modern religious foundation of the same name near Collon.)

Counties Monaghan and Cavan are a countryside of drumlins and lakes. The drumlins account for the 'basket of eggs' type of scenery with its little rounded hills in clusters, and correspondingly winding little roads. Inishkeen was the home territory of Patrick Kavanagh, and the Monaghan landscape is evoked in many of his poems. The lakes are a delight for coarse fishing. Killykeen Forest Park, near Killeshandra, is just one of the places where you can take full advantage of the trees and the water; on the shores of Lough Oughter, it has picnic sites, a restaurant in season, holiday chalets which blend very well with the landscape, walks, and fishing facilities.

County Leitrim lies near the head waters of the Shannon (the actual source of which is a disappointing little pool, known as the Shannon Pot, in County Cavan on the slopes of the Cuilcagh Mountains, not far from Glangevlin). Carrick-on-Shannon is a picturesque and popular centre for cruising on Ireland's largest river; in the north of the county, Lough Melvin is a large fishing lake not far from Bundoran.

County Sligo is full of interest. The county town is noted for its annual Feis Shligigh, which attracts singers and musicians of a very high calibre as competitors; it also hosts the Yeats Summer School. Yeats' grave, with its injunction to 'Cast a cold eye, on life, on death', is in Drumcliffe churchyard, on the Bundoran road. Lough Gill with its 'Lake Isle of Innisfree' and Lissadell, the home of the Gore-Booth family, open to the public, are within easy reach of Sligo town. So too are the hills of Knocknarea and Ben Bulben, which afford magnificent views over Sligo Bay, where Rosses Point and Strandhill are two of the little resort villages. The prehistoric tombs at Carrowmore, on the way to Strandhill, and Carrowkeel, in the Bricklieve hills near Castlebaldwin, should not be missed.

Donegal suffers from being virtually cut off from the rest of the Republic. It may, of course, be reached via Ballyshannon and Bundoran, travelling by Sligo, but this is a long way round if you're bound for the northern part of the county. In fact, you would have to be exceedingly unlucky to encounter anything other than a courteous welcome when travelling direct through the North to cross into Donegal at Strabane or Derry. Donegal is one of the largest and loveliest of the Irish counties. Its coast line, from Malin Head in the north round to the Slieve League cliffs in the south, is most spectacular. Inland, Glenveagh Forest Park, with its lake, trees, castle, and deer herds, is well worth a visit, as is the Grianán of Aileach, the restored fort of the local kings at the foot of the Inishowen peninsula, near the Derry border. The ruined friary in Donegal town is associated with the seventeenth-century 'Annals of the Four Masters'. Killybegs, on the northern shore of Donegal Bay, has a big fishing harbour where some of the country's largest trawlers may generally be seen. A visit to one of the tweed factories throughout the county is likely to tempt you into some expenditure!

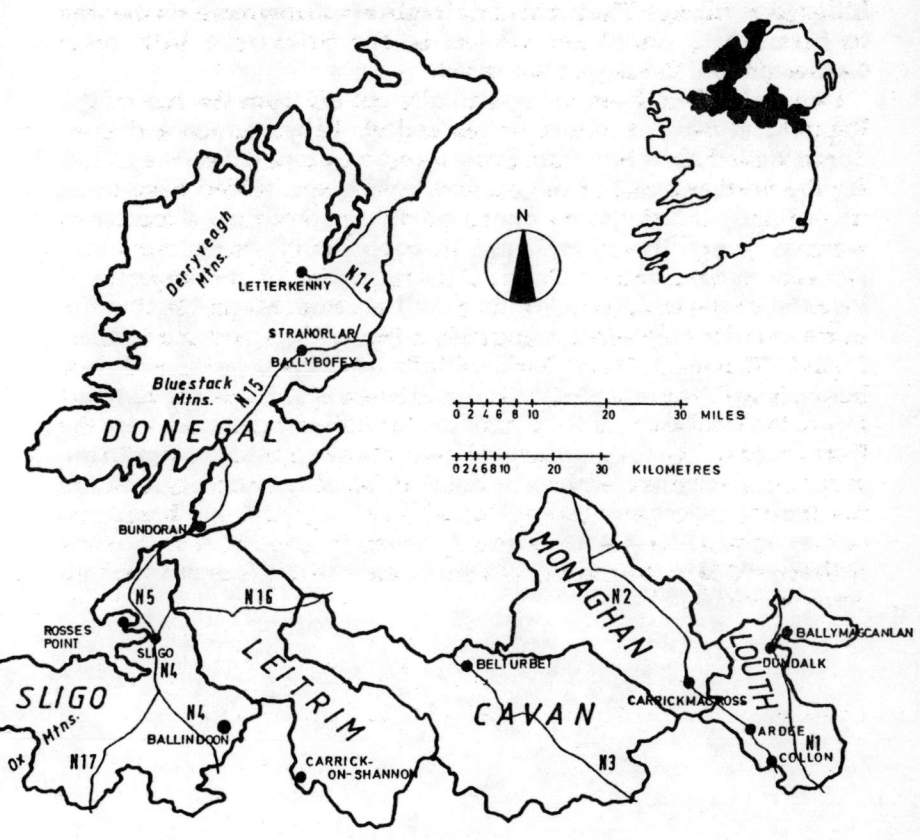

Co. Cavan

BELTURBET

ERNE BISTRO
The Lawn, Belturbet, Co. Cavan.

Tel. 049-2243 ££ Service nil
Open 19.00-23.00 weekdays, 12.30-14.30 Sun. *Closed* bank holidays.

This is part of a bar/lounge/disco complex near a jetty on the Erne. The dining-room is tastefully decorated, and has a well stocked and maintained aquarium along one wall.

Reporters had both Sunday lunch and dinner there. For lunch, seafood cocktail and vegetable soup were starters; chicken in wine sauce and trout were the main dishes, with fresh fruit salad and sherry trifle as desserts. For dinner, there were avocado with prawns and mushrooms as starters, with fillet and peppered steaks as main dishes, and much the same desserts as at lunch.

Piat d'Or wine, 'nice, very well chilled', was drunk at both meals. Cooking was excellent, and service professional, speedy, and friendly.

•*Drinks* full licence •*Meals* lunch (T d'H Sun), dinner (AC) •*Cards* none

Co. Donegal

BALLYBOFEY/STRANORLAR

KEE'S HOTEL (TAPESTRY RESTAURANT)
Stranorlar, Co. Donegal.

Tel. 074-31018 ££ Service nil
Open 12.30-14.15/17.15-21.30 daily. *Closed* two days at Christmas.

The two neighbouring towns of Ballybofey and Stranorlar are virtually one, and this hotel is in the main street of Stranorlar. The outside is not impressive, one reporter saying: 'I doubt that we would have gone in to eat there only someone recommended it'. There is a large car park. The Tapestry Restaurant is comfortable, with pairs of tables enclosed in booths, candles and silver cutlery on the tables, and small tapestries decorating the walls. There is also bar food available, and a full range of light snacks.

Both lunch and dinner in the restaurant were the subject of reports. For lunch, described as 'exceptionally good value', there was seafood cocktail, beef Stroganoff, and fresh fruit salad. Starters at dinner included corn on the cob, barbecued spare ribs, and broccoli cream soup. Some of the main dishes were scampi, baked trout, pork à la crème, and steak, which one enthusiast claimed was 'one of the best ever tasted'. Some reporters had no room for desserts, but others sampled cheesecake, fresh fruit salad, and Black Forest gâteau. Few drank wine with the meal, but Bernkastel was good. Coffee earned praise.

Cooking was generally excellent; 'our main course was as good a main course as we have ever set to', one report said; but in one case vegetables, at lunch, were overcooked.

Service was good, even when the restaurant was full to capacity.

•*Drinks* full licence •*Meals* breakfast, lunch (AC + T d'H), dinner (AC + T d'H), bar food, tourist menu daily 12.30-14.15/18.30-20.00 •*Cards* Access, Visa, Diners, American Express •*Cater for* children (high chairs provided)

BUNDORAN

IMPERIAL HOTEL
West End, Bundoran, Co. Donegal.

Tel. 072-41507 ££ *Service* 10%
Open 13.00-14.30 1 Jun-31 Aug, 19.00-23.00 1 May-31 Oct. *Closed* 1 Nov-30 Apr.

The food must be good here, because our reporters, who highly recommended this hotel, agreed that its exterior was drab and the interior dull although lightened by a nice fire in the foyer.

They had both lunch and dinner there, with soup as a starter, roast pork and roast lamb as main dishes, and pavlova for dessert. Their meals were accompanied only by water, with coffee to finish.

Cooking for both meals was excellent, and service very good.

•*Drinks* full licence •*Meals* lunch (T d'H 1st June-31st Aug), dinner (AC) •*Cards* Access

Co. Leitrim

CARRICK-ON-SHANNON

COUNTY HOTEL
Bridge Street, Carrick-on-Shannon, Co. Leitrim.
Tel. 078-20042   ££   Service nil
Open 08.00-10.00 breakfast, 12.00-15.00/18.00- 22.00 daily. *Closed* two days at Christmas.

The outside of this hotel has been described as 'clean and sober' but not otherwise inviting. Its dining-room is functional rather than decorative; the windows are high up and one cannot see out through them. In addition to the restaurant, food is served in the bar, and there is a coffee shop. Breakfast is served to non-residents.

All reports dealt with lunch. Prawn cocktail and melon were starters, with turkey and ham, fish, and roast beef as main dishes. Strawberries and cream, crème caramel, and sherry trifle were desserts. The hotel has a full licence, but our reporters did not drink at lunch. Cooking was very good, service pleasant and quick.

•*Drinks* full licence •*Meals* breakfast, lunch (AC + T d'H), dinner (AC + T d'H), bar food •*Cards* Access, Visa, American Express •*Cater for* children, wheelchair

Co. Louth

ARDEE

THE GABLES HOUSE AND RESTAURANT
Dundalk Road, Co. Louth.
Tel. 041-53789   ££   Service 10%
Open 19.00-23.00 Tues-Sat. *Closed* first two weeks June, first two weeks November.

This is an old house, with an attractive area of grass and flowers in front. It is quiet, warm, and comfortable. Patrons are made to feel welcome, and each one receives the personal attention of the proprietor. The restaurant specialises in French country cooking, using local herbs, vegetables, game, and fish.

It is an evening restaurant, so all reports dealt with dinner. Some of the starters selected were escargots in garlic, smoked salmon, prawn cocktail, and pâté maison. Main dishes chosen from a varied menu were sole bonne femme, peppered steak, and Indonesian chicken, the last described as 'scrumptious'. Crème de menthe ice cream, crème brulèe, and chocolate mousse were among the desserts. Coffee was very good, 'and plenty of it if wanted'.

Nuits-St-Georges and white house wine were 'easy to drink'. Cooking was excellent — 'vegetables crisp', 'sauces very light, nothing overcooked'.

As to service, there was personal attention at all times, but 'there was no hurry to move you so that somebody else might use your table.'

•*Drinks* full licence •*Meals* dinner (AC + T d'H) •*Cards* all major •*Cater for* overnight accommodation

COLLON

FORGE GALLERY RESTAURANT
Collon, Co. Louth.

Tel. 041-26272　　　　　　　££　　　　　　　Service nil
Open 18.30-22.30 Tues-Sat.

This restaurant is situated in the main street of Collon with a car park behind it and another across the road. Pre-dinner drinks are taken on a gallery overlooking the dining-room. The walls of the restaurant are adorned with paintings by local artists, which are for sale, as are the antiques displayed in the reception area. A feature of this restaurant, one reporter said, is that there is nearly always one 'imaginative' vegetarian main dish available. It serves evening meals only.

Some of our reporters' starters were seafood pasties, crab salad, melon in port wine, and seafood lasagne. Rack of lamb — 'tender and juicy' — turbot, tournedos steak, and sole stuffed with walnut were main dishes.

Brandy snaps and cream, strawberries in orange liqueur, and lime mousse were desserts. The brandy snaps were the only item criticised in any report; they 'tasted like toffee.' Red and white house wine were good.

The cooking was highly rated. One person said that 'they are especially proud of their vegetables,' and that there was 'always nicely underdone meat, tender, and fresh'. Service was attentive without being overpowering.

•*Drinks* wine licence •*Meals* dinner (AC + T d'H) •*Cards* Access, Visa

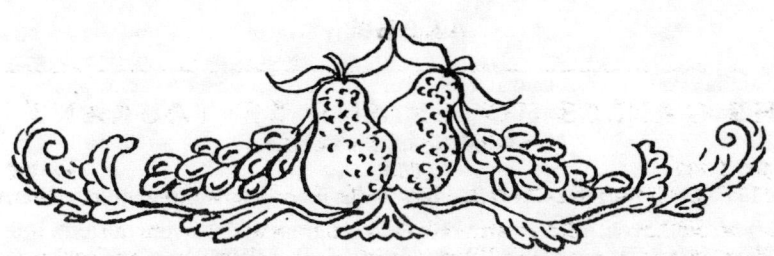

DUNDALK

BALLYMASCANLON HOUSE HOTEL
Dundalk, Co. Louth. (1.6km off Dublin-Belfast N1 road.)
Tel. 042-71124   ££   Service 10%
Open 07.30-21.30 daily. Closed two days at Christmas.

This hotel is north of Dundalk, on the road to Carlingford and Greenore (signposted off the main Belfast road). It has a parkland setting. It may be mentioned that for anyone wishing for a short walk before or after a meal, the enormous Proleek dolmen a short distance away through the grounds is worth viewing. To return to the hotel, the dining-room is comfortable, and beautifully decorated.

Our reporters had lunch there, and also — an unusual feature in our reports — high tea for a party of twelve, including nine hungry fifteen-year-olds.

The high tea (£84 for 12 people) consisted of bacon, egg, sausage, turkey, and stuffing, with tea, chips, bread, butter, jam, and ice cream to finish. For lunch, starters were orange juice and vegetable soup; main dishes were roast pork and deep-fried plaice, with fruit salad and apple pie to follow. House wine was very good.

Service was very courteous — a little slow to begin with for the fifteen-year-olds. Cooking was good for both meals.

•*Drinks* full licence •*Meals* Breakfast, lunch (AC + T d'H), dinner (AC + T d'H), snacks, afternoon tea •*Cards* Visa, Access, Diners, American Express •*Cater for* children, wheelchair

CELLARS RESTAURANT
Clanbrassil Street, Dundalk, Co. Louth. (In Backhouse Centre.)
Tel. 042-33745/35684   £   Service nil
Open 12.00-14.30 Mon-Fri. Closed one week at Christmas.

This restaurant-cum-bar serves lunches only. It is in a basement, and would be easy to miss. The interior is somewhat dark, but it is clean, with tables in long rows, and efficiently run, with a friendly atmosphere. Vegetarian food is available; there is a salad bar, with a wide selection. Desserts are home-made.

Salads were chosen by all our reporters, including one who had a vegetarian salad as a main dish. Lentil soup was a starter, and roast beef and lasagne other main dishes. There was a selection of sweets on a dessert table, and people selected a mixture. The house wine was good.

Cooking was very good — salads and desserts came in for special mention both for content and presentation. Service was friendly and efficient; the proprietress herself works in the restaurant and is anxious to please.

•*Drinks* full licence •*Meals* lunch (AC + T d'H) •*Cards* none •*Cater for* children

QUAGLINOS
Clanbrassil Street, Dundalk, Co. Louth.

Tel. 042-38567 ££ Service nil
Open 18.30-23.30 Mon-Sat. Closed 24-26 December, New Year's Day.

This is an upstairs restaurant, with a pleasant colour scheme and a relaxed ambience. It serves evening dinner only, specialising in French cuisine and home-made pasta dishes, using unusual fish such as shark, swordfish, and red snapper when available.

Our reporters' starters included smoked salmon stuffed with prawns, and melon with kiwi. Some of the main dishes were roast duckling, salmon in filo pastry, beef Stroganoff, steak Diane, and chicken suprême. Desserts were summer pudding and fresh fruit salad. There is a wide selection of French wines, with some Italian; the white house wine was very drinkable.

Cooking was excellent. Service was friendly and helpful, but not obtrusive.

•*Drinks* wine licence •*Meals* dinner (AC + T d'H) •*Cards* American Express, Access, Visa

Co. Monaghan

CARRICKMACROSS

NUREMORE HOTEL
Carrickmacross, Co. Monaghan. (On N2 Dublin road.)

Tel. 042-61438 ££ Service nil
Open 12.45-14.45/18.00-21.45 daily. Closed three days at Christmas.

This hotel is a modern building approached by a drive way, adjacent to woodland, a lake, and a golf course. It has a pleasant, comfortable dining-room overlooking the lake. It specialises in fresh vegetables, local produce, and seafood, using no frozen foods.

Reporters had both lunch and dinner there. For lunch, the starters chosen were avocado vinaigrette, home-made vegetable soup, shrimp cocktail, and egg mayonnaise. Roast beef — 'beautifully rare' — was the most popular main dish; there was also veal chasseur, thought rather tasteless. Helpings were generous. Desserts included pavlova and chocolate mousse.

For dinner, starters included frogs' legs in tomato sauce, pilaff, pâté, and melon in crème de menthe. Some of the main dishes were quail, rack of lamb, lobster, steak, and fresh salmon. Desserts included fresh fruit salad, lemon mousse, and raspberry meringue. House white wine was good.

Cooking was generally excellent. 'Care obviously taken' was one comment. 'Vegetables in particular properly cooked', 'the taste of the food was not spoiled by too much or too strong accompaniments' were others.

Service was in the main highly commended, with the exception of a party there for lunch who thought it 'very hurried and unfriendly'.

•*Drinks* full licence •*Meals* breakfast, lunch (AC + T d'H), dinner (AC + T d'H), bar food •*Cards* Access, Visa, American Express, Diners •*Cater for* children, wheelchair

Co. Sligo

CASTLEBALDWIN

CROMLEACH LODGE
Lough Arrow, Castlebaldwin, Co. Sligo.
(5.5km off Boyle-Sligo road — N4 — signposted at Castlebaldwin.)
Tel. 071-65155　　　　　　　　£££　　　　　　　　Service 10%
Open 18.00-21.30 Tues-Sat. *Closed* 23-31 December.

This restaurant is a modern country house, with a car park. It overlooks Lough Arrow and there are views of the lake from the dining-room. It has a quiet, relaxed atmosphere. Reservations should be made; as it accepts only twenty bookings a night there is no hurry for people to finish their meals. Locally grown herbs and vegetables are used whenever possible.

Evening dinner only is served. Some of the starters were broccoli and apple soup, crab stuffed mushrooms, garlic mussels, melon in port wine, seafood chowder, and avocado and prawns. Main dishes included breaded veal, pheasant, wild Donegal salmon, steak, monkfish, turbot, and Cordon Bleu chicken. Desserts were Black Forest gâteau, crème de menthe ice cream, raspberry pavlova, white chocolate mousse and coffee meringue.

There was an extensive wine list, and the house wine was pronounced 'quite satisfactory'. Wine was served at the correct temperature.

The cooking was praised in every report received. Some of the comments were: 'Excellent in the French style', 'everything came with lovely light sauces', 'vegetables were crisp.'

Service was unobtrusive but attentive and friendly.

•*Drinks* wine licence •*Meals* dinner (T d'H) •*Cards* American Express, Access, Visa •*Cater for* children under 10 before 19.00

ROSSES POINT

REVERIES RESTAURANT
Rosses Point, Co. Sligo.
Tel. 071-77371 ££ Service 10%
Open 19.00-22.00 Mon-Sat.

This house in the seaside village of Rosses Point has a modern all-glass extension which affords views of Sligo Bay. Inside, it is decorated in modern style, and has linen tablecloths and napkins, with flowers on the tables. It serves evening dinner only.

For starters, reporters had melon with blackcurrant sorbet, seafood vol-au-vents, and cheese in pastry. Beef Wellington, quails, wild duck, fish, pheasant, and steak were among the main dishes; lemon sorbet with passion fruit, chocolate gâteau, and mince meat ice cream were desserts. The house wine was 'fine'.

Cooking was highly rated, except by the people who had wild duck and found it very tough; the other members of that party were pleased with the cuisine. Service was efficient and friendly.

•*Drinks* wine licence •*Meals* dinner (T d'H) •*Cards* Access, Visa

SLIGO TOWN

GULLIVER'S RESTAURANT
23/24, Grattan Street, Sligo.
Tel. 071-42030 £ Service nil
Open 10.00-24.00 daily.

The exterior of this restaurant is framed in wood, and inside it has the character of a ship, with portholes set in the walls and nets hanging from the ceiling. It is 'well run, with emphasis put on friendliness and hygiene', and does a big local business. There is an extensive salad bar.

Reporters had dinner and a snack there. Prawn cocktail and melon were two starters. Steak, chicken Maryland, trout and chicken Hibernia (using a whiskey sauce) were main dishes, and for dessert pavlova was chosen — other reporters were too full! House wine at £1.40 a glass was good.

Cooking was considered very good — 'the food is always excellent,' said one reporter. Service was quick, and more than one report specially mentioned the friendliness of the waitresses.

•*Drinks* full licence •*Meals* lunch (T d'H 12.00-14.30), dinner (AC 14.30 on)
•*Cards* all major

STRANDHILL

KNOCKMULDOWNEY HOUSE
Culleenamore, Co. Sligo.
(5km from Strandhill on Ballisodare-Strandhill road.)
Tel. 071-68122 ££ *Service* nil
Open 19.30-21.30 daily. *Closed* early November-mid March.

This is a Georgian country house under the southern flank of Knocknarea, the prominent hill crowned by the huge cairn which is the legendary grave of Queen Maeve. It is furnished and decorated in keeping with the style of the house as far as possible. There is a sitting-room with a log fire for perusal of the menu and for pre-dinner drinks. The atmosphere is friendly, with great attention paid to guests' wishes and tastes. All vegetables and fruit are home grown.

All reporters had dinner — it is an evening restaurant only. Starters included aubergines au gratin and seafood crêpes. Roast lamb and sirloin steak were some of the main dishes, and among the desserts were egg-nog pie, banana splits, raspberry pavlova, and chocolate mousse.

House wine (Muscadet) was served at the correct temperature. Cooking was 'expert', 'all perfectly cooked'. Vegetables were particularly good.

Service was courteous and obliging.

•*Drinks* wine licence •*Meals* dinner (AC + T d'H) •*Cater for* children, wheelchair (not to toilets)

MIDLANDS

*Counties Laois, Longford, Offaly,
Roscommon, Westmeath*

LAOIS, ONE OF THE FIRST counties to spring to mind as part of the Midlands, is not just flat fields and bog dotted with a few towns. The Slieve Bloom Mountains, basically a high moorland ridge broken up by deep glens, have been opened up in recent years as a recreation area, with forestry, picnic sites, marked walks, and a signposted system. Arderin, the highest point, gives far-reaching views; it is not, however, very accessible and the Wolftrap Mountain, much nearer traffic roads, is a good alternative. The roads in the Slieve Blooms are not broad highways, and call for careful driving, particularly as you may be lucky enough to see a deer cross your path at any turn. One of the roads across from the Mountrath-Portlaoise side comes down at Kinnity, not far from Birr, and if you are in that region the opportunity should be taken to visit Birr Castle Gardens, open to the public throughout the year.

The extent of the Midlands bogs may be seen from the ridge of the Slieve Blooms. An immense area of Offaly and Westmeath is worked by Bórd na Móna (the Peat Production Board), the far stretching brown patches broken only by the occasional splash of yellow machinery, the shine of plastic covers, like sheets of water at a distance, and the characteristic cooling towers of the turf-fuelled electricity stations. Near Tullamore, the county town of Offaly, is a base for cruising boats on the Grand Canal, navigable from there to Shannon Harbour, where it enters the river. Upstream on the banks of the Shannon lies Clonmacnoise. These famous monastic ruins on a slope beside the river, where careful restoration work has been carried out, well repay the effort of travelling off the beaten track.

Athlone is the nearest large town to Clonmacnoise. It is busy, with narrow streets which become congested with the volume of Dublin-Galway traffic that they have to carry, but it is in a favourable situation on the banks of the Shannon, with attractive walks beside it. John McCormack, the singer, was born here; in fact the house is now a restaurant, featured in this Guide. In the middle of Westmeath, around Mullingar, are several large lakes — Lough Ennel, Lough Owel, and, further north, Lough Derravarragh and Lough Lene. Near Lough Lene are the ruins of Fore Abbey, a National Monument.

North of Athlone, over the Longford border, is Ballymahon, the centre of Oliver Goldsmith's country. More than one small village in this district claims to be the original of his 'Sweet Auburn'. North of that again is Mostrim or Edgeworthstown, the home of Maria Edgeworth who wrote *Castle Rackrent*. Lanesboro' is at the head of Lough Ree; not far from there is Clondra, with the attractive little basin of Richmond Harbour, still accessible from the Shannon and formerly the terminus of the Royal Canal.

A long bridge spans the Shannon at nearby Tarmonbarry, leading into County Roscommon. Roscommon town has an imposing ruined castle, and ruined friary. In the north of the county is Lough Key, one of the loveliest of the lakes accessible from the Shannon Navigation.

Lough Key Forest Park is on its shore; it has well laid-out picnic, camping, and caravan sites, which are discreetly located among the trees and shrubbery of what was once the Rockingham estate. Not far from Boyle, the town near the forest park, is Keadue, where the bard-harpist Turlough O'Carolan lived and is buried. His music has enjoyed a revival in recent years. On the slopes of the nearby Slieveanerin Mountains at Arigna are the last coal mines to be worked in Ireland.

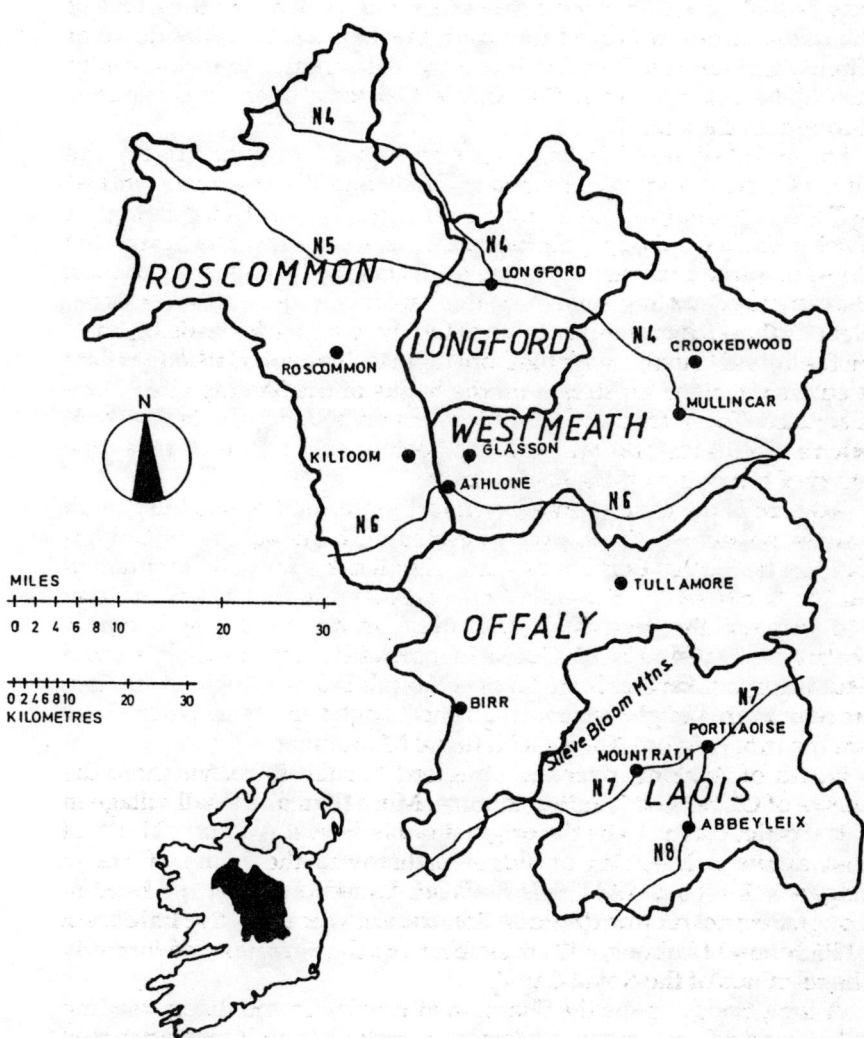

Co. Laois

ABBEYLEIX

HIBERNIAN HOTEL
Main Street, Abbeyleix, Co. Laois.
Tel. 0502-31252   ££   *Service* nil
Open 12.00-15.00/18.00-23.00 daily, breakfast 08.30,bar food 11.00-21.00 daily. *Closed* two days at Christmas.

The hotel tones in with the general architecture of this old De Vesci estate town. As the main Dublin-Cork road passes its doors, it is well situated as a stopping place on the journey. Inside, it boasts nothing remarkable in the way of decor, but is pleasant and comfortable. It serves lunch and an evening meal; all reports here relate to lunch.

Tomato soup was home-made and very good. Fruit juice was also available. Trout was one main dish, as was beef, which was cooked exactly as ordered, with well presented vegetables. Sherry trifle, pronounced first-class, was one of the desserts, with pavlova and Black Forest gâteau. Wine was good, and reasonable in price. Cooking was very good, using good local produce, and service was friendly and efficient.

•*Drinks* full licence •*Meals* breakfast, lunch (T d'H), dinner (AC + T d'H), bar food, tourist menu 12.00-15.00 Mon-Sat •*Cards* Visa, Access, Diners •*Cater for* children, wheelchair, non-smokers

MOUNTRATH

ROUNDWOOD HOUSE
Mountrath, Co. Laois. (5km from Mountrath on the road to Kinnity, signposted from the town in the direction of the Slieve Bloom mountains.)
Tel. 0502-32120   ££   *Service* nil
Open 20.30 Tues-Sat, 13.30 Sun. *Closed* Christmas Day.

This is a small family-run country house hotel. It is set in parkland and is comfortably furnished in period country-house style, with a log-fire in the drawing room where one has pre-dinner drinks.

The restaurant serves only pre-booked dinner, at 20.30, and pre-booked Sunday lunch at 13.30. Children are welcome to the lunch, but not to dinner.
People who had dinner there were well pleased with their meals. Home-made soups (potato and tomato and apple) with savoury and fish pancakes and salmon pâté, were starters. Beef Wellington, grilled salmon steak, and fondue fillet of pork and sirloin beef, with three different sauces, were main dishes. Soufflé, home-made ice cream, profiteroles and crème brûlée were among the desserts. Both red and white house wine were very good.
Cooking and service were excellent.
• *Drinks* wine licence • *Meals* Sunday lunch (T d'H), dinner (T d'H) • *Cards* Access, Visa, American Express

Co. Longford

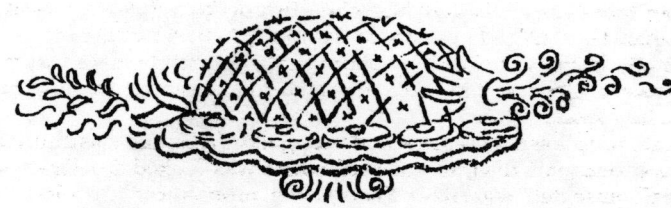

LONGFORD TOWN

LONGFORD ARMS HOTEL
Longford.
Tel. 043-46296   ££   Service nil
Open 12.30-15.00/18.00-21.00 daily. *Closed* Christmas Day.

The Longford Arms is in the centre of Longford town, a commercial centre for the area and a popular stop on the Dublin-Sligo road. The outer appearance of the hotel is not very striking, and the signposting of the car park not very prominent. The dining-room is upstairs; it has a quiet atmosphere, and linen cloths on the tables.

Reporters had both lunch and dinner. As the menus and conditions were virtually interchangeable, they are dealt with together here. Home-made soup and consommé were starters. Main courses were roast beef, roast pork, lamb cutlets, and turkey and ham. Desserts included coffee and strawberry gâteau, éclairs, pavlova, and fresh fruit salad. The hotel is, of course, fully licensed, but it so happens that none of our reporters sampled either wine or spirits with their meals.

Cooking and presentation were generally good. Service was prompt, with attention to detail at lunch-time, even when the restaurant was crowded; at dinner there was a rather long wait between courses.

• *Drinks* full licence • *Meals* lunch (AC + T d'H), dinner (AC + T d'H) • *Cards* all major • *Cater for* children, wheelchair

Co. Offaly

BIRR

DOOLEY'S HOTEL
Emmet Square, Birr, Co. Offaly.

Tel. 0509-20032   ££   *Service* nil
Open 12.30-14.30/18.30-21.30 daily. *Closed* Christmas Day.

This hotel is an old coaching house. Emmet Square, where it is located, is one of Birr's principal parking areas, also serving the hotel, and tends to be crowded. The hotel has been refurbished in recent years, and is well decorated. It has a welcoming reception area and a rather ornate dining-room. As well as table d'hôte lunch and dinner in the dining-room, lunches are served in the bar.

All our reporters had dinner there. Some of the starters chosen were corn on the cob, melon, and prawns in wine sauce, followed by soup. Salmon stuffed with prawns, chicken princess, and entrecôte steak were some of the main dishes. There was a good selection on the dessert trolley, from which Bailey's cheesecake, trifle, and Irish Mist gâteau, were sampled. The house wine was very good.

Cooking received high praise; all dishes were cooked to the customers' liking. Service was efficient and obliging.

•*Drinks* full licence •*Meals* lunch (AC + T d'H), dinner (AC + T d'H) •*Cards* all major •*Cater for* children (not in bar after 19.00 hrs), wheelchair

THE STABLES
Oxmantown Mall, Birr, Co. Offaly. (Outside the gates of Birr Castle, not far from the town centre.)

Tel. 0509-20263   ££   *Service* nil
Open 19.30-22.30 Wed-Sat. *Closed* one week at Christmas.

This restaurant is in an old converted stable. It is open only from Wednesday to Saturday inclusive, and serves evening dinner only. It has a cosy atmosphere, with a fire at which one can sit and chat. The restaurant specialises in seafood and home-made pâtés. Starters included seafood cocktail and mushroom soup. The main dishes chosen by our reporters were stuffed pork, fillet steak, and chicken Kiev. There was a wide selection on a dessert trolley, with pavlova and fresh fruit salad as two of the choices. While a bottle of German wine was good, the house wine was criticised as too dry.

Cooking was overall very good, but chicken Kiev was 'very dry, just like breaded chicken'. Steaks were well cooked, and vegetables were fresh.

Service was very satisfactory.

•*Drinks* wine licence •*Meals* dinner (T d'H) •*Cards* Access, Visa, American Express, Diners •*Cater for* wheelchair

TULLAMORE

THE BRIDGE HOUSE
Bridge Street, Tullamore Co. Offaly.
Tel. 0506-21704/21718 ££ Service nil
Open 12.30-14.30/17.30-21.30.

This is a pub-cum-restaurant. It has no car park of its own, but is quite near some of the town's public parking places. It has an unremarkable exterior; inside, it is nicely decorated, with a warm relaxing atmosphere which 'makes you want to stay longer'. In addition to lunches and dinner in the dining-room, there is a self-service lunch available in the bar. This is good value, but if one has to sit on a high stool at a small high table it is not very comfortable.

Reporters had both lunch and dinner in the dining-room. Starters at lunch included egg mayonnaise and chicken and mushroom vol-au-vents, with veal, beef, and pork among the main dishes, and Irish Mist gâteau, sherry trifle, and strawberry soufflé as desserts. At dinner, some of the starters were melon slices, prawn cocktail, duck pâté, and home-made vegetable and potato soup. Main dishes included roast duckling, fillet steak, sirloin steak, Bridge House chicken, and prawn Mornay. Broccoli, spinach, cauliflower, and mushrooms were some of the vegetables. Desserts chosen were pavlova, Bailey's soufflé, and fresh fruit. The house wine, white and red, was acceptable.

Cooking was generally very good, although the veal served to one person at lunch was stringy, and there was some overuse of salt in sauces. The staff were very pleasant; service was unobtrusive and, on the whole, prompt.
• *Drinks* full licence • *Meals* lunch (AC + T d'H), dinner (AC + T d'H) • *Cards* Access, Visa, American Express • *Cater for* children, wheelchair

Co. Roscommon

KILTOOM

NEWPARK HOUSE HOTEL
Kiltoom, Co. Roscommon. (On the Athlone-Roscommon road, 8km west of Roscommon.)
Tel. 0902-89130/89124 ££ Service nil
Open 12.30-14.30 Sun only, 19.00-21.30 daily. *Closed* Christmas Day.

This is a small hotel overlooking Lough Ree serving evening dinner and Sunday lunch. The interior is decorated in pine. There is a warm friendly atmosphere, and several instances of the readiness of management and staff to accommodate customers' needs have been mentioned in reports. At lunch, children's half-size portions of main course dishes were very generous, and the adults' wine glasses were topped up without extra charge. At dinner, people were allowed to choose their main dish from the à la carte menu while paying only table d'hôte prices for the meal.

Corn on the cob and home-made vegetable soup with cream and croûtons were lunch starters, with roast pork and roast beef as main dishes. A selection from the dessert trolley included cream slices with raspberries, cheesecake, brandy trifle, and chocolate éclairs. For dinner, chowder — 'almost a meal in itself' — was a starter, with vegetable soup. Beef Stroganoff and chicken Marengo were main dishes, and, as with lunch, there was a wide selection from the dessert trolley. French house wine was good.

On the whole, cooking was excellent for both meals; meat was just right, and desserts freshly made. Vegetables were not overdone, the only exception being carrots, which were mashed.

There was no delay in service, and the staff were friendly and obliging.

•*Drinks* full licence •*Meals* Sunday lunch (T d'H), dinner (AC + T d'H)
•*Cards* Access, Visa •*Cater for* children, wheelchair, non-smokers

ROSCOMMON TOWN

ABBEY HOTEL RESTAURANT
Roscommon. (Off the Roscommon-Galway road.)

Tel. 0903-26240 ££ *Service* nil
Open 12.45-14.30/18.00-22.00 daily. *Closed* two days at Christmas.

The hotel, standing in its own grounds, is an eighteenth-century turretted mansion. There is an open fire off the bar, and an air of general welcome in the foyer. The dining-room is on a raised level and has candles on the tables. Freshly cooked local produce is used.

Reporters had lunch and dinner there. Grapefruit and mandarin cocktail was a starter at lunch, with chicken Cordon Bleu (breast of chicken wrapped in cheese and ham and pan-fried) and peach melba. At dinner, egg mayonnaise was a starter, with a generous mixed grill and minute steak for the main course. Ice cream sundae and strawberry soufflé were desserts. Nobody had wine at either meal, but the hotel has, of course, a full wine list.

The cooking was fairly good. Chips, at lunch, could have been crisper, and the minute steak could have been more succulent.

The staff took a personal interest in the patrons, but there was some delay in serving on two occasions due to a staff shortage.

•*Drinks* full licence •*Meals* lunch (AC + T d'H), dinner (AC + T d'H), tourist menu (Mon-Fri 12.45-14.30) •*Cater for* children (but not in bar), wheelchair

Co. Westmeath

ATHLONE

COUNT JOHN'S RESTAURANT
The Bawn, Athlone, Co. Westmeath. (Just off main street,
on the same side as Church of Ireland church.)
Tel. 0902-74362 £ *Service* nil
Open 12.00-22.00 daily. *Closed* Good Friday.

This restaurant is just off Athlone's major traffic route, so that car parking is best sought in one of the public car parks. It is from the singer Count John McCormack that the name is derived — the house was his birthplace. It has an unremarkable shop-front entrance; inside, it is comfortable and well decorated, with more accommodation than one thinks on first entering. Lunch, dinner, and à la carte meals are available.

Lunch was the subject of our reports. Mushroom soup, good, was a starter, with roast lamb and cold meat and salad as main dishes, and apple tart and sherry trifle desserts. Coffee was one of the weak points for one party; it was instant, and not very hot.

Cooking was in the main good; meat had both good flavour and good texture. Of the vegetables, turnip was somewhat tough.

Service was quick and courteous, even when the restaurant was busy.

One of our reporters found it remarkable that so good a four-course lunch was available for £3.60 a head.

•*Drinks* soft •*Meals* lunch (AC + T d'H), dinner (AC + T d'H) •*Cards* none

GLASSON VILLAGE RESTAURANT
Glasson, Athlone, Co. Westmeath. (8km from Athlone
on the Longford/Cavan road.)
Tel. 0902-85001 ££ *Service* nil
Open 19.00-22.30 Tues-Sat, 12.30-14.30 Sun only. *Closed* four days at Christmas.

This is a restored nineteenth-century stone cottage, which was formerly a Royal Irish Constabulary barracks, near Lough Ree, in the village of Glasson. It is furnished and decorated in a cosy cottage style. It serves evening dinner only from Tuesday to Saturday inclusive, with lunch on Sunday, specialising in the use of local herbs, vegetables, lamb, venison, and trout.

Reports related to both dinner and Sunday lunch. For the latter, starters were kedgeree and home-made cauliflower soup with cream. Roast lamb and oriental beef curry with rice and poppodums were main dishes; crème de menthe syllabub and ice cream with butterscotch sauce, desserts. Portions were generous, and second helpings offered.

Some of the starters at dinner were seafood cocktail, home-made French onion soup, deep-fried squid, crabs' claws, smoked cod roe, melon in port wine, mussels, and dolmades (meat balls served in vine leaves). Main dishes included sirloin steak, pork stuffed with pâté, salmon in garlic butter, and roast lamb. Choices from a dessert trolley with a good selection of high quality included lemon soufflé, kiwi pavlova, fresh fruit salad, and apple crumble. House wine, red and white, was good, and served in generous glasses. Sherry, claret, and port were also appreciated.

Cooking was of a very high standard. 'One could nearly lick the plates,' one enthusiastic reporter said.

Service was very personal, prompt and courteous.

•*Drinks* wine licence •*Meals* Sunday lunch (T d'H), dinner (AC + T d'H) •*Cards* Access, Visa, Diners •*Cater for* wheelchair

MULLINGAR

CROOKEDWOOD HOUSE

Crookedwood, Mullingar, Co. Westmeath. (13km south of Mullingar, on Castlepollard road.)

Tel. 044-72165   ££   *Service* nil
Open 19.30-22.00 Tues-Sat, 12.30-14.00 Sun. *Closed* bank holidays, two weeks late November.

This large old country house is off the beaten track, near Lough Derravarragh. The house is well maintained; the dining area, in a basement, is nicely decorated and furnished, with linen tablecloths and napkins, but could be a trifle cold in winter. The waiting area is a comfortable sitting room with an open fire. The restaurant serves only evening dinners from Tuesday to Saturday, with lunch on Sunday. It uses local produce, including organically grown vegetables.

All our reporters had dinner there. There was a wide choice of starters. Soups were home-made, and included dill and cucumber, carrot and orange, and chowder. Other starters were pan-fried chicken livers in raspberry sauce, seafood pancakes, éclairs stuffed with salmon mousse, and kiwi sorbet. Some of the main dishes were roast goose with apple and ginger sauce, fillet steak, and scallops in a bed of rice. Various home-made ice creams, including Bailey's, brown bread, and coffee, were the favourites among a very good selection of desserts. There was unlimited coffee after the meal.

The wine list was extensive. Liebfraumilch, one of the less expensive, was adequate, and the house wine was fair.

Cooking was described as first-rate throughout; vegetables, particularly, were cooked to perfection.

Service was natural, courteous, and efficient, the chef normally coming to a table for a few moments to inquire if the meal was to the customer's liking.

•*Drinks* awaiting wine licence •*Meals* dinner (AC + T d'H) •*Cards* Visa, Access, American Express, Diners •*Cater for* children (over 12 for dinner)

FOR YOUR USE WHEN NEXT EATING OUT

Report Form

**To The Consumer Choice Guide to Restaurants in Ireland
FREEPOST, 45 Upper Mount Street, Dublin 2.**

Restaurant name and address:

I had lunch / dinner on _____ 1989. (Delete as appropriate.)

The bill amounted to £ _____ for _____ people.

I would rate this establishment (out of 20) ____ /20.

I would / would not recommend this establishment to my friends. (Delete as appropriate.)

Character (outside and inside): _____

_____

_____

Overall impression: _____

_____

_____

Any unusual aspect: _____

_____

_____

Please describe the dishes you (and your companions) had:

to start: _____

_____

for main course: _____

_____

to finish: _____

_____

drinks: _____

_____

Please comment in detail on each of the following:

Quality of cooking:_____

_____

_____

Quality of service:_____

_____

Quality of wine (or other drink): _____

_____

YOUR DECLARATION

'I am not connected with the owner(s) or management of this establishment. This report is my independent assessment, based on my own experience.'

Signed: _____ Date: _____

Your name and address: _____

_____

FOR YOUR USE WHEN NEXT EATING OUT

Report Form

To The Consumer Choice Guide to Restaurants in Ireland
FREEPOST, 45 Upper Mount Street, Dublin 2.

Restaurant name and address:

I had lunch / dinner on _____ 1989. (Delete as appropriate.)

The bill amounted to £ _____ for _____ people.

I would rate this establishment (out of 20) ____ /20.

I would / would not recommend this establishment to my friends. (Delete as appropriate.)

Character (outside and inside): _____

_____

_____

Overall impression: _____

_____

_____

Any unusual aspect: _____

_____

_____

Please describe the dishes you (and your companions) had:

to start: _____

_____

for main course: _____

_____

to finish: _____

_____

drinks: _____

_____

Please comment in detail on each of the following:

Quality of cooking:_____

_____

_____

Quality of service:_____

_____

Quality of wine (or other drink): _____

_____

YOUR DECLARATION

'I am not connected with the owner(s) or management of this establishment. This report is my independent assessment, based on my own experience.'

Signed: _____ Date: _____

Your name and address: _____

_____